THE FORMATION
OF THE
RESURRECTION
NARRATIVES

REGINALD H. FULLER

FORTRESS PRESS
PHILADELPHIA

REVERENDO PATRI IN DEO
RICARDO
OLIM COLLEGAE SEMPER AMICO
THEOLOGIAE SACROSANCTAE
NUPER PROFESSORI
NUNC EPISCOPO CLOCHERENSI
IN ECCLESIA HIBERNAE

First Fortress Press edition 1980
Second printing 1983

Library of Congress Cataloging in Publication Data

Fuller, Reginald Horace.
    The formation of the Resurrection narratives.

    Includes bibliographical references and indexes.
    1. Jesus Christ—Resurrection—Biblical teaching.
I. Title.
BT481.F84   1980   232.9′7   79-8885
ISBN 0-8006-1378-3

743J83   Printed in the United States of America   1-1378

Contents

Contents

Preface

WHEN I WROTE the first edition of this work during the years 1969–70 I could say with confidence that very little had been written on the resurrection narratives since World War II (see p. 6). Since 1970, however, the situation has radically changed, and in fact the appearance of my book coincided with the beginning of a spate of books on the Easter accounts, in English (both British and American) as well as in French and German. My intention here is to note points of consensus in which my book shares and to point up issues on which I differed and continue to differ with the positions of others in these recent works.

There is general agreement that if one wishes to inquire into the earliest traditions about what happened at the first Easter one has to look not at the Easter stories at the ends of the Gospels but, as I did, to 1 Corinthians 15:5–8. The only partially dissenting voice here is Willi Marxsen's. For him, the whole appearance tradition has a single origin in Peter's post-Easter experience. The other experiences are simply ways of saying that through Peter's witness others came to share his Easter faith. Further than that, for Marxsen Peter's statement that he had "seen Jesus" is reduced to his having come to believe.[1] I would still contend that Peter's believing is the *result* of his seeing, not identical with that seeing. For biblical faith is always response to revelation. The third and major point Marxsen makes is that the resurrection is merely a way of saying that "the cause of Jesus continues"—"Die Sache Jesu geht weiter." This is again to confound cause and effect. Of course Easter means that everything that Jesus stood for, the cause on which he staked his all, continues despite the disaster of Good Friday. But it continues only and precisely because God raised Jesus from the dead, as the earliest kerygma asserts and as every page of the New Testament presupposes. I continue to hold, as Schniewind held in his debate with Bultmann,[2] that something happened between God and

Jesus on Easter Day, and not only between God and the disciples (i.e., the production of their faith).

The abrupt ending of Mark continues to be much debated. There seems to be general agreement that Mark did end his Gospel at 16:8, and that consequently there is no "lost ending." But the reason I gave for this, viz., that Mark had no appearance narratives available for the simple reason that at the time of writing such narratives had not yet developed, but only lists of appearances such as that in 1 Corinthians 15, has not made much impression. And it has been indirectly assailed by those who hold that the transfiguration story is a post-resurrection appearance story retrojected by Mark for redactional reasons into the earthly ministry. Along with this they argue further that Mark 16:7 points toward the parousia rather than a resurrection appearance (a view put forward many years ago by Ernst Lohmeyer. And further still they connect this with Mark's alleged redactional purpose in setting up the Twelve as representatives of a false *theios anēr* (divine man) Christology. All I need say here is that these scholars have never refuted C. H. Dodd's form-critical analysis of the post-resurrection appearance stories, in which he showed among other things that an essential feature of all such stories is the initial absence and subsequent appearance of the Risen One. In the transfiguration story the presence of Jesus from the beginning is integral to the narrative. One can only reiterate Dodd's position and challenge these scholars to answer it.[3] At the same time I am now more inclined to agree with Raymond Brown[4] that the miraculous draft of fishes is an original post-resurrectional story retrojected into the earthly ministry by Luke. This, however, does not affect my position that *Mark* had no post-resurrectional appearance stories at his disposal.

I remain convinced that in 16:7 Mark is pointing not to the parousia but to appearances in Galilee. Perrin's argument that the verb *opsesthe* invariably points to the parousia is weighty but not conclusive, for other tenses of this verb are used of resurrection appearances (1 Cor. 9:1; Matt. 28:17; John 20:18, 25). I believe myself that Mark's plot requires the rehabilitation of the disciples in an Easter appearance, for otherwise the charge (Mark 9:9) that they are to keep secret the messiahship of Jesus until after the resurrection remains unfulfilled.

Perhaps the most widespread point of disagreement is over the historicity of the empty tomb. One might almost speak of a critical consensus in favor of Bultmann's view that the empty tomb is a late legend. This consensus extends beyond Germany (Marxsen) to Britain (C. F. Evans, Lampe) and the United States (the J. M. Robinson and

Perrin schools). Support for my view comes almost entirely from Roman Catholic[5] and conservative evangelical[6] circles. There are, however, a few exceptions in Protestant critical circles, for instance Ulrich Wilckens, a member of the German Pannenberg school,[7] and John A. T. Robinson in England.[8] Robinson is even prepared to give some credence to the shroud of Turin![9] For myself, I would not want to rely upon such evidence, though I must admit that it has recently become more and more intriguing and I think we should be open-minded about it. I still believe that the Marcan tomb story has a long history behind it. Indeed, in his book on the resurrection posthumously published, Norman Perrin failed to carry out his own principle enunciated earlier,[10] that in dealing with any pericope we need to write a history of the tradition. I would maintain that this is just what I have done in this book, and that as a result I have not indeed proved the historicity of the empty tomb, but at least have shown that the earliest accessible tradition is the report of the women (or at least Mary Magdalene) to the disciples that they (or she) had discovered the tomb empty. More than that a historian cannot be expected to achieve.

Since writing this book I have been reinforced in this opinion by the observation that the tradition of the women's report to the disciples has multiple attestation, being found in the Special Lucan tradition (Luke 24:10, 23), in the Johannine tradition (John 20:18), and in the (to my mind) early and independent tradition preserved in Pseudo-Mark 16:10–11. I would also be prepared to argue that the finding of the empty tomb has multiple attestation, being preserved independently in Mark 16:1–8 and John 20:1, 11–13.

My colleagues on the Lutheran-Catholic task force on Peter in the New Testament were not convinced by the distinction I drew between the church-founding and mission-inaugurating appearances listed in 1 Corinthians 15.[11] I still believe this distinction can be justified exegetically for the respective appearances, though with one exception, namely that to James. My suggestion that he was a kind of head of the board of missions is perhaps overpressing the evidence of the later chapters of Acts. It may be that there is more to be said for the older view that James appears as an alternative to Peter as the foundation apostle of the church.

Finally, there is the question whether the term *historical* can be appropriately applied to the resurrection. As we have noted, Marxsen asserts that the only historical fact about Easter is that the cause of Jesus continued after Good Friday (as Bultmann has said that the only historical fact about Easter was the rise of the Easter faith). Conservative scholars of various kinds continue to insist on the historical nature of the resurrection, as might be expected.[12] More surprising perhaps is the view of the Pannenberg school that the resurrection is a historical act of God, though not open to historical investigation.[13] Quite apart from the usual arguments against its being appropriately called historical, there is, as I have pointed out in this book, an important theological reason for its not being "historical" in the proper sense of the word, and this is because, as the Pannenberg school itself has so strongly insisted, it is by definition eschatological. I thus draw the opposite conclusion from Pannenberg, who thinks that the historian cannot rule out the resurrection's historicity precisely because it is unique. Being eschatological, resurrection occurs at the end of history, at the point where history is transcended. This however does not mean that nothing happened. What "happened" at Easter "happened" in the same sense in which the parousia will "happen," an event transcending time and space as we know them now.

REGINALD H. FULLER

Virginia Theological Seminary
Alexandria
Holy Cross Day, 1979

Preface to the First Edition

THE PRESENT WORK had its beginnings in a course of lectures delivered at the summer session at Union Theological Seminary in 1967. They were subsequently expanded and rewritten. Parts of them were delivered orally on several occasions during my sabbatical leave in Europe in 1969: at Professor C. F. D. Moule's seminar in the Divinity School at Cambridge, to the departments of theology in the Universities of Birmingham, Nottingham, and Lancaster, at Handsworth Theological College, at the meeting of the Studiorum Novi Testamenti Societas in Frankfurt am Main, and at the New Testament Congress at Christ Church, Oxford. I wish to thank numerous members of my audiences on these various occasions for their helpful criticisms and suggestions which, when possible, have been incorporated into the text. One of these helpful critics was the Reverend Professor R. P. C. Hanson of Nottingham, now Lord Bishop of Clocher, to whom this book is dedicated.

I wish further to thank the publishers, The Macmillan Company, their religion editor, Clement Alexandre, and Will Davison for his help with the manuscript. It has been an unexpected pleasure to find myself working with these two gentlemen once more and in quite a different context.

It will be noted that the manuscript was completed before the appearance of Professor C. F. Evans's study of the resurrection narratives.

REGINALD H. FULLER

Union Theological Seminary
New York City
Tuesday after Pentecost, 1970

Abbreviations

SB   H. L. Strack and P. Billerbeck, *Kommentar zum Neuen Testament aus Talmud und Midrasch*

SBA   Sitzungsbericht der Berliner Akademie der Wissenschaften

SBT   Studies in Biblical Theology, London

SHA   Sitzungsbericht der Heidelberger Akademie der Wissenschaften

S.N.T.S.   Studiorum Novi Testamenti Societas

SNU   Seminarium neotestamenticum Upsaliense

S.P.C.K.   Society for the Promotion of Christian Knowledge

TDNT   *Theological Dictionary of the New Testament* (E.T. of *TWNT* by G. W. Bromiley, 1964–   )

ThZ   *Theologische Zeitschrift*, Basel

TNT   R. Bultmann, *Theology of the New Testament*

TWNT   G. Kittel (ed.), *Theologisches Wörterbuch zum Neuen Testament*

USQR   *Union Seminary Quarterly Review*, New York

West. Comm.   Westminster Commentary

ZNW   *Zeitschrift für die neutestamentliche Wissenschaft*, Giessen, Berlin

ZThK   *Zeitschrift für Theologie und Kirche*, Tübingen

CHAPTER ONE

Introduction:
The Riddle of Easter

A GENERATION AGO the greatest New Testament scholar of this century, Rudolf Bultmann, in an epoch-making essay entitled "New Testament and Mythology," spoke of the "incredibility of a mythical event like the resuscitation of a corpse."[1] He did not himself think that this was the major problem of the Easter faith, but it is certainly the problem that looms largest in the eyes not only of the man in the street but also of the man in the pew.

Bultmann did not wish to eliminate the resurrection from the Christian faith, but rather to interpret it correctly. According to him, the real meaning of the resurrection message is not that a certain incredible event occurred on Easter Sunday morning, but that the cross is permanently available to us in the church's preaching as the saving act of God.

We need not concern ourselves about the adequacy of this interpretation of the resurrection to the intention of the New

Testament. Clearly, the New Testament asserts that something over and above the Good Friday event happened in the experience of the first disciples, something more than their coming to a new assessment of the meaning of the event of Good Friday. Even the most skeptical historian has to postulate an "x," as M. Dibelius called it,[2] to account for the complete change in the behavior of the disciples, who at Jesus' arrest had fled and scattered to their own homes, but who in a few weeks were found boldly preaching their message to the very people who had sought to crush the movement launched by Jesus by disposing of its leader.

What is the precise content of this "x"? What really happened at Easter? Can the historian go any further than leaving it as an insoluble problem? The New Testament itself is quite clear on what the "x" was: the tomb of Jesus was discovered empty on Easter Sunday morning, and Jesus appeared to his disciples as one risen from the dead.

There are so many discrepancies between the reports of these stupendous events that, even if we grant (as we might on a priori grounds) that they were unique and involved a unique person—something so incredible as the "resuscitation of a corpse"—the stories themselves appear incredible on the grounds of their palpable inconsistencies. The best way to discredit a witness in court is for the cross-examiner to tie him up in knots and make his evidence appear to be such a tissue of inconsistencies that the jury becomes convinced he is entirely untrustworthy. One does not need to be a scientific New Testament scholar to do that with the resurrection narratives.

In its original form, Mark—the earliest Gospel—contained no resurrection appearances, though the writer seemed to know of such appearances, apparently to Peter and the others in Galilee. It *relates* only the discovery of the empty tomb by two women named Mary and one named Salome. They are charged by a "young man"—apparently an angel—to tell the disciples to go into Galilee, where they will see the risen Lord. But they disobey, failing to deliver the message out of fear. At this point Mark comes to an abrupt end.

Matthew follows Mark down to the point at which the women (only two of them, both named Mary) leave the tomb after their discovery that it is empty, but this Gospel has the Risen One meet the two women in person while they are on the way to tell the disciples of their discovery. Here the Risen One appears as an earthly figure whose feet they can grasp, yet, at the same time, as a divine being, whom they worship. The Risen One repeats the angel's charge (Matthew expressly identifies Mark's young man as an angel) for the disciples. Nothing is said of the women's subsequent silence, as in Mark; presumably they deliver the charge. This would seem to be further indicated by the fact that the disciples go to Galilee, where they see the Risen One on a mountain in a form which apparently implies that he is already ascended.

Luke's Gospel gives a very different account. The discovery of the Easter events of the tomb is certainly much the same, though there are minor discrepancies when this Gospel is compared with the other accounts. Thus three women—one of them Mary Magdalene, but two of them with different names from those given by Mark and Matthew—make the discovery. There are *two* men, apparently angels, at the tomb. They charge the women, not to tell the disciples to go into Galilee, as in Mark and Matthew, but to remind the disciples how Jesus while in Galilee had predicted that he would be raised on the third day after his crucifixion. The women obediently deliver the message, nothing being said of their fearful silence as in Mark. Here, according to some texts of Luke, Peter goes to the tomb to check the women's story.

Next follow two appearances, both located in Jerusalem and neighborhood. (Luke is completely silent about appearances in Galilee.) The appearances are to two disciples on the road to Emmaus and to the eleven, seemingly in a house in Jerusalem. It is characteristic of these Lucan appearances that the Risen One walks with his disciples and eats with them. The appearance to the eleven concludes with his leading them out to Bethany, where he finally departs from them and, according to some texts, ascends to heaven. Whether this is part of the authentic text or not, Luke leaves no room for any appearances in Galilee.

John is different again. Mary Magdalene goes to the tomb (no other women being present), discovers that it is empty, and reports her discovery to Peter and an unnamed disciple, who then go together (not Peter alone as in some manuscripts of Luke) to check out Mary Magdalene's story. There is no angel at the tomb in John, and therefore no message to the disciples to go to Galilee, as in Mark and Matthew, nor any reminder of the passion and resurrection prediction, as in Luke. There is however an appearance to Mary Magdalene, somewhat reminiscent of that to her and the other Mary in Matthew, but it occurs at a slightly different point in the narrative. Mary is not, as in Matthew, on her way to tell the disciples about her discovery, for she has already met Peter and the unnamed disciple and told him. Instead, she is still tarrying outside the tomb when the Risen One appears to her—Peter and his companion having already gone back home. Jesus does not give her a charge about the disciples going to Galilee, as in Matthew, but grants her a personal manifestation of himself, including the enigmatic command *noli me tangere* and a perplexing reference to his impending ascension. There is no further allusion to, or account of, the ascension, as in Luke, but since Thomas is eight days later commanded precisely to touch the Risen One, it seems by implication to have taken place sometime between the appearance to Mary Magdalene and the appearance to the eleven with Thomas present. Like Luke, John has an appearance to the disciples in a room, but there were ten, not eleven, because Thomas was absent. This appearance does not end with the ascension at Bethany, as in Luke. A week later there occurs another appearance at which Thomas is present and at which the Risen One overcomes Thomas's doubt. This story apparently concludes the appearances, for the book seems to end at John 20:31, with no room for any appearances in Galilee, as in Matthew and Mark. But the narrative is unexpectedly resumed at John 21:1, and proceeds to relate an appearance of Jesus by the lake of Galilee (not on a mountain, as in Matthew) to seven disciples (not to eleven, as implied in Mark and as stated in Matthew, where there are also others present). Then follow two scenes: the first includes both the draft of fish (a story similar to one which Luke had located in the earthly ministry at the call of the first disciples) and a meal of fish by the lakeside (whereas in Luke the meal of fish took place at Jerusalem); the second scene includes the commissioning of Peter to feed the sheep as well as a prediction of the martyrdom of Peter and the fate of the unnamed disciple.

There are thus hosts of minor discrepancies, and two major ones, in the resurrection narratives of the four Gospels. The major ones are: first, Mark implies, while Matthew and John 21 state, that the appearances are located in Galilee but, in Luke and John 20, the appearances take place in Jerusalem. Second, in Matthew and in John 21 (and perhaps also by implication in Mark), the appearances seem to be manifestations of an already risen and ascended One and of a more "spiritual" kind, whereas the appearance to the women on the way from the tomb in Matthew, the Lucan Emmaus story, and the Christophany to the eleven in Luke and in John 20 are of a risen but not yet ascended Lord whose corporal manifestation is emphasized (he is touched and he eats). John throws the picture into further confusion by implying that the ascension took place between the appearance to Mary Magdalene and the encounter with Thomas. Yet Thomas is invited to touch him. One would expect touching to be characteristic of the preascension Christophanies, as in Luke, but John has a different view. For him Christ apparently ascends between the appearance to Mary Magdalene and the appearance to the disciples a week later.

It is no wonder that many have found these discrepancies a major obstacle to belief in the resurrection. In his autobiographical novel *The Way of All Flesh*, the Victorian novelist Samuel Butler tells us that it was precisely through the discovery of these discrepancies that his hero, a clergyman's son (in reality, Butler himself), lost his Christian faith and became an agnostic. More recently, the late Bishop James A. Pike confessed that the same "discovery" led to his abandonment of the orthodox Chris-

tian belief in Christ's resurrection.[3] Perhaps, however, it is the scientific, philosophical, and theological objections to belief in the
resurrection that loom larger today. Not only is the assertion
of the resuscitation of a corpse incredible, as Bultmann pointed
out, but still more pressing is the question, So what? Suppose a
first-century Jewish prophet did in fact, incredible though it
may seem, rise from his grave. What difference can that make
to my existence, or to the social, political, and environmental
problems of contemporary man? Is it possible to retrieve something out of the debris of New Testament Christianity which can
be both credible and relevant to modern life? If so, would not
the resurrection of Jesus have to go or, at least, have to be
reduced to a mere symbol for some other idea more acceptable
to the contemporary world, such as Albert Schweitzer's "rever-
ence for life"? Or was the apostle Paul right when he said, "If
Christ be not risen, then is your faith in vain" (1 Cor. 15:17)?
It is the task of the systematic theologian to wrestle with the
scientific, philosophical, and theological problems posed by the
New Testament message of Christ's resurrection, but it is the
task of the New Testament scholar to probe the historical basis
of this proclamation. This is a preliminary task which must be
undertaken before the scientific, philosophical, and theological
questions of the contemporary church and world—with regard
to the Easter faith—can be broached. It is this task which the
present work has set itself—a critical study of the resurrection
narratives.

Such a work has not been undertaken in the English-speaking
world for over a generation. The only books written in English
on this subject in the present century are those by Kirsopp Lake
and P. Gardner-Smith.[4] These books use the tools of source
criticism alone. Much has happened in the critical study of the
Gospels since that time. Although the pioneering works in form
criticism had already been written when Gardner-Smith published
his book, they had not yet been assimilated in English-speaking
scholarship. Since then form criticism has matured into the
broader discipline of traditio-historical criticism and can be used
with far greater assurance as a tool to reconstruct the history

of the Gospel traditions. And during the last decade or so the development of redaction criticism offers, in conjunction with source and tradition criticism, the tools for defining the theology of the evangelists by exposing their treatment of the traditions that came down to them. As a result the creativity of both the community and the Evangelists is now being given equal weight in the history of tradition. The time is therefore ripe for a re-examination of the resurrection narratives with the use of the new critical tools that were not available to Lake or Gardner-Smith.

Some years later than Gardner-Smith, M. Goguel published a study of the resurrection narratives.[5] This work, though rather neglected by present-day scholars, is still of considerable value. It uses insights both of earlier form criticism and of the history of religions. It also includes consideration of the resurrection narratives in the apocryphal Gospels, an aspect of the subject which should not be neglected, as well as the question of possible resurrection narratives retrojected into the earthly ministry of Jesus. However, even Goguel antedates the later developments of traditio-historical and redaction criticism.

Many essays on the resurrection, using the newer methods, have appeared in German,[6] and one complete study of the resurrection narratives.[7] The present work takes note of these German contributions. It is often indebted to them, yet at the same time follows its own independent line on certain major issues, notably on the place of the empty tomb in the history of the tradition.

Our plan is to start with the earliest record of the Easter traditions, in 1 Corinthians 15, and then to apply the tools of tradition and redaction criticism to the Easter narratives of the four Gospels. In doing so our purpose will be to reconstruct the history of the tradition from its earliest recoverable form in allegedly factual reports (beyond this the historian cannot go) through its successive developments in the preliterary and literary stages. In the process we shall seek to lay bare the motivations behind the developments and shaping of the narratives into their final form. By this method we shall hope, not to smooth away the discrepancies and iron out the inconsistencies, but to discover the reasons which gave rise to them and perhaps more importantly the secret of that artless indifference of the New Testament writers which allowed these to stand side by side.

The result of these investigations should have an important bearing on Christian faith, for resurrection faith then becomes not a matter of believing in the historical accuracy of these narratives but of believing the proclamation which these narratives, for all their differences, enshrine. A final chapter will therefore discuss what New Testament belief in the resurrection really involves, what faith the resurrection narratives proclaim, and how the Easter pericopes can be used in preaching today.

CHAPTER TWO

The Earliest Easter Traditions

THE RESURRECTION NARRATIVES of the Gospels are by no means the earliest tradition of the Easter events which we have in the New Testament. Writing in the middle of the first century A.D. to the Christian community at Corinth, Paul reminds the Corinthians of the traditions which he had delivered to them when he had established the community there in A.D. 49–51:

³For I delivered to you as of first importance what I also received, that Christ died for our sins in accordance with the scriptures, ⁴that he was buried, that he was raised on the third day in accordance with the scriptures, ⁵and that he appeared to Cephas, then to the twelve. ⁶Then he appeared to more than five hundred brethren at one time, most of whom are still alive, though some have fallen asleep. ⁷Then he appeared to James, then to all the apostles. ⁸Last of all, as to one untimely born, he appeared also to me.   (1 Cor. 15:3–8)

It is almost universally agreed today that Paul is here citing tradition. He did not compose this passage either at Corinth for the occasion or prior to his visit there. He had, he says, "received" it from others who were Christians before him. This was established first by the presence of non-Pauline words and phrases in the passage,[1] and secondly by the words "I received" and "I delivered" (*parelabon* and *paredōka*, which are the Greek equivalents of the technical rabbinic terms *qibbel min* and *masar le*).[2]

At this point, however, agreement stops. There are other unsolved questions about the formula: (1) when and where did Paul receive it? (2) how much of the material in verses 5–8 belongs to the original formula and how much has Paul subsequently added? (3) is it one formula or a combination of a plurality of formulae?

Paul could have received the formula at any time or place between his conversion near Damascus (Gal. 1:17; cf. Acts 9:3; 22:5; 26:12) and his arrival in Corinth *ca.* A.D. 49. The most favored possibilities are at Antioch before A.D. 50 or at Damascus before A.D. 40.[3] Another possibility is at Jerusalem *ca.* A.D. 36, at the time of Paul's first postconversion visit (Gal. 1:18f.). Indeed, it is hardly conceivable that he should have received the formula any later than this, for it contains the names of the two leaders, Cephas (Peter) and James, whom he saw on that visit. The real question is whether the formula is the product of Hellenistic Christianity or of the earliest Aramaic-speaking community. In favor of an Aramaic origin, J. Jeremias has produced a series of arguments[4] from the style and language of the formula, which, he claims, point to an Aramaic origin.

His arguments have provoked a debate in which P. Vielhauer[5] and H. Conzelmann[6] have sought to rule out the arguments for Semitisms. Jeremias has replied with a defense of his original position.[7] The upshot of the argument seems to be that while the alleged Semitisms *could* be Semitisms, they are not necessarily so. They are equally explicable as "Septuagintalisms." Moreover, Jeremias himself has been unable to come up with a Semitic equivalent of *kata tas graphas* ("according to the scriptures"), a turn of phrase which, it appears, is possible only in Greek. The safest conclusion for the moment seems to be that the tradition as Paul received it was originally Palestinian, but that it has subsequently passed through a Hellenistic Jewish milieu, and that it was this Hellenized form that Paul received. Although Hellenized, the content of the formula is certainly Palestinian in origin. It was in that milieu that the title "Christos" was first associated with the passion.[8] It was there, too, that the atoning interpretation of Christ's death was first developed (Mark 10:45; 14:24). It was there that the statement about Christ's burial is most likely to have originated. It was there apparently that the resurrection of the Christ was first proclaimed. It was there that the apologetic which asserted that Christ's death took place in fulfillment of scripture originated, and it was with Palestine—specifically with Jerusalem—that Cephas, the Twelve, and James were associated. While Paul probably received the formula, or much of it at least, from the Hellenistic Christian community at Damascus, it represents a Hellenized form of a tradition whose substance goes back to the earliest Aramaic-speaking church.

Thus far we have been assuming that it was a single formula which Paul received. There are further problems. If it was a single formula, how far did it extend? Or do we have here a plurality of formulae which have been combined in some stage of the history of the tradition?

It is obvious that Paul would not have "received" from others the tradition of the appearance to himself (v.8). This passage, if nothing else, is clearly a Pauline addition to the traditional material. The same must be true of the note which states that the majority of the five hundred were still alive, though some had died (v.6b). This looks like a comment added by Paul when writing to the Corinthians. It speaks of the situation as it was, not when Paul received the formula, but as it was at the time when he wrote 1 Corinthians.[9] We are left with 1 Corinthians 3b–6a and 7 as the original pre-Pauline tradition.

But was this a single formula? In a celebrated article A. von Harnack[10] called attention to the parallelism between two parts of the tradition:

I	II
he appeared to Cephas, then (*eita*) to the twelve	he appeared to James, then (*eita*) to all the apostles

and suggested that we have here two competing lists of appearances. These lists came into being, suggested Harnack, from the (alleged) rivalry between the Peter-party and the James-party in the early Jerusalem community. The earliest formula therefore, according to Harnack, must have run from verses 3b through 5 and comprised the statements about the death, burial, and resurrection, and the appearances to Cephas and to the Twelve. Prior to Paul, the appearance to the five hundred and the alternative list of primary appearances headed by James would also have been added. Harnack's reconstruction of the earliest tradition has found wide acceptance, at least in Germany, even from those who would reject his particular theory of rivalry between the two parties.[11] There are, however, several difficulties in this reconstruction. First, the appearances to Cephas and the Twelve are tacked on to statements about the death, burial, and resurrection but the appearances to James and to all the apostles, if they existed separately, are left dangling on their own without any prior mention of the death, burial, and resurrection. The parallelism is not complete.

Second, on Harnack's analysis, the appearance to the five hundred is left in isolation, belonging neither to the Cephas formula nor to the James formula. In either position it would destroy the parallelism between the two formulae and can only be explained either as an independent tradition or as a Pauline insertion. Third, the theory of an outright rivalry between a Peter- and a James-party is speculative. There is no real evidence for this in the New Testament. Galatians 2:11 shows that there were for a time differences between Peter and James on the interpretation of the "gentlemen's agreement" (Gal. 2:9–10), but to speak of a rivalry goes beyond the facts. There is, it is true (and this is the abiding worth of Harnack's analysis), a parallelism between the formulae "Cephas—the Twelve" and "James—all the apostles" which requires some explanation, though it cannot be explained satisfactorily in terms of the rivalry theory. Finally, it is clear

from the careful use of chronological adverbs, *eita . . . epeita
. . . epeita . . . eita* (then . . . then . . . then . . . then), that
the formula intends to give the appearances in chronological
succession: the appearances to James and all the apostles occurred after those to Cephas, the Twelve, and the +500,[12] but
in strict succession. And it is clear, from the way that he introduces the appearance to himself: "last of all" (v.8), that Paul
himself also understood the formula in a chronological sense.

The first important breach in the Harnackian "consensus" occurred when E. Bammel offered an alternative analysis, dividing
the tradition of 1 Corinthians 15:3ff. into three (rather than
two) formulae:[13] (1) Christ died—was buried—was raised—
appeared; (2) (he appeared) to Cephas and the Twelve; (3) he
appeared to James and all the apostles. In formula 1, Bammel,
like Jeremias, saw a *parallelismus membrorum.* The two other
formulae represented for Bammel, as for Harnack, two *alternative* lists of the same primary appearances. The major problem
in this analysis is the overlapping of formulae 1 and 2. As will
be observed from the above summary, the word "appeared"
(*ōphthē*) has to do double duty, serving both as the conclusion
of the first and as the beginning of the second formula. Either
formula 1 must have lost its conclusion or formula 2 its introduction. The alleged poetical character (*parallelismus membrorum*)
is also open to question, as is the thesis of two *alternative* lists of
appearances. Nevertheless, Bammel was on the right lines when
he sought a plurality of traditions behind 1 Corinthians 15:3–7.

Any cogent analysis of this text must do justice to the peculiar
grammatical features of the passage. Here the recent analysis
of U. Wilckens[14] is by far the most convincing. He draws particular attention to the curious repetition of the particle *hoti*
(that). This word is repeated four times: before each of the
statements about the death, burial, resurrection, and the appearances. Most previous scholars had been content with E. Norden's
explanation[15] that the repeated *hoti* is characteristic of credal
formulae. The only example of such credal use that Norden gave
was 1 Thessalonians 4:13–17, containing three occurrences of
hoti. But, as Wilckens has pointed out, this passage combines

three quite separate elements: a credal formula in 4:13, a dominical logion in 4:15, and an apocalyptic elaboration on the logion
in 4:16. *Hoti* is used in 1 Thessalonians 4:13ff. and therefore in
1 Corinthians 15:3ff. to combine *different* traditions, and serves
the same function as the modern use of quotation marks (cf.
hoti recitative in the Gospels). From this it would seem to follow
that we have in 1 Corinthians 15:3ff. a combination of at least
four different traditions, each introduced by its own *hoti*—

Formula I: "Christ died for our sins in accordance with the
scriptures."

Formula II: "He was buried."

Formula III: "He was raised the third day in accordance
with the scriptures."

Formula IV: A list of appearances.

If we accept this analysis, it will reopen several questions.
First, the question of provenance. If the tradition represents a
combination of four formulae, it is not necessary to suppose that
all should have been derived by Paul from a single source. The
first three formulae are of a different character from the fourth.
They are summaries of three basic incidents in the event of
salvation: "he died," "he was buried," and "he was raised,"
whereas the fourth formula is a list of appearances which vali-
dates the last of the three statements, rather than an event of
salvation in its own right. Since the basic kerygmatic materials
are composed in a Semitized Greek, explicable either as translation from Hebrew/Aramaic or influenced by the Septuagint
(though, as we have noted, one phrase "in accordance with the
scriptures" has apparently no Hebrew or Aramaic equivalent),
we are directed for their provenance toward a Hellenistic Jewish
community in close touch with Palestine and, therefore, as the
first community with which Paul came into contact, to Damascus.
The appearance formula, on the other hand, containing as it does
the two names Cephas and James, whom Paul contacted on his
visit to Jerusalem two or three years after his conversion, would
be just the kind of information he would have received on that
occasion.

Let us now examine each of the four formulae in turn.

Formula I: The death (1 Cor. 15:3b)

The formula "Christ died for our sins in accordance with the scriptures," taken by itself, is a summary of the passion tradition. It states not merely the fact of the Messiah's death, but also its theological significance. This is expressed in two phrases:

  a. for our sins
  b. according to the scriptures.

That Christ died according to the scriptures is the principal motif of the primitive passion narrative[16] which appears to underlie the three passion narratives of the Gospels, the Marcan-Matthean, the Lucan, and the Johannine. That Christ died "for our sins," however, is a motif absent from this primitive passion narrative. It is found first in the Marcan eucharistic tradition (Mark 14:24; cf. Mark 10:45b, which probably also has liturgical associations).[17] In the two Marcan passages, the reference to the "many" seems to be a clear allusion to Isaiah 53.[18] It is less clear that "for our sins" in 1 Corinthians 15:3b is based on Isaiah 53, and more likely that it is from the somewhat earlier interpretation of the death of Jesus in terms of the post-Maccabean concept of the atoning value of the death of martyrs.[19] These considerations suggest that the phrase "in accordance with the scriptures" should be taken, not with the phrase "for our sins," but primarily with "died." This formula will, therefore, antedate the attempt to discover Old Testament prophecies of the *atoning* significance of the Messiah's death, a consideration which will be important for the interpretation of the resurrection formula in verse 4b.

Formula II: The burial (1 Cor. 15:4a)

There has been much discussion about the place and function of the statement "he was buried" within the kerygmatic formula. Should it be taken closely with the previous statement "he died," as in the common phrase, "he died and was buried"? If so, its function would be to underline the conclusive reality of Jesus' death.[20] Or should it on the other hand be taken closely with the following statement "he was raised"? In this case its function would be to imply the empty tomb.[21]

Now it must be noted that the phrase "he was buried" occurs within its own *hoti* clause and must be taken therefore as an independent statement standing on its own and summarizing an earlier form of the burial pericope found in a later and developed form in Mark 15:42–46. The history of the burial tradition will be investigated in the next chapter. All that is relevant for us to notice at present is that it cannot be used to imply a knowledge by Paul or by the pre-Pauline tradition of the story of the empty tomb.

There is no evidence that the reality of Jesus' death was ever doubted in the early years after the event. It is noteworthy that, when Jewish tradition resorts to counterpropaganda against the Christian claim of the empty tomb, it replies by the thesis of the theft of the body (Matt. 27:64; 28:13–14), not by the thesis that Jesus has not really died. The thesis of the nondeath of Jesus arose later in docetic circles, and the only possible New Testament allusion to it is in I John 5:6, with its insistence that Jesus came "by blood" as well as "by water," i.e., he underwent a real death as well as a baptism.[22] The tradition of the burial antedates all such notions. For the significance of the burial we must look elsewhere.

Formula III: The resurrection (1 Cor. 15:4b)

Whereas formulae I and II appear to be summaries of other material, the statement about the resurrection cannot be, for never in the New Testament is there any actual narrative of the resurrection as such, only of its accompanying phenomena: the empty tomb and the appearances. In the early community the resurrection was not narrated, but proclaimed (e.g., 1 Thess. 1:10). In the Gospel tradition, similarly, statements of the resurrection occur, not in narrative form, but in predictions (e.g., Mark 8:31), in the angelic announcement at the tomb (e.g., Mark

16:6), and in the report of the eleven to the Emmaus disciples (Luke 24:34). Formula III must therefore be a summary of the resurrection kerygma.

The verb *egēgertai*, "was raised," is a reverential passive, denoting an interventive act of God: *God* raised Jesus (cf. *ēgerthē* in Mark 16:6; Luke 24:34). This language of God's "raising" the dead is the language of the Jewish apocalyptic, which occurs in the following Old Testament passages:

Thy dead shall live, their bodies shall rise (*yeqûmûn*, LXX *anastēsontai*),

O dwellers in the dust, awake (*haqîsû*, LXX *egerthēsontai*). (Isa. 26:19)

And many of those who sleep in the dust of the earth shall awake (*yaqîmû*, LXX *anastēsontai*). (Dan. 12:2)

The righteous will arise from sleep. (En. 92:3)

It is to be noted, first, that there is no essential difference between the intransitive ("will arise") and the passive ("will be raised") forms. This is clear from the LXX version of Isaiah 26:19 where the two forms occur in synonymous parallelism. A second point to be noted is that this resurrection is conceived as a resurrection from the grave, as the reference to the "dust of the earth" in the Daniel passage shows. This point is more explicitly stated in a fragment of early Christian, perhaps even of pre-Christian Jewish, apocalyptic which has survived in John 5:28:

All who are in the tombs
will hear his voice
and come forth.[23]

The language of "rising" or "being raised" is derived from the daily experience of awakening from sleep. In these apocalyptic contexts, however, it is used to indicate a transition from one mode of existence (existence in this age) to another (existence in the age to come). This is important. Resurrection, in these apocalyptic contexts, is not a restoration to the former mode of existence nor a mere prolongation of the former mode of existence. This difference in the mode of the risen existence is indicated pictorially:

And those who are wise shall shine like the brightness of the firma-
ment; and those who turn many to righteousness, like the stars for
ever and ever.   (Dan. 12:3)

A similar conception is presupposed in Enoch 51.

Thus the synoptic tradition follows the pattern of the apocalyptic
hope when it ascribes to Jesus in the pericope of the Sadducees'
question the words:

For when they rise from the dead, they neither marry nor are given
in marriage, but are like angels in heaven.   (Mark 12:25 par.)

The apocalyptic resurrection hope was not, as has frequently
been alleged, a purely this-worldly materialistic hope of the
resuscitation of corpses, but the hope of the raising of the dead
to a new, utterly transformed existence. When the kerygmatic
summary of 1 Corinthians 15:4b asserted that Jesus "was raised"
it therefore means, not that his body was resuscitated, but that
his whole self in his entire psychosomatic existence was transformed and entered thereby into the eschatological existence.[24]
    Christ's resurrection depends—at least so far as language in
which it is expressed is concerned—on the validity of the apocalyptic hope. This explains Paul's surprising statement:

But if there is no resurrection of the dead, then Christ has not been
raised.   (1 Cor. 15:13)

We should have expected him to put it the other way round
and to say that "if Christ has not been raised from the dead, there
is no resurrection of the dead," which is what he does say in
the next verse (v.14). His point in verse 13 is that the very possibility of Christ's resurrection depends on the abstract validity of
the apocalyptic hope that there will be such a resurrection. The
apocalyptic hope provides the cultural and linguistic context in
which the resurrection of Christ could be proclaimed in the
kerygma of the early Christian community.
    Paul's interpretation of the resurrection of the faithful, which
is expounded on the basis of the kerygmatic assertion of the resurrection of Christ, shows that he clearly understood the Christ

not to have been resuscitated in his old bodily existence, but to have been raised to the wholly new mode of eschatological existence. In the ensuing argument (1 Cor. 15:12–50) he is combatting the Corinthian gnostics who asserted that the believers were raised already, and that there was therefore no further need of a future eschatological resurrection.[25] The presupposition of Paul's argument is that there is a constitutive and organic relationship between the resurrection and the future resurrection of the believers. The two are inseparably linked (vv.12,13,16). Christ's resurrection was the beginning of the eschatological process of resurrection. He is raised from the dead as the "first fruits of those who have fallen asleep" (v.20). When, therefore, Paul goes on to define the nature of the resurrected existence, what he says about it will apply equally to Christ:

> What is sown is perishable,
>   what is raised is imperishable.
> It is sown in dishonor,
>   it is raised in glory.
> It is sown in weakness,
>   it is raised in power.
> It is sown a physical body,
>   it is raised a spiritual body.
>   (1 Cor. 15:42–44b)

and again:

> We shall not all sleep,
>   but we shall all be changed. . . .
> the dead will be raised imperishable,
>   and we shall be changed.
>   (1 Cor. 15:51,52)

It is at first sight a little curious that Paul does not begin his argument by asserting the transformation of the old bodily existence of Jesus into the new bodily existence of the eschatological order, and then inferring from Christ's resurrection that the resurrection of the believers will be of the same order, namely, a bodily transformation. Instead, he argues (vv.35–41) from natural analogies (the sowing of seed and the various types of "bodies") and then quotes the traditional language of apocalyptic (vv.51–55). On these grounds it has been argued by H. Grass[26] that since Paul does not draw any analogy from Christ's resurrection to the resurrection of the believers, we cannot draw any inferences for the resurrection of Christ from what Paul says about the resurrection of the believers. Paul's actual conception of the resurrection of Christ, Grass goes on to argue, is rather to be seen from 2 Corinthians 5:1ff., according to which we have a body awaiting us in heaven, a body in total discontinuity with our present bodily existence. Hence (Grass concludes) for Paul, Christ's new postresurrection bodily existence was not a transformation of the old bodily existence (for neither the pre-Pauline tradition of 1 Corinthians 15:1–8 nor Paul himself knew anything of the empty tomb), but a wholly discontinuous new bodily existence awaiting him in heaven, as in 2 Corinthians 5:1.

Against this we must assert:

1. Grass's interpretation of 2 Corinthians 5:1ff. is itself highly problematical. Some think that the exegesis of 2 Corinthians 5:1ff. should rather be conformed to that of 1 Corinthians 15.[27] Others hold that, between 1 and 2 Corinthians, Paul changed his mind (or developed his thought) in a Platonic direction.[28] In any case, it seems more natural to interpret the statement about Christ's resurrection in 1 Corinthians 15:4b in the light of the argument in verses 35ff., since the latter passage occurs in the same chapter, and was written at the same time, rather than in the light of 2 Corinthians 5:1, which was written later than 1 Corinthians 15:4b.

The Achilles' heel of Grass's thesis is of course Philippians 3:21, where Paul argues directly from the resurrection body of Christ to the future resurrection body of the believers: "who will change our lowly body to be like his glorious body." This clearly indicates that, for Paul, Christ's glorious body was a transformation of his lowly body. An analogy between Christ's resurrection and the future resurrection of the believers is similarly, though less clearly, drawn in Romans 8:11: "If the Spirit of him who raised Jesus from the dead dwells in you, he who raised Jesus Christ from the dead will give life to your mortal bodies also through his Spirit which dwells in you." The same conception seems also to be presupposed in Paul's baptismal exhortation in Romans 6:4: "We were buried therefore with him by baptism into death, so that as Christ was raised from the dead by the glory of the Father, we too might walk in newness of life" (cf. Col. 2:12). It is the "Spirit" or the "glory" of God that transforms the lowly body of Christ and of the believers. Since the Romans passage was written later than 2 Corinthians 5 and exhibits the same conception as 1 Corinthians 15, it would seem reasonable to interpret the former passage in accordance with 1 Corinthians 15, as Goudge does. Why then did Paul not argue in 1 Corinthians 15:35ff. from the resurrection of the Christ to the resurrection of the believers? Perhaps the answer is that he interpreted both the resurrection of Christ and the resurrection of the believers in terms of the apocalyptic hope, and that his argument in 1 Corinthians 15:35ff. is an argument for the correctness of the apocalyptic hope. If so, we may conclude that "he was raised," in 1 Corinthians 15:4b, was interpreted both by Paul and by the pre-Pauline tradition in the sense of a transformation into a new mode of existence, exactly in the way in which it was understood in the apocalyptic texts which we have already cited. That there should have been this continuity of perspective from the Book of Daniel through the later Pauline writings should occasion no surprise.

In the argument which follows 1 Corinthians 15:1–11 Paul says that Christ was raised as the "first fruits of those who have fallen asleep" (1 Cor. 15:20). By this he means more than the fact that Christ was the first instance of eschatological resurrection (though he does mean that too, as our argument from the nature of the apocalyptic hope of the resurrection from the dead to the nature of the Christ's resurrection has throughout presumed). As he makes clear in the Adam/Christ typology in verses 45–49, Christ's resurrection was also the determinative resurrection, just as Adam's disobedience was determinative. He was not only the first to make the eschatological breakthrough; his breakthrough made it possible for the elect later to follow him. In other words, Christ's resurrection also differed from the later resurrections which were to occur in the general resurrection in that it had an exclusive, christological-soteriological significance. From all that we know of the most primitive stratum of early Christianity, the same belief was present from the outset. It was expressed by the use of christological titles dating from the resurrection. In the most primitive Christology of all[29] this was expressed by the identification of the Risen One with the coming Son of man. At a slightly later (Hellenistic Jewish) stage, the Risen One was identified from the resurrection as the exalted Kyrios (Acts 2:36). Neither title appears in the formula of 1 Corinthians 15:4b. The title Christos was originally attached only to Formula I, the death formula of 1 Corinthians 15:3a. No doubt, by combining the formulae Paul has made Christos the subject of the verb *egēgertai*, "was raised." This would preserve the christological interpretation of the resurrection, despite the fact that neither title, "Son of man" or *kyrios*, is used. We may assume that this christological understanding of *egēgertai* ("he was raised") was already present in Formula III when it existed separately prior to the Pauline combination.

There has been much discussion as to whether "he was raised" is a "historical" assertion, that is, whether the resurrection was a "historical" event. If our interpretation of *egēgertai* as the fulfillment of the apocalyptic hope is correct, then the resurrection is an event which occurs precisely at the *end* of history, at the point where history comes to an end, at the point of exit from history. This is why the resurrection itself was not accessible to witnesses. For such witnesses would have still been standing within history, and that which is at the end of history is not open to direct observation. That too is why the resurrection as such cannot be narrated but only proclaimed. If it were narrated, it could be narrated only as a this-worldly historical event (e.g., as a legend or as an otherworldly, supernatural event, i.e., as a myth). Instead, the New Testament, at least in its earlier strata— for Matthew's narrative additions to the empty tomb pericope, see below, pp. 74–77—is content simply to affirm the resurrection kerygmatically. This is why, against both traditional conservativism[30] and against the more sophisticated assertions of the Pannenberg school[31] that the resurrection itself was a "historical" event, we must assert its meta-historical character.

By this we do not mean to suggest that nothing transpired between God and Jesus,[32] but rather that what took place between God and Jesus took place at the boundary between history and meta-history, between this age and the age to come. As such, the resurrection leaves only a negative mark within history: "he is not here" (Mark 16:6). The positive aspect, "he was raised," is not an event within history, but an event beginning at the end of history, and extending into the beyond-history. It is an event which can be known, not by direct observation, but only, as we shall see, by indirect revelatory disclosure within history.

The precise function of the phrase "on the third day" has been much debated. Here are the main possibilities:

First, it refers to something historical. Since the resurrection as such, as we have seen, is not "historical" in the sense that it occurred as an observable event, the phrase "the third day" cannot date the actual resurrection itself chronologically. Conceivably, the negative side of the resurrection itself could have been dated at the point when it became true that "he is not here." But no observer was present at the grave to pinpoint that moment. Consequently, attempts have been made to tie the third day to two events that did occur (or at least that could, in principle, have occurred) within history, namely, to the discovery of the empty tomb (Mark 16:1ff.) or, alternatively, to the first appearance to Peter (Luke 24:34). Each of these has its problems, which will be discussed later. These problems would make a historical reference difficult, if not impossible. A more telling point against a historical interpretation of the "third day" is that it occurs in the third (*egēgertai*) formula, not in the fourth (*ōphthē*) formula. It is tied, therefore, to the meta-historical event, "he was raised," and neither to the discovery of the empty tomb (which is not mentioned) nor to the first appearance (which is mentioned, but in a separate clause). It is arguable, of course, that since the resurrection was itself, from the human perspective, an inference from the discovery of the empty tomb and/or the first appearance, the chronology was similarly an inference, but there is no *a priori* reason why the raising should not have been thought to have "occurred"[33] at any specific point of time after the entombment, if indeed the early Christians would have thought of an eschatological event as datable. These considerations have led to attempts to look for a doctrinal rather than historical origin to the phrase "on the third day." One suggestion which commands fairly wide assent[34] is that it derives from Hosea 6:2:

After two days he will revive us;
     on the third day (LXX: *tē hēmerā tē tritē*, as in 1 Cor. 15:4b)
he will raise us up.

The difficulty with this suggestion is that there is no un-equivocal evidence anywhere for the use of Hosea 6:2 among the *testimonia* or proof texts in the early Christian community.[35] This suggestion would be strengthened if the phrase "in accord-ance with the scriptures" were taken closely with "on the third day." But the same reasons hold good for taking it primarily[36] with the verb as in the death formula (I). That is to say, there is abundant evidence that the resurrection (and exaltation) of Jesus was a subject for scriptural proof, just as his death was. The primary texts which were used in this connection were Psalm 118:22, Psalm 110:1, and Daniel 7:13. It is to such texts as these that the phrase "in accordance with the scriptures" would seem to refer, but none of these texts allude to the third day. For this reason, we are unconvinced by a derivation of the reference to the third day from Hosea 6:2. It has occasionally been proposed as an alternative that the phrase was suggested by the sojourn of Jonah for three days and three nights in the belly of the sea monster, cited as an analogy to the burial and resurrection of Jesus in Matthew 12:40. But there is no indica-tion that the Jonah episode was used as proof text or type of the resurrection prior to this comparatively late date in the growth of the synoptic tradition. And in Matthew 12:40 it is introduced as an attempt to interpret the enigmatic "sign of the prophet Jonah," perhaps an attempt originating with the Evangelist himself.

Not too much should be made of the argument that *graphai* implies a plurality of scriptures, rather than a single scripture passage. For *graphai* was equivalent to our modern use of the word Bible. It means no more than "as it says in the Bible," leaving open the question whether the reference is to one or more passages of scripture.

Occasionally, a cultic origin for the "third day" has been sought: the resurrection was dated on the third day because the Christians met for worship on a Sunday. Now the first implicit allusion we have to Sunday as the Christian day of worship is in 1 Corinthians 16:2, where Paul urges the Corinthian community to lay aside money for his collection for the Jerusalem saints each week on the first day of the week, implying that that was the day of the assembly. In the sub-apostolic age such references become more frequent (e.g., Acts 20:7, a passage which may be derived from the diary of one of Paul's companions, then in Revelation 1:10 and *Didache* 14:1). There is no evidence that Sunday was the day of assembly in primitive Palestinian Judaism, and we may suppose that they met like their fellow-Jews on the sabbath. The Lord's Day appears to be a Hellenistic Christian institution, perhaps originating in Antioch. The reference to the third day in Formula III therefore probably antedates the observance of Sunday as the Christian day of worship, a custom which more likely arose from the tradition of the resurrection on the third day than vice versa.

H. Gunkel proposed a derivation of "on the third day" from the history of religions.[37] According to him, there was a widespread myth, of which there are other hints in the Bible, of a belief in the three days' triumph of evil. Other writers, on dubious evidence, have contended that the myths of dying and rising gods provide some sort of parallel in their references to the interval between the death and the god's return to life.[38] But the parallels are by no means exact, and in any case such material is too remote from the New Testament. The proximate source for New Testament concepts in the history of religion is Judaism. In this area we find a popular idea that the soul finally leaves the body on the third day, and that this is the point at which decomposition sets in. Basing their argument on the use of

Psalm 16:8–11 in Acts 2:25 and 13:35, the advocates of this thesis argue that the third day would be the *terminus ad quem* for a resurrection.[39]

But the use of Psalm 16:8–11 is not attested in any unimpeachably primitive stratum of the New Testament. It does not occur either in the Pauline homologoumena or in the synoptic tradition. Also, in both places in Acts the psalm is quoted in the LXX version, which makes it less likely that Luke is following a tradition going back to the Aramaic. The emphasis on the non-occurrence of decomposition appears to reflect a stage in the history of the tradition when the resurrection was being thought of in terms of a resuscitation rather than of a transformation. All of this suggests that Psalm 16:8–11 came into the testimonial tradition at a later stage.

After examining these possibilities, Goguel proceeds to make a suggestion which has received little attention:

> There are several Talmudic texts (cited by Str.-Bill. I, p. 747) where the idea occurs that the general resurrection will occur three days after the end of the world. This conception, which is not without some analogue and some relationship to the idea of the morning of the third day as a critical moment, receives confirmation from the passage of Hosea which we have quoted [i.e., Hos. 6:2]. We have seen that in the conceptions of primitive Christianity, there is a close and direct relation between the resurrection of the Christ and the general resurrection expected on the last day, a relation which is expressed by the epithet, *prōtotokos tōn nekrōn* (firstborn of the dead) as applied to the Christ (Rom. 8:29; Col. 1:18; Rev. 1:5). . . . In these conditions, it is natural that the resurrection of the Christ was placed in a chronological rapport with his death similar to that which was thought would occur between the end of the world and the general resurrection.[40]

Of course, the Talmudic evidence taken by itself is late, but the Hosea quotation makes it quite possible that we have here a long-standing apocalyptic expectation not otherwise attested. Such a source for the phrase "on the third day" in 1 Corinthians 15:4b would be the natural one to look for, since apocalyptic was the matrix of the earliest Christian kerygma and colors every part of these primitive formulae. If this position is tenable, then we may conclude that "on the third day" is not a chronological datum, but a dogmatic assertion: Christ's resurrection marked the dawn of the end-time, the beginning of the cosmic eschatological process of resurrection.

Formula IV: The appearances (1 Cor. 15:5–7)

The five appearances listed in this formula are to:

Cephas (Peter)

The Twelve

+500

James

All the apostles.

Many, perhaps the majority of German scholars in recent times, have followed Harnack's view that there are two lists here, headed by Peter and James respectively,[41] whether they subscribe to Harnack's rivalry theory or not. It must be agreed that there is a certain parallelism between Cephas–the Twelve, James–all the apostles: in each instance a named figure and prominent leader is followed by a group of unnamed leaders. In addition, the careful use of connecting particles (*eita* "then," and *epeita* "afterward"), unfortunately obscured by RSV which translates them promiscuously by "then," gives the list a definitive articulation:[42]

1. He *appeared* to Cephas, *then* to the Twelve
2. *Afterward* he *appeared* to the +500
3. *Afterward* he *appeared* to James, *then* to all the apostles
4. *Afterward* he *appeared* to me

As the above tables show, the lists use *ōphthē*, "he appeared," with each *group* of appearances (the appearance to the +500 and also the appearance to Paul forming "groups" by themselves).

The second and third "groups" are connected to the preceding "group" with the particle "afterward" (*epeita*), while connection within the groups (in the case of the first and third) is achieved by means of "then" (*eita*). From this, we conclude that the list combines three separate traditions of appearances:

1. Cephas–the Twelve
2. The +500
3. James–all the apostles

to which Paul has added:

4. The appearance to himself.

But (*contra* Harnack) Paul gives no indication that he understands 1 and 3 as rival lists. His use of chronological particles "then," "afterward" indicates that he considers the lists to be following a chronological order. We may reasonably infer that Paul had three separate informants, Peter for the first list, James for the third, and one or more of the +500 for the second. His careful use of chronological particles suggests that he checked the relative order of the series. It may be reasonably supposed he acquired this information when he went up to Jerusalem to enquire (*historēsai*) of Cephas (Gal. 1:18), and when he also saw James (vv.18–19). Interestingly enough, this suggests a solution to the issue debated by Jeremias and Conzelmann as to the provenance of 1 Corinthians 15:3–7: while Formulae I, II and III probably derive from the Hellenistic Jewish Tradition (Damascus), Formula IV derives, somewhat later, from Jerusalem. This would also indicate an entirely different character for Formula IV from that of the first three. Formulae I-III are kerygmatic, cultic and catechetical summaries of traditions which were used in various activities of the primitive communities. Formula IV by contrast consists of individual items of information which Paul collected for himself on his own initiative. From this, an important conclusion emerges. The appearances formed no part of the primitive kerygma or catechesis either in the form of lists or in the form of narratives. The earliest church did not "prove" the reality of the resurrection from the appearances. It simply affirmed it kerygmatically, and asserted its eschatological character by stating that it took place "on the third day" and in fulfillment of the scriptures. Paul, by attaching formula IV to the resurrection Formula III, apparently began the use of the appearances as *evidence* for the resurrection, a procedure he was led to by the attack on his own status as an apostle. Here we touch upon the debate between Barth and Bultmann over the function of the list as witnesses to the appearances in 1 Corinthians 15:5–7. Barth, eager to maintain the supra-historical character of the resurrection, held that Paul could not have intended the list of eye-witnesses to serve as "proof" of the resurrection. As a supra-historical event the resurrection could not be proved.[43] As Barth interprets it, the eye-witnesses are cited to prove that Paul and the other witnesses preached essentially the same gospel message. Bultmann, on the other hand, recognized that Paul intended to "prove" the resurrection, but stigmatized Paul's procedure as "fatal."[44] Paul thus initiated the "fatal" process of historicizing the resurrection, a process which was further developed in the later Easter narratives of the canonical Gospels, and which reached its apogee in the apocryphal Gospels. That Paul intends to cite eye-witnesses for an evidential purpose is clear from his added gloss on the appearance to the +500. If you want to check up on these witnesses, most of them are still alive and you can ask them (v.6b). But they are eye-witnesses, not of the resurrection, but of the visions. They are cited as proof, not for the resurrection itself, but for the appearances. What then is the function of the appearances in the combination of traditional formulae which Paul cites? Why, contrary to the pattern of the earliest forms of the kerygma (e.g., 1 Thess. 1:9), which proclaimed the resurrection but not the appearances, does Paul tack on the appearances? Because—and this is the point at which Barth is right—his primary concern in the immediate context is with the identity of his gospel and that of the earliest disciples (1 Cor. 15:11). This identity substantiates Paul's claim to be as much an apostle as the Jerusalem leaders. Both proclaim a Christ crucified and risen, the inauguration of the eschatological reality. It was in the appearances that both the Jerusalem preachers and Paul himself received the revelation of the death, burial and resurrection as eschatological events. The Corinthian "gnostics," who held that there was no future resurrection for the believers, maintained this was what apostles other than Paul had preached (cf. "I am of Cephas," etc., 1 Cor. 1:12 and also 3:4). The Corinthians interpreted Christ's resurrection not as an anticipation of the future resurrection of the believers at the end, but as the opening up of a new existence into which by baptism they were completely initiated. There was therefore no need for any further future resurrection, no element of "not yet." Against this, Paul recalls the Corinthians to the tradition which he had handed to them, a tradition which was identical with the gospel proclaimed by the earlier apostles, a gospel which placed Christ's resurrection firmly within the eschatological scheme.

THE MEANING OF THE APPEARANCES

The appearances are characterized by the verb *ōphthē*, literally "was seen" (so KJV), but, when used with the dative, "appeared." This is often the meaning of *ōphthē* in the LXX, where it represents the niph'al of *ra'ah* ("see") with *lᵉ* ("to"). In the Old Testament the verb appear is used in connection with appearances of angels, as in Exodus 3:2: "And the angel of the Lord appeared (*ōphthē*) to him [Moses]" at the burning bush. It is used also of theophanies, as in Exodus 6:3: "'I appeared (*ōphthēn*) to Abraham, to Isaac and to Jacob, as God Almighty (*El Shaddai*).'" The emphasis rests on the revelatory initiative of the angel of God, who desires to make himself manifest, not upon the experience of the recipient. Thus the question as to how they see, whether with the physical eye or with the eye of the mind or the spirit, is left entirely undetermined and unemphasized;[45] it lies entirely outside the horizon of interest. W. Michaelis notes that such appearances frequently introduce verbal communications in such statements as "Yahweh appeared to him . . . and said to him," followed by a statement giving the content of the verbal communication (e.g., Gen. 12:7). What is seen and what is heard can only be described as "revelation." These are disclosures not of something which is visible or discernible within this world or age by ordinary sight or insight: they are disclosures that come from "heaven above" to this world, or (as takes place with increasing emphasis in Jewish apocalyptic) from the eschatological future to the present. Such disclosures often include a preview of the end. It is in such a context that we must place the *ōphthē* of 1 Corinthians 15:5–7 (cf. Luke 24:34; Acts 13:31; 9:17; 26:16). They designate not necessarily physical seeing, not necessarily visions in a subjective sense (involving, for example, ecstasy or dreams), but a revelatory self-disclosure or disclosure by God of the eschatologically resurrected Christos.

More light is thrown upon the understanding of these revelations by the passages in Paul where he alludes to his own Damascus road appearance. In 1 Corinthians 9:1, he uses the active word *heōraka* ("I have seen"). This is an ambiguous word, for it could denote physical or ecstatic sight, as well as the reception of a revelation. It emphasizes the subject in an abnormal way. Indeed, it may be characterized as Paul's "lowest" statement about his Damascus road experience. Michaelis suggested that the reason for this "low" statement is purely stylistic: the subject of the two previous questions is Paul himself and so the clause about Paul's resurrection appearance must have the same subject. More significant is the reference in Galatians 1:16, "[God] was pleased to reveal his Son to me." This confirms what we have already said about *ōphthē*, namely, the emphasis is on the transcendent subject, whether it be God, an angel, or, as in 1 Corinthians 15:5–7, the risen Christ, rather than upon the experience of the recipient. By his use of the verb *apokalyptein* Paul brings out what we have already suspected with regard to *ōphthē*, namely, it is to be interpreted in an eschatological-apocalyptic_sense. It is such a disclosure, not so much "from heaven above" as from the eschatological future. God reveals his Son as the One who has been raised in order that he may later appear as eschatological regent. Thus *ōphthē*, interpreted by *apokalyptein*, includes the thought, not only that the resurrection of Christ is revealed in the resurrection appearances (we may argue from the appearance to Paul to the earlier appearances, since he arranges them in a continuous series), but that these appearances also disclosed that the future general resurrection would occur through Christ. In this way the argumentation of 1 Corinthians 15:22ff. will be seen to draw out the implication of the *ōphthē* of 1 Corinthians 15:5–7.

THE NATURE OF THE APPEARANCES

The word *ōphthē* suggests a vision. Yet Paul never calls his Damascus experience a vision (*horama* or *optasia*; for the latter cf. 2 Cor. 12:1). He distinguishes it clearly from the kind of visionary experience to which he alludes in 2 Corinthians 12:2–4. This experience was ecstatic as he shows by the phrases "caught up to the third heaven," "out of the body" and "caught up into Paradise." Here the emphasis is on the side of the recipient, on *his* experiences, even though Paul refuses to enlarge upon them. The fact is he is here adopting the subjective language of his syncretistic opponents.[46] The language of the resurrection appearances, on the other hand, as we have seen, accentuates not the experience of the recipient, but the revelatory action of Christ or God. "I have seen" (1 Cor. 9:1), as we have argued already, is no real exception. This is perhaps why Paul avoids using a noun like *horama* or *optasia* or even the noun *apokalupsis* in reference to them. They are not to be objectified and considered as experiences to be analyzed for their own sake.[47] They can only be described verbally, as acts in which Christ, or God in Christ, acts in self-disclosure. On the whole, the later tradition adheres to this usage. The semitizing verb *ōphthē* continues to be the favorite term in references to the appearances (Luke 24:34; Acts 9:17; 13:31; 26:16). Verbal, rather than nominal, equivalents occur in the later New Testament strata which attempt a more idiomatic Greek: e.g., "he presented himself alive" (Acts 1:3), "God . . . made him manifest" (*emphanē genesthai*, Acts 10:40); and the good Hellenistic verb *phaneroun*, "to manifest," in the reflexive at Pseudo-Mark 16:12,14 and in the passive in

John 21:1 (*bis*). It is remarkable that with all the development of presentation in the resurrection narratives (which we shall examine later) this basic understanding of the Easter experiences as revelatory events remains constant. The only exception to this is the nominal definition of Paul's Damascus encounter as a "vision" (*optasia*) in Acts 26:19. But this single instance is doubtless to be set to the account of the author of Luke-Acts, and represents part of his re-interpretation of the Damascus event so as to downgrade Paul (see below). It is not inconsistent with Luke's preservation elsewhere of the older *ōphthē* terminology, since that also could be interpreted as an ordinary vision (cf. "a vision appeared (*ōphthē*) to Paul in the night," Acts 16:9).

It is, therefore, impossible to categorize the Easter appearances in any available this-worldly language, even in that of religious mysticism. It is not really satisfactory to call them "objective visions," for that introduces a nominal form which the New Testament, apart from the otherwise explicable exception in Acts 26:19, is careful to avoid. The ultimate reason for this difficulty is that there are no categories available for the unprecedented disclosure of the eschatological within history. One may resort to the language of metaphor, myth, legend, mysticism, or to the elaborate, but rather clumsy, device of the messianic secret, as in Mark. All such language is analogical. Language was made for the description of events in this age; the New Testament has the problem of conveying events which belong to the eschatological age, but which are disclosed through this-worldly, historical events. The farthest we can get perhaps is to say that the *events through which* the Easter revelations were conveyed were visionary, but to describe them as visions, even as "objective visions,"[48] is not entirely felicitous. The word vision, at best, denotes the this-worldly event through which the eschatological event is mediated. "Objective" points to the divine act of disclosure mediated by the vision, but does not indicate that what was disclosed was eschatological. Similarly, Selwyn's "veridical" (see last note) suggests the disclosure of timeless truths, rather than of future, eschatological reality. If we speak of the Easter appearances as visions it must be clear that we are speaking only of their this-worldly, historical aspect, of the

medium of the revelation, not of the revelation in its eschatological reality.

THE APPEARANCES TO CEPHAS AND TO THE TWELVE

As we have seen, the appearances to Cephas and to the
Twelve form a closely linked group. A single *ōphthē* ("he appeared") functions for both appearances, and the particle *eita*
("then"), used in verses 5–7 to join two items within a single
group, connects these two appearances. Two main problems call
for discussion. The first is the historical question of the date and
location of these appearances, and the second their theological
significance.

As to the historical question, the particle tells us nothing about
the dating except that the appearance to Cephas was the very
first, and that the appearance to the Twelve took place after the
appearance to Cephas (cf. Mark 16:7; also Luke 24:34, where,
however, the order is disrupted by the prior insertion of the
Emmaus story). We have already rejected the possibility that
"on the third day" reflects the date of the appearance to Cephas,
preferring to interpret that phrase in a theological rather than
chronological sense. To some extent, the dating will depend on
the location. The tradition in 1 Corinthians 15:3 tells us nothing
of this, either. Mark, the next earliest tradition, seems to imply
that the appearance to Peter as well as that to the Twelve, took
place in Galilee (Mark 16:7—for a discussion of this verse, see
below). This, seemingly, involves the assumption that after the
disciples forsook Jesus and fled, they immediately made their way
to Galilee, a view which has been stigmatized by M. Albertz as
a "Legende der Kritik."[49] Even if we assume that the disciples
remained hidden in Jerusalem until after the sabbath, as Mark
seems to suppose, yet according to the earliest available tradition
(Mark) it was in Galilee that the first appearances took place.
If John 16:32 ("The hour is coming, indeed it has come, when
you will be scattered, every man to his home [*ta idia*]") is
derived from the pre-Johannine passion narrative,[50] this would
support the view that after the arrest of Jesus the disciples fled

straight to Galilee, whether they stopped off and rested on the sabbath en route or in their fear ignored the sabbath command and continued their journey. Peter, as indicated by the undoubtedly authentic tradition of the denial, must have detached himself from the main party, fleeing to Galilee some hours later. The appearance to Peter could have taken place before he actually reached Galilee and while he was still in flight.[51] We may conjecture that upon arriving back in Galilee, Peter proceeded to assemble the disciples for the second appearance. Luke contains a hint that this was the procedure: "'When you [singular] have turned again, strengthen your brethren'" (Luke 22:32).

Turning now to the theological significance of the appearance to Peter, we find this indicated by the use of the name Cephas. In the resurrection appearance, Simon Bar-Jonah receives the name Cephas (Aramaic: *kepha*, rock; Greek: *petros*), appointing him to be the foundation upon which the eschatological community is built (Matt. 16:17–19).[52]

Note that in thus interpreting the appearance to Cephas we are still firmly within the eschatological-apocalyptic perspective that is characteristic of the earliest community's interpretation of the Easter events.

Whether or not the Twelve already existed as a body prior to the crucifixion need not now concern us. In any case they now, as a result of the resurrection appearance of which they were the recipients, embark on their eschatological regency, signalized in the words, "You . . . will also sit on twelve thrones, judging the twelve tribes of Israel" (Matt. 19:28).

Once again, we are within the orbit of primitive Christian eschatological-apocalyptic thought. Once again, the establishment of the community is viewed eschatologically. We conclude, therefore, that the appearances to Peter and to the Twelve share a common function. In these appearances the Risen One initiates the foundation of the eschatological community: they are "church-founding appearances." As such they must be distinguished from the later appearances, whose function is the call and sending of apostles to fulfill a mission. This point will be developed below.

THE APPEARANCE TO THE +500

The traditional formula indicates nothing about the significance of this appearance. Previous discussion has revolved around the question whether this appearance is to be equated with the Pentecost narrative in Acts 2:1ff.[53] The usual argument against this identification is that 1 Corinthians 15:6 reports a Christophany, whereas Acts 2:1ff. describes an incident of glossolalia (so e.g., Kümmel). This is certainly true of Acts 2:1ff. as it now stands, but the pericope clearly has a long history behind it. In the Lucan redaction it has been transformed from a genuine description of glossolalia into a description of the eschatological reversal of Babel, or of the reversal of the rejection of the Law at Sinai by the seventy (or seventy-two) nations. Could it not be that, at an earlier stage of the tradition, the pericope narrated an appearance of the Risen One in which he imparted the Spirit to the +500, as in the appearance to the disciples in John 20:19–23? (see below, p. 140). If this is a possibility, then the appearance to the +500 belongs, like the appearances to Cephas and the Twelve, to the church-founding series. It could in that case also be located at Jerusalem like the Pentecost story in Acts. When then is it listed separately from the first two appearances? The answer, perhaps, is that whereas in the first two appearances Peter and the Twelve were chosen to be instrumental in founding the community, it was with the appearance to the +500 that their church-founding function came into operation. The +500 are the first-fruits of the church-founding function of Peter and the Twelve after their return from Galilee to Jerusalem.

THE APPEARANCE TO JAMES

There can be little doubt that this is the James identified by Paul in Galatians 1:19 as the brother of the Lord (cf. 1 Cor. 9:5). Had it been James bar Zebedee, who died an early martyrdom (Acts 12:2; cf. Mark 10:39) at the hands of Herod Agrippa

I, who himself died in A.D. 44, Paul would surely have commented (as he does in the case of the +500) that James had "fallen asleep." James, the son of Alphaeus, mentioned in the lists of the Twelve (Mark 3:18 parr.; Acts 1:13), is so obscure as to be out of the question. This leaves us with James, the brother of the Lord. According to the synoptic (Mark 3:21, 31–4) and the Johannine (John 7:5) traditions, this James had not been a disciple of Jesus during the earthly ministry. As an individual he appears on the scene relatively late in the history of the early community (Acts 12:17; but cf. 1:14), yet soon after he is found playing a leading role (Gal. 2:1–10, 12; cf. Acts 15:13 and 21:18). It might be said that if there were no record of an appearance to James the Lord's brother in the New Testament we should have to invent one in order to account for his post-resurrection conversion and rapid advance.

What is the significance of the appearance to James? That it had a personal meaning to him is obvious, for it betokened his conversion. In this it was like the appearances to Peter, the Twelve and Paul, which also had a personal significance for the recipient: in the case of Peter it was his restoration after his denial (cf. Luke 22:32; John 21:15–17), and in the case of the Twelve it was their acceptance after they had forsaken Jesus at the arrest; in the case of Paul, his conversion from being a persecutor of the church. In all these cases the appearance involved an act of forgiveness. The traditions of 1 Corinthians 15:3–7 and Paul's own statement in verse 8, however, are not primarily concerned with the personal meaning of the appearances, but with their meaning in salvation history. The meaning of the appearance to James seems to be determined by its relation to the appearance to "all the apostles," for it bears a relation to that appearance analogous to the relation of the appearance to Cephas with that of the Twelve.[54] At first sight this is surprising, for we tend to think of James as a stationary figure —the head of the Jerusalem church and first "Bishop of Jerusalem," as he became in later church tradition. The Pauline epistles, and indeed the Book of Acts, give a somewhat different impression. James appears there to have an intimate concern with the missionary outreach of the church. It is James, as well as Cephas, that Paul visits after his conversion (Gal. 1:19). This reference gives the impression that at this time (*ca.* 35), Peter was still the leading figure, since Paul mentions him first and James as an afterthought. But at Paul's second visit for the so-called "apostolic conference" (Gal. 2:1–10), it is James[55] who is mentioned first, followed by Cephas and John. It was James who was in the forefront at the conference, which was concerned with a major problem in the mission of the church. Finally in Galations 2:12, it is James who sends inspectors to the missionary church of Antioch to see how the Gentile Christians are observing the agreement reached at the conference. The same impression is created by the narrative of Acts. Here again, James plays the leading role at the apostolic conference (Acts 15:13ff.), while Paul later reports to him to reassure him about his policies in the Gentile mission (21:18).[56]

Viewed thus, James looks more like the chairman of the Central Board of Missions than the Bishop of Jerusalem. This may explain why the appearance to James heads the group in which the appearance to the "apostles" follow. From this it is evident that the meaning of the appearance to James in salvation history is the inauguration of the mission outside of Jerusalem. This mission was conceived initially as a mission to Israel. It is the mission attested, perhaps, in the saying of Matthew 10:23, and in the missionary charges of the synoptic tradition as a whole, as also in Paul's reference to its failure in Romans 10:21.

Since the result of the appearance to James is that he came to preside over the Jerusalem community and over the mission emanating from Jerusalem, it would be consistent if the appearance itself were located at Jerusalem. It would not, of course, have been impossible for the appearance to have occurred in Galilee, since that was where James had lived previously (Mark 3:31; 6:3; John 7:3). The origin of the tradition, in John 7:8 and 10, that the brothers of Jesus went to Jerusalem when Jesus began his Jerusalem ministry, is highly uncertain. If it has a sound historical basis, it would further support a Jerusalem location of the appearance to James.[57]

THE APPEARANCE TO ALL THE APOSTLES

There has been much discussion as to the identity of "all the apostles." Four positions have been held: (1) that the apostles and the Twelve were identical; (2) that "all the apostles" included the Twelve and others as well; (3) that it included some of the Twelve and others as well; (4) that it included none of the Twelve and was an entirely different group. Let us see whom we can identify as *apostoloi*. Of the Twelve, we know from Paul for certain that Peter was an apostle (Gal. 1:18). The only other member of the original Twelve to be named by Paul is John, whom he includes with Peter (and James) among the "pillars," not as an apostle. The term pillar suggests a complex of ideas[58] associated with the first (church-founding) group of appearances. One would expect Peter and John to be *stuloi*, but not James. From this, we may infer that the term *stulos*, which designated the function of the Twelve and therefore belonged properly to Peter and John, has "rubbed off," as it were, onto James. The second problem about the status of James is whether he should be included among the apostles. The two Pauline passages which associate him with the apostles are both ambiguous:

I saw none of the other apostles except (*ei mē*, but only) James the Lord's brother. (Gal. 1:19)

Do we not have the right to be accompanied by a wife, as the other apostles and the brothers of the Lord and Cephas? (1 Cor. 9:5)

On the whole, there is more to be said for including James and (in the second passage) the brothers of the Lord among the apostles than for excluding them. In Pauline usage, *ei mē*, which occurs in the first passage, normally means "except" rather than "but only" (Gal. 1:7). In the second passage Cephas was certainly an apostle in the eyes of Paul (Gal. 1:18f.), which suggests that we could paraphrase this passage as: "the other apostles, including the brothers of the Lord and Cephas." A further consideration is the parallelism between the two sets of appearances, Peter–the Twelve, and James–all the apostles. Since Peter is included among the Twelve, and therefore was a recipient of the second appearance as well as the first, we may perhaps legitimately infer that James was one of "all the apostles" to whom the fifth appearance occurred.

Although in the account of the apostolic conference Paul seems to subordinate Barnabas to himself (Gal. 2:1, "I with Barnabas") and to avoid including Barnabas in the Jerusalem church's recognition of his (Paul's) own apostolate in 2:8, the wording of 2:9 "gave to me and Barnabas the right hand of fellowship that we should go to the Gentiles" suggests that Barnabas was, in fact, acknowledged by the Jerusalem church as an apostle. In 1 Corinthians 9:5f. Paul similarly associates Barnabas very closely with himself as an apostle, almost suggesting that he was, yet refraining from saying so outright. Perhaps Paul was reluctant to admit this after the fracas at Antioch (Gal. 2:13; cf. Acts 16:39, which also reports their estrangement after the conference, though attributing it to the dissension over Mark). At Acts 14:4,14, inadvertently, in view of his theology of the "Twelve apostles" (unless indeed the author reinterprets "apostle" here in the sense of "apostle of the churches"), Luke has allowed the ascription of "apostle" to both Paul and Barnabas in his source to stand.

In Romans 16:7, Paul refers to Andronicus and Junias as "men of note among the apostles" who were "in Christ before me." Although this may mean that the original apostles had a high regard for these two, it seems more likely that Paul is intimating that they preceded him in the apostleship. There is no question of their being "apostles of the churches" (2 Cor. 8:23) rather than apostles of Jesus Christ, since the latter held only a temporary commission, like the Jewish *shaliach*. Now it is interesting to note that both of these men have Greek names. This suggests that there were Hellenistic Jewish as well as Aramaic-speaking missionary-apostles in the pre-Pauline church. Were these perhaps the missionaries referred to in Acts 11:19, who embarked upon a mission to Hellenistic Jews in Phoenicia, Cyprus and Antioch? Were the seven of Acts 6 originally part of the group consisting of "all the apostles"? If so, we may conclude that there were two groups among the apostles, Aramaic-speaking Jewish Christians and Hellenistic Jewish Christians. This offers us an interpretation of the "all" in the phrase "all the apostles." It includes both groups, the Aramaic-speaking and the Hellenistic Jewish ones, too.

The mission-inaugurating function of the appearances to James and to all the apostles should help us to date them. These appearances clearly occurred prior to Paul's conversion. They must have coincided with the inauguration of both the Aramaic-speaking mission in Palestine and of the Hellenistic Jewish Christian mission in Phoenicia, Cyprus and Antioch. They thus marked the point at which the earliest community began to move outward from Jerusalem. A date halfway between the earliest appearances (Peter, the Twelve and the +500) and the appearance to Paul would be a safe conjecture.

In the appearance to James and to all the apostles we have a second group of appearances whose function is different from that of the first group, those to Peter and the Twelve. Whereas the first group had a church-founding significance, the second had a mission-inaugurating significance. As will be seen later, it is this type of resurrection appearance which became normative for the later appearance narratives (Matt. 28:16–20; Luke 24:47; Acts 1:8; John 20:21; and perhaps John 21:6, for which cf. Luke 5:6–7). This circumstance has given rise to the widespread opinion that the sending of apostles was the one essential feature of all the resurrection appearances listed in 1 Corinthians 15:3ff. Too little attention has been paid to the fact that the appearances to Peter and to the Twelve have a different function, namely that of founding the eschatological community.

Two problems yet remain in connection with the appearance to all the apostles. First, was this a single appearance or a series of appearances? The appearance to the +500 is stated to have occurred "at one time" (verse 6). Since this qualification is not made in connection with the appearance to "all the apostles" it might be argued that it was not necessarily a single appearance to "all the apostles." It may even mean that there was a series of individual appearances to each of the apostles in turn. This is possible but unlikely, since the other appearances listed are either to groups or to named individuals. Since, however, the apostles included both Aramaic-speaking and Hellenistic Jewish missionaries, it is possible that there were two appearances, one to each group. This subject will be taken up further at a later stage (see below, p. 84).

The second problem is the question of the location of the appearance or appearances to all the apostles. Since the early Christian mission emanated from Jerusalem, it is reasonable to suppose that these appearances occurred in that city.

THE APPEARANCE TO PAUL

This is obviously the appearance to Paul which took place in the neighborhood of Damascus (cf. Gal. 1:17, "I returned to Damascus").[59] It is this experience, as we have seen, that Paul refers to elsewhere (Gal. 1:12; 1 Cor. 9:1), in passages which serve to illuminate for us the character of the earlier appearances as eschatological revelation. Here we are concerned with the appearance to Paul for its own sake. Paul says that this was the "last of all" the appearances (*eschaton de pantōn*, v.8). Attempts have been made to prove that Paul was mistaken about this. While it may have been the latest appearance to date, the argument runs, there were others later (e.g., the appearance to John the Seer in Rev. 1:10,12–20). When, however, we consider the salvation-historical significance of the two types of appearances (founding of the eschatological community; inauguration of the Christian mission), any later appearance seems excluded on principle. With the founding of the church at Jerusalem and with the inauguration of the mission to Israel, Aramaic-Palestinian and Hellenistic-Jewish, and finally to the Gentiles (Paul), the post-Easter period of salvation history prior to the parousia has been decisively set in motion. These events complete the *eph' hapax* of the Christ event, to which the appearances belong. There may be future adjustments of salvation history (e.g., the emergence of early catholicism in the sub-apostolic age). However, these do not require a fresh resurrection appearance to set them in motion, since they consist of a response to the revelation that has already occurred. Of course, there can be, and presumably have been, "visions" of the glorified Christ in church history subsequent to Paul's conversion, the latter's own visions included (2 Cor. 12:1ff.), and the vision of the Seer of the Apocalypse. We must therefore conclude that Paul means not only that he knew of no other appearances during the past twenty years or so after his own,[60] but also that any such appearances were ruled out in principle by the proper understanding of salvation history. The next, new salvation-historical event will be the parousia.

Paul goes on to say that the appearance occurred to him as "one untimely born" (RSV). If this is the correct translation, it would reinforce our interpretation of "last of all"—that the appearances were, in principle, long closed when the appearance to Paul occurred. Unfortunately, that is not what the Greek word *ektrōma* means. It cannot mean one born *later* than he should have been, but either one born *earlier* than he should have been (which was not the case with Paul), or a monstrous birth, a deformity. Since this is the only remaining possibility, we should prefer the NEB rendering, "though this birth of mine was monstrous."[61] The use of this word is explained in the clause that immediately follows, which should not be separated (so NEB) by a period from the preceding clause, but by a comma: "This birth of mine was monstrous, for I had persecuted the church of God." Harnack's suggestion that *ektrōma* was a term of abuse directed at Paul by his opponents may be right; at least it has some support from the article before it: they called him not "a" but "the" monstrosity.

The importance of Paul's statement can hardly be overestimated. Here we have a first-hand statement by one who himself was a recipient of an appearance, deliberately placed by him in the series of appearances. What we know of Paul's appearances (enlarged by his other references to it) can be applied, as we have already done, to the interpretation of the earlier appearances. But it is also important to remember that he had been in direct personal contact with at least two of the earlier recipients, Cephas and James. Yet can we get beyond these tantalizingly enigmatic references by Paul himself to the appearances? Can we, for instance, use the three narratives of Paul's conversion in Acts to fill out the statement of 1 Corinthians 15:8? Looking at these three narratives we see that the first of them (Acts 9:1–22) is in the form of a report, while the other two (Acts 22:3–21; 26:1–23) are in what purport to be autobiographical speeches. The older, literary-critical analysis of the interrelation of these three accounts was done by E. Hirsch,[62] who concluded that Acts 26 was closest to Paul's own references in Galatians 1:12,16. This speech occurs in a "we-section," and exhibits the following parallels to Paul's own references:

Acts 26:10,11/Gal. 1:12,13—close connection between the persecution and conversion.

Acts 26:6/Gal. 1:14—emphasis on Paul's Jewish upbringing.

Acts 26:17/Gal. 1:16—the appearance was Paul's call to the apostolate.

Acts 26:18/Gal. 1:16—it was Paul's call to the mission to the Gentiles.

Moreover, in neither Acts 26 nor Galatians 1 (cf. 1 Cor. 15) is there any reference to the part of Ananias as there is in both Acts 9 and 22.

According to Hirsch and others of the pre-form-critical period, the account in Acts 9 is written from the standpoint of the Damascus community, and may therefore be ascribed to a Damascus source. The account in Acts 22 represents the combination of the accounts in Acts 9 and 26 by the author of Acts.

This neat literary analysis was challenged by M. Dibelius in a form-critical analysis of the speeches of Acts.[63] According to Dibelius, the speeches in Acts are deliberate compositions of the author. The differences between the three accounts of Paul's conversion are to be explained from Luke's theological purposes. There is much truth in this contention, but it requires qualification. While the speeches are in the main Lucan compositions, they do employ earlier traditions (e.g., the christological form-

ulae) which are worked into the speeches.[64] While we are prepared to agree that the three accounts of Paul's conversion in
Acts are the compositions of the author, it would seem that he
uses traditional materials. Such materials are identifiable as
those which are in conformity with Paul's own presentation of
his Damascus call in the genuine letters. Material, on the other
hand, which contradicts the evidence of the letters must be
assigned to Lucan composition. That being the case, it would
seem to rule out *a priori* the possibility that Acts could add anything to our knowledge of the circumstances and character of
Paul's call. However, it is worth investigating whether there are
features in the Acts accounts, which, though additional compared with the Pauline information, are not incompatible with
it and which are, on the other hand, immune from any expression of the peculiar *Tendenz* of Luke-Acts.

The basic *Tendenz* of Luke's treatment of Paul in Acts is to
downgrade him. He is not an apostle (despite Acts 14:4,14),
but one who stands in apostolic succession.[65] For Luke, an
apostle must satisfy the strict requirements of Acts 1:21–22, so
that Paul, who did not accompany the earthly Jesus, cannot be
an apostle. Consequently his Damascus experience could not
be for Luke a resurrection appearance or an apostolic call, but
precisely a conversion, a term which Paul never uses when referring to it. For Luke it is merely a post-resurrection vision,
precisely an *optasia* (Acts 26:19). Paul carefully avoids using
this word for it. As we have seen, he admits that he did have
such *optasiai*, but he sharply distinguishes them from his apostolic
call (2 Cor. 12:1ff.). Luke puts the conversion in a series, not
with the earlier resurrection appearances, but with Paul's subsequent visions (Acts 26:16: "the things in which you have seen
me and . . . those in which I will appear to you"). The utmost
Luke can bring himself to call Paul is a "servant and witness"
(*huperētēs* and *martus*, Acts 26:16 NEB; RSV has converted these
nouns into verbs). For Luke, Paul is not an apostle in the full
sense, though something of Paul's original understanding of the
Damascus experience still shines through in the verb "send"
(*apostellō*, Acts 26:17).[66] In this account Luke comes closest to

Paul's understanding of his call. In the other accounts, the call to mission (as distinct from the conversion) is mediated to Paul through Ananias, in flat contradiction to Galatians 1:1 and 12. In Acts 26 it is given to him directly but piecemeal, partly in the conversion vision and partly in subsequent visions (v.16). In Acts 9:17 and 26:16, Luke also preserves the Pauline verb for "appear" (*ōphtheis, ōphthēn*). As we have seen, this word is in itself neutral, and could be used for any visionary experience without necessarily carrying a strongly objective sense as in 1 Corinthians 15:3ff. That Luke understands it in the sense of an ordinary vision is shown by the use of the same verb in reference to Paul's post-conversion vision in Acts 26:16c. Luke also records the outward details of the vision: there was a light (*phōs*, Acts 9:3; 22.6; 26:13; in the last passage the light is stated to have been brighter than the sun). In Acts 9:4; 22:7 and 26:14, a *voice* (*phōnē*) is also audible and in all three accounts the utterance of the voice is given: "Saul, Saul, why do you persecute me?" In each account the voice continues in a self-disclosure of the Risen One: "I am Jesus, whom you are persecuting" (Acts 9:5; 22:8; 26:15). The notorious contradiction over the effect of the incident on Paul's companions (9:7, they heard the voice, saw no one, but remained speechless; 22:9, they saw the light but heard no voice; 26:14, the light had the effect of forcing them to the ground) has often been noted. Less frequently noticed is the common element in all these minor variations: the real meaning of the event is invariably hidden from Paul's companions, a trait which accords with the Pauline interpretation of the event as eschatological revelation. All three accounts, therefore, agree that in the Damascus road encounter there was a visionary element and an auditory element, and that the inner meaning of the encounter was apprehended by Paul alone. It would be safe to infer that these three common elements are pre-Lucan, not redactional.

Let us now compare the three common elements (light, voice, concealment of the encounter from the companions) in turn with the Pauline data.

Paul states that he saw "the Lord," not a light. Yet, without seeming contradiction, the voice in Acts states, "I am Jesus," while in two of the accounts we are told that it was Jesus who appeared (Acts 9:17; 26:16). Paul does not mention the light in the first chapter of Galatians or in 1 Corinthians 15, yet there is another Pauline passage which commentators have referred to the Damascus road experience:[67] "For it is the God who said, 'Let light shine out of darkness,' who has shone in our hearts to give the light of the knowledge of the glory of God in the face of Christ" (2 Cor. 4:6). Grass also compares the reference to the "glory" of the risen body of Christ in 1 Corinthians 15:43 and Philemon 3:21.[68] From this we would suggest, very tentatively, that the form which the self-disclosure of the Risen One took for Paul (and therefore presumably, also for the recipients of appearances prior to him) was the form of a vision of light.

In alluding to his apostolic call in Galatians 1:16, Paul seems to imply that it was not simply a visual experience of some sort, but that it also involved a communication of meaning: God revealed his Son (i.e., Jesus in his eschatological-christological significance) to Paul. God called him to be the apostle of the Gentiles. Paul does indeed speak of an auditory element in his other post-resurrection visions. In them, he heard "things that cannot be told, which man may not utter" (2 Cor. 12:4). However, he did utter, in his christological proclamation and in his assertion of his own apostolate, the meaning conveyed in his apostolic call.

Paul clearly understood that the Damascus encounter was not an ordinary experience capable of ordinary apprehension or neutral observation, but a revelatory event (*apokaluptein*, Gal. 1:15). The extraordinary nature of this encounter still shines through in the stories of his conversion in Acts, in the circumstance that the incident is not fully apprehended by his companions.

We would argue, then, that while Luke regarded the Damascus road experience not as a resurrection encounter (Luke understood resurrection appearances very differently, as we shall see when we come to the Lucan resurrection narratives), he nevertheless left much of the early understanding of the nature of a resurrection appearance undisturbed. Such appearances, we may conclude, involved visionary experiences of light, combined with a communication of meaning. They were not in their innermost essence incidents open to neutral observance or verification, but revelatory events in which the eschatological and christological significance of Jesus was disclosed, and in which the recipient was called to a particular function in salvation history. In the case of the appearances to Cephas and to the Twelve it was a call to be the instruments of the founding of the eschatological community. In the case of the +500 it was the call to be the nucleus of that community. In the case of James it was the call to preside over the church in the second phase of its history, the phase of missionary expansion beyond Jerusalem and its immediate environs. In the case of the "apostles" it was the call to carry out the mission to Israel beyond Judea, both Aramaic- and Greek-speaking. And finally, in the case of Paul, it was to carry that mission to the Gentiles.

The oldest available traditions of the Easter events are to be found not in the stories at the end of the Gospels, but in 1 Corinthians 15:3-8. From this passage we learn that within a few years of the events concerned (within five years at the very latest) the following points were accepted parts of the tradition:

1. The resurrection of Jesus from the dead was the central claim of the church's proclamation. There was no period when this was not so.

2. The resurrection of Jesus was conceived as the first and determinative (and therefore christological) instance of the general resurrection of apocalyptic hope involving translation into an entirely new mode of existence. As such, it was not a "historical," but an eschatological and meta-historical event, occurring precisely at the point where history ends, but leaving its mark on history negatively in the empty tomb ("He is not here") and positively in the appearances.

3. The empty tomb is neither narrated nor proclaimed in this kerygma but a resurrection from the grave is implied by the

statement, "God raised Jesus," since the apocalyptic conception of resurrection is precisely resurrection from the grave.

4. The appearances are best defined theologically as "revelatory encounters." Their outward, historically definable form is a vision (perhaps a vision of "light"), accompanied by an audition (i.e., a communication of meaning). The meaning conveyed is invariably both a disclosure of Jesus as resurrected in the apocalyptic sense of the word, i.e., as translated into eschatological existence, and a call of the recipient to a specific function in salvation history. In the case of the first three appearances (Cephas, the Twelve, and +500), this salvation-historical significance is concerned with the foundation of the church as the eschatological community, while the three later appearances, those to James, to all the apostles and to Paul, are concerned with the inauguration of the apostolic mission of the church beyond Jerusalem and Judea, to the Aramaic-speaking Jews in Palestine, to the Hellenistic Jews in Palestine and in the diaspora and finally to the Gentiles.

5. The appearances occurred over a period of some three years or so, the last and definitive one being that to Paul. As such, they belong to the *eph' hapax* of the Christ event. In the earliest tradition, they are not located geographically. But the appearances to Cephas and to the Twelve probably took place in Galilee, the appearance to the +500 (especially if it is the origin of the later Pentecost story) at Jerusalem, the appearance to James perhaps at Jerusalem (since he is so strongly associated with the leadership of the Jerusalem community subsequent to its initial founding), the appearance to all the apostles at Jerusalem as the center from which the mission radiated, and the appearance to Paul certainly on the Damascus road.

CHAPTER THREE

The Resurrection Narrative
of Mark

Mark 16:1–8

¹And when the sabbath was past, Mary Magdalene, and Mary the mother of James, and Salome, bought spices, so that they might go and anoint him. ²And very early on the first day of the week they went to the tomb when the sun had risen. ³And they were saying to one another, "Who will roll away the stone for us from the door of the tomb?" ⁴And looking up, they saw that the stone was rolled back; for it was very large. ⁵And entering the tomb, they saw a young man sitting on the right side, dressed in a white robe; and they were amazed. ⁶And he said to them, "Do not be amazed; you seek Jesus of Nazareth, who was crucified. He has risen, he is not here; see the place where they laid him. ⁷But go, tell his disciples and Peter that he is going before you to Galilee; there you will see him, as he told you." ⁸And they went out and fled from the tomb; for trembling and astonishment had come upon them; and they said nothing to any one, for they were afraid.

Many objections have been raised against the plausibility of Mark's account of the discovery of the empty tomb on the first Easter morning. In examining these objections we shall begin at the end of the story and work backward.

The pericope ends with the statement that the women said nothing to anyone of what they had seen because they were afraid.[1] This is curiously inconsistent with the previous verse (7) in which the angel[2] had charged the women to tell the disciples and Peter that the Risen One was going before them to Galilee. The contradiction, it has been maintained, not only indicates that verse 7 is a redactional insertion of the Evangelist, but also gives a clue to the history of the tradition: Mark had received a passion narrative which concluded not with a story of the discovery of the empty tomb, but with a narrative of the two first appearances to Peter and the disciples. In order then to accommodate the new empty tomb pericope in his Gospel, Mark composed verse 7.[3] Hence the empty tomb story belongs not to the primitive stratum of the Gospel material, as does the passion narrative, but to a much later stratum. This, it is held, is borne out by other considerations. Some critics[4] (though not all) explain the statement about the silence of the women as a device by which the Evangelist seeks to explain the recent origin of the empty tomb story: nobody had heard about it earlier because of the silence of the women.

The difficulties do not end here. The angelophany is patently a legendary feature, as is the miraculous rolling away of the stone (the passive *anakekulistai*, v.4, is perhaps reverential—it had been rolled away by God or by the angel acting as his agent; cf. Matt. 28:2). The perplexity of the women as to who should roll away the stone is inexplicable as a historical fact: why did they not think of this difficulty earlier? But it is entirely explicable as legendary feature: it heightens the tension and prepares for the astonishing discovery of verse 5. The statement about the motive of the women in verse 1, that they had come to anoint the body of Jesus, presents several difficulties. First, the embalming of bodies was apparently not in accord with contemporary Jewish custom.[5] Second, the completion of the burial rites on a Sunday morning after burial on Friday night is inconceivable in the Palestinian climate, in which decomposition would already have set in (cf. John 11:39). Third, and of decisive importance, the intention of the women to complete the burial rites in 16:1 is inconsistent with the statement in 15:46, according to which Joseph of Arimathea had carefully buried the body, and had apparently done all things required by Jewish law and custom. Finally, the list of the women is doubly curious (16:1). It does not quite tally with the lists in 15:40 and 47 as will be seen from the following table:

15:40	15:47	16:1
1. Mary Magdalene	1. Mary Magdalene	1. Mary Magdalene
2. Mary, mother of James *mikros* and Joses	2. Mary (wife?) of Joses	2. Mary (wife?) of James
3. Salome		3. Salome

The fresh start at 16:1 has been taken as evidence that 16:1 is the beginning of a wholly separate tradition, unconnected with what precedes.

All these problematical features seem to lead to one conclusion: the empty tomb story is a later legend, introduced by Mark for the first time into the narrative. The absence of any reference to the empty tomb in the pre-Pauline formula, its ostensible incompatibility with the burial story and with the earlier tradition of Galilean appearances, its materialistic concept of the resurrection as contrasted with the pre-Pauline tradition, the ignorance about Jewish burial customs—all seem to force upon the critic this ineluctable conclusion.

It is not our immediate intention to try and rescue some nucleus of facticity from this story, but to attempt a reconstruction of the history of the tradition.

The empty tomb (Mark 16:1–6,8)

Again, working from the end of the pericope back to the beginning, we start at verse 8. The silence of the women can hardly be explained as the Evangelist's device to account for the recent origin of the story; that is altogether too modern and rationalistic an explanation, and assumes that the early church was concerned, like the modern historical critics, with conflicting historical evidence. The early church expounded its traditions anew in new situations: it did not investigate them historically in order to discover their origins and *Sitz im Leben*. There is another explanation of verse 8 which lies closer to hand and which is thoroughly explicable from the milieu in which these stories originated. Trembling and ecstasy (*tromos kai ekstasis*, v.8) are the usual biblical reaction to an angelophany (cf. Luke 1:12,29), and such reaction can also take the psychosomatic form of temporary aphasia (Luke 1:22). Verse 8 is no indication that the whole of the empty tomb pericope is of recent origin, or that the Evangelist has inserted it in order to account for this fact.[6]

Verse 7, we may readily agree, is a Marcan interpolation. Its precise import as an expression of Marcan theology will be discussed later in this chapter. This verse overweights the angelic proclamation and, when removed, allows a smooth transition from verse 6 to verse 8. The angelophany then has the immediate effect, as is usual in the Bible, of producing amazement. Verses 6 and 8 are so intimately connected that they must belong to the same stratum of the tradition. The function of the angelophany is to announce the resurrection. As such, it plays a vital role in the passion narrative, for that narrative must end, not with the death of Jesus, but with the resurrection. Since the early community did not narrate the actual resurrection, and since, too (if our thesis is correct), there existed at the beginning no appearance narratives, the angelophany, asserting as it does that the resurrection was made known by revelation, was a natural device for achieving that end. From this we may conclude that the angelophany was inserted into the empty tomb pericope at the time when that pericope was added as the conclusion of the passion narrative—probably for the purposes of cultic recitation.

It is hard to be certain about the statement that the stone

was rolled away. On the one hand it is closely connected with the angelophany. Its function in the narrative is to enable the women to test the angel's statement "He is not here." So it might be held to belong to the same stratum of tradition as the angelophany. Verse 3 (the women's question) could be assigned also to the same stratum of tradition. But this would reduce the narrative to a torso. Further, the Johannine form of narration (John 20:1) states quite clearly that Mary Magdalene found the stone rolled away from the sepulcher, and this in a context wholly independent of the angelophany. From this we should probably conclude that the rolling away of the stone belongs to the earliest form of the tradition.

We come now to the problems of verse 1. The apparent inconsistency between the burial and the empty tomb pericopes, noted above, is perhaps susceptible of an entirely different explanation. At first sight, the story of the burial of Jesus by Joseph of Arimathea looks perfectly straightforward and plausible. Even Bultmann, in an oft-quoted statement, found nothing in it to suggest a legend.[7] But the presentation of Joseph's burial of Jesus as an act of charity by a friendly-disposed outsider is hardly compatible with the earlier tradition about the burial. This tradition is at first quite neutral on the character of the act: it simply states "he was buried" (1 Cor. 15:4a), without mentioning who did it or for what motive. But in Acts 13:29, in a missionary speech attributed to Paul, we have a surprising statement:

"They [sc., "those who lived in Jerusalem and their rulers," v.27, i.e., the same parties who had initiated the crucifixion of Jesus in v.28] took him down from the tree, and laid him in a tomb."

According to this interpretation, the burial of Jesus was the "last act of the crime,"[8] the final insult done to him by his enemies. It was the culmination of the Jews' No to Jesus, providing the nadir out of which the triumphal Yes of God was uttered: "But God raised him from the dead" (v.30, which already implies [see John 5:25–28] from the tomb).

Which tradition is earlier, Acts or Mark? It seems easier

to account for the change of the burial from an act of hostility into an act of charity than vice versa. It must have been a scandal to the disciples that none of them had been present to pay the last honors to their Master—only a few women, apparently, watched helplessly from afar. If the Sanhedrin was the agent of Jesus' burial—a hasty burial lest the hanging of the dead body on the cross should profane the sabbath—the easiest way out for Christian piety was to make one of the councilors, Joseph of Arimathea, do it not as an act of hostility but as an act of charity. Why Joseph of Arimathea? Was he a pure invention? Possibly, but perhaps not. Perhaps he was in fact the member of the Sanhedrin who had, as the final hostile act, taken charge of the disposal of the body. Perhaps he disposed of the body in a tomb provided by himself. But on that we can only speculate. All we would argue is that Mark or the tradition used by him—which designated Joseph as "a respected member of the council who was looking for the kingdom of God," and which makes him provide, not a hasty interment, but a burial carefully carried out according to Jewish law and custom, not as for executed criminals but as for one who died a normal and respectable death—signalizes the beginning of the Joseph legend. This legend is developed further in the later Gospels. In Matthew Joseph becomes "a disciple," in Luke he is Hellenized as a good and upright man, while in John he is *secretly* a disciple.[9] This last circumstance opens up another aspect of the problem. The statement that Joseph was "secretly" a disciple would perhaps be more appropriate to Nicodemus (cf. John 3:2), who also figures as a somewhat supernumerary character. It has been plausibly suggested that either the Evangelist or the pre-Johannine tradition has combined two different accounts of the burial—one in which Joseph and one in which Nicodemus played the friendly role. If so, it looks as though we have here alternative legendary corrections of the original tradition of the burial of Jesus as the final act of ignominy. It is thus the Marcan burial story not the empty tomb, which is responsible for the inconsistency between the two pericopes.

This brings us to the statement about the motive of the women (to complete the burial rites). Because of the discrepancy with the burial pericope, many commentators prefer Matthew here (according to Matthew they came simply to see the tomb).[10] If, however, the account of Joseph's action is later and legendary, the discrepancy disappears and there is no reason why, if the body of Jesus had been cast into the grave by his enemies without proper burial, the women should not have gone to the tomb with the intention of giving Jesus a proper burial if they could.

The slight discrepancy in the names of the women becomes intelligible if the name of Mary Magdalene (which is the one constant feature of all traditions) stood originally alone. In that case the names of the other Mary and Salome will have been added to square with 15:40, after the empty tomb pericope was taken up into the passion narrative. That originally Mary Magdalene was the sole visitor to the tomb appears to be borne out by the independent version in John 20:1.[11]

Our analysis suggests that this is the earliest form of tradition: As soon as possible after the sabbath, Mary Magdalene visited the tomb to give Jesus a proper burial, but discovered the stone rolled away and the tomb empty. This version is so formless that it is hardly a pericope, but merely a report on the basis of which the pericope with the angelophany was constructed. What is the origin of this report? All we can say for certain is that it stands right at the beginning of the history of the tradition and is doubtless very early. We may surmise, with U. Wilckens,[12] that when the disciples returned from Galilee to Jerusalem after their visions of the Risen One they received from Mary Magdalene a report that she had visited the tomb and discovered it empty. The disciples welcomed this report as wholly congruous with the belief which they had come to share as a result of their visions, that God had raised Jesus from the grave. They took up Mary's report and by means of the angelophany attached it to the passion narrative as a vehicle for the cultic proclamation and celebration of the resurrection.

Let us take another look at the angelophany. It is commonly thought that the empty tomb pericope presupposes a materialistic conception of the resurrected existence—that the Risen One walks about on earth in a quasi-physical mode of existence. But there is nothing to suggest this in the Marcan pericope. There is no narrative of the Risen One's egress from the tomb. Rather, the implication is that the resurrection of Jesus was conceived here in apocalyptic terms—not as the resuscitation of a corpse, but as the transformation of the body into an eschatological mode of existence and his immediate assumption into heaven. This is indicated by the angelic proclamation, "He has risen, he is not here." He is no longer on earth: he has been translated into heavenly existence.[13]

This concept of a translation from the grave into a heavenly (or eschatological) existence survives in a number of later Christian legends, as Goguel has shown.[14] It also appears to underlie some of the apocalyptic ideas about the ascension of Enoch, Moses and Elijah. The primitive conception of Jesus' resurrection was not that of an "ascension from the cross" as G. Bertram claimed in a celebrated essay[15] but rather of a resurrection (or ascension) from the grave.[16]

The reunion in Galilee (Mark 16:7)

We have already assigned 16:7 to the Evangelist's redaction. It poses a number of exegetical problems.

The first problem is the phrase "his disciples and Peter." Why this order, if, as is generally agreed, the allusion is to the two primary appearances to Cephas and the Twelve listed in 1 Corinthians 15:5? Are we to conclude from this that Mark has telescoped the appearances to Peter and to the Twelve into a single appearance?[17] If so, why then is Peter singled out for special mention? Did Mark intend to suggest that the special appearance to Peter occurred *after* the general appearance to the disciples? This is hardly likely in view of the continued survival, as late as Luke 24:34, of the early tradition that the first appearance was to Peter (1 Cor. 15:5). Accordingly, we would agree with the judgment of Wilckens when he says (my translation): "The formulation in Mark 16:7 does not place Peter after the disciples but before them by giving prominence to

Peter as the only one referred to by name."[18] The phrase *kai
Petro* singles out Peter for special mention, and we may para-
phrase the command thus: Go tell his disciples, and especially
Peter whom he will see first.

The next problem is raised by the phrase "he is going before
you" (*proagei*). What does *proagei* mean? The same verb occurs
in 14:28, which reads: "After I am raised up, I will go before
you (*proaxo*) to Galilee." To this earlier verse the Evangelist has
provided a cross reference in 16:7, "as he told you." Both passages must therefore be taken together.

The usual meaning given to *proagein* in both verses is "to
precede." In some mysterious manner the Risen One is to precede
the disciples on their journey to Galilee, so that he is ready
to appear to them when they arrive.

This interpretation was questioned by J. Weiss.[19] He pointed
out that the verse immediately preceding 14:28 depicts the Lord
under the image of a shepherd with the aid of a prophecy from
Zechariah:

> And Jesus said to them, "You will all fall away; for it is written, 'I
> will strike the shepherd, and sheep will be scattered.' "

The Risen One will later lead the disciples as a shepherd in
person to Galilee. For what purpose? Says Weiss: in order to
establish the kingdom of God or to await its coming. As an unfulfilled prophecy, 14:28 has therefore, according to Weiss, good
claim to authenticity; it is certainly very primitive.

Apparently quite independently of Weiss, E. C. Hoskyns in
an early essay[20] proposed a similar interpretation. He, too, took
proagein to mean "lead," arguing that Mark 14:28 should be
read in close conjunction with Mark 10:32, where the same verb
occurs in a context which makes it clear beyond all doubt that
it means "to lead": "And they were on the road, going to
Jerusalem, and Jesus was walking ahead of them (*proagōn*)."
Hoskyns then concludes:

> The two passages may therefore be paraphrased: The Son of man
> led his disciples to Jerusalem in order that they might witness the
> rejection of the Messiah and his crucifixion by the chief priests—in

fact, in order that they might see the end of the old covenant; and he promised that he would rise again and lead them, perhaps still against their will, out of the doomed city of fossilized and now superseded Jehovah worship—into Galilee (p. 149).

Hoskyns now poses the question of the significance of Galilee. His answer is that it stands for the inauguration of the mission to the Gentiles. He appeals to the changes made to the Marcan narrative by Matthew and Luke. Both add appearances accompanied by missionary charges to evangelize the Gentiles (Matt. 28:16–20 and Luke 24:46,47), while Matthew explicitly interprets Galilee as "Galilee of the Gentiles" (Matt. 4:15) by invoking the prophecy of Isaiah 9:1.

Hoskyns' final conclusion is:

We are driven, first to accept the historicity of these sayings, and secondly, to discard the literal interpretation of the Galilee sayings as giving no adequate meaning. There appears, therefore, no alternative left but to interpret Galilee from the Isaiah passage (viz., Isa. 9:1, cited by Matthew at 4:15), and to draw the conclusion that our Lord proclaimed his resurrection as leading to the establishment of the new covenant in which the sovereignty of God and his kingdom would be extended to include Gentiles (p. 152).

Hoskyns' interpretation was taken up by one of his pupils, C. F. Evans.[21] Evans showed that in Mark *proagein* never means "to precede." That meaning is more characteristic of Matthew. Where it is used transitively in Mark it always means "to lead." Like J. Weiss, Evans is most emphatic that neither Mark 14:28 nor Mark 16:7 can be used to support the theory of resurrection appearances in Jerusalem in Luke 24 and John 21. Then having eliminated a literal interpretation of Galilee, he concludes with Hoskyns that "the word Galilee must be taken as a symbol of the Gentile world." But he has certain hesitations: That the word "Galilee" could have carried this more than geographical content for Jesus is, of course, incapable of proof, if only because this is the sole occasion in the Gospels that it is found on his lips (p. 13).

This interpretation of 14:28 and 16:7 has much to commend

it, particularly its insistence that *proagein* in 14:28 and 16:7 must be interpreted in the light of its meaning in 10:32, and its association of Galilee with the mission, a point which we shall take up in a somewhat different way later. However, it has its weaknesses. In the first place, neither Hoskyns nor Evans offers a clear analysis of the history of the tradition in 14:28 and 16:7. They assume too readily that the whole logion in 14:27–8 is of one piece, and that as such it is authentic to Jesus. Hoskyns rightly emphasizes the importance of the fact that verse 27 quotes Zechariah 13:7, but too hastily deduces from this the fact that *Jesus himself* consciously and deliberately interpreted the whole of his passion in terms of the Old Testament. The impregnation of the passion narrative with Old Testament testimonies and allusions has to be seen, however, precisely as the work of the early Christian community. It has the apologetic function of mitigating the scandal of the events narrated, and the positive function of proclaiming these events as eschatological acts of God.[22]

Verse 27 must be assigned to the primitive community. Verse 28 is a still later insertion, as can be seen from the way in which Peter's reply to Jesus, "Even though all fall away . . ." picks up the words of verse 27b, "You will all fall away," while curiously ignoring the stupendous promise of verse 28. Remove verse 28, and verse 29 follows smoothly upon verse 27. There is no question that verse 28 is not an authentic logion of Jesus, for it contains an obvious *vaticinium ex eventu:* "after I am raised up." Historically, Jesus proclaimed the imminent event of the eschatological kingdom of God apocalyptically conceived, and therefore also by implication the resurrection of the elect. Their acceptance into the kingdom of God depended upon acceptance of his own eschatological message (and therefore of his person as the bearer of this message). But the prospect of his own resurrection, as a distinct and separate event prior to the general resurrection of the elect, represents a post-Easter adjustment of the salvation-historical perspective.[23] We therefore conclude, with W. Marxsen,[24] that 14:28 is a redactional insertion of the Evangelist, made in order to keep the passion narrative, like the empty tomb narrative, open-ended toward the dénouement of the messianic secret in the resurrection appearances.

What then of 16:7? That verse, too, as we have seen, was inserted by the Evangelist. But it is not his free composition, for it echoes the pre-Pauline list of the primary appearances, and the probable location of these appearances in Galilee.[25]

The second problem in the Weiss–Hoskyns–Evans interpretation of 14:28/16:7 is their unclear conception of what is involved by Jesus "going ahead" of the disciples into Galilee. While it is clear that the verb *proagein* must be interpreted in the light of 10:33, it is by no means clear that this is meant to suggest that the Risen One is to march ahead of the disciples from Jerusalem to Galilee precisely as the earthly Jesus had marched ahead of them on their pre-Easter journey from Galilee to Jerusalem. This would entail the picture of the Risen One as an earthly wanderer, in the manner of the later resurrection narratives (cf. especially the Emmaus story). But here is no indication that Mark conceived the appearances in this way. The words of the angel in 16:6, "He is not here," suggests rather that Mark conceives the Risen One as already "in heaven," and his appearances as taking place "from heaven." Accordingly, it is best to take *proagein* in all three passages, 10:33, 14:28 and 16:7, in the sense of "to precede." In the first instance Jesus precedes, as the context indicates, by literally walking ahead of his disciples. In the latter two cases, the Risen One precedes the disciples in the sense that when they reach Galilee, they will find him waiting to appear to them there "from heaven."

The third problematical feature of the Hoskyns–Evans interpretation (this objection does not apply to J. Weiss) is the failure to provide cogent evidence that Mark (as opposed to Matthew) explicitly understood Galilee as "Galilee of the Gentiles." Evans goes a little further than Hoskyns in trying to establish this point. He appeals to the argument of G. H. Boobyer.[26] There are *several* Old Testament passages (not just Isaiah 8:23), especially in the LXX version, which use the designation "Galilee of the Gentiles" or speak of Galilee as inhabited by Gentiles.[27] But even with the help of Boobyer, Evans has failed to demonstrate conclusively that Mark, as opposed to Matthew, attaches this particular significance to Galilee.[28] This can be established neither by reference to the LXX prior to Mark, nor from conditions in Galilee in Mark's time, nor from Matthew's redactional alterations to Mark. All these factors are extraneous to Mark himself. The case can only be argued from the Marcan redaction.

Special importance therefore attaches to an essay by J. Schreiber who has attempted to do just this.[29] He has assembled[30] relevant passages in which references to Galilee occur (1:14; 1:16; 1:28; 1:39; 3:7; 7:30; 9:30), and endeavored to show that Mark regards Galilee precisely as a Gentile land, which includes within it such Gentile places as Tyre and Sidon (3:7; 7:31), Gerasa (5:1), Decapolis (7:31), together with Bethsaida and Caesarea Philippi. I believe this is going beyond the evidence. There is nothing in any of the passages cited by Schreiber to indicate that Mark actually locates any of these places *in* Galilee. Rather, they are places *contiguous* to Galilee. Mark represents Galilee, not as the place where Gentiles are evangelized, but as the place *from which the mission goes out to the Gentiles*. We would therefore accept the Hoskyns–Evans thesis with this modification: Galilee is to be the place from which the mission is to go forth. But this is Marcan theology not a prediction of the historical Jesus.

Now this has a very important bearing on our understanding of 14:28 and 16:7. Mark opens up the view that the primary purpose of the resurrection appearances to Peter and to the Twelve in Galilee was to send them out on a mission which was to lead them beyond the confines of Israel (of which, for Mark, Galilee was still a part) to the neighboring Gentile countries.

In the mid-1930s Lohmeyer inaugurated yet another interpretation of Mark 16:7.[31] It looks forward, he maintained, not to a resurrection appearance (the normal interpretation) nor to the triumphant progress of the Christian mission among the Gentiles (Weiss, Hoskyns) but to the parousia. "You will see me" (*opsesthe*) means "You will see me returning as the Son of man." This interpretation has been taken up by several other scholars, notably R. H. Lightfoot,[32] W. Michaelis,[33] and W. Marxsen[34] and developed further.

There is much to be said in favor of Lohmeyer's interpretation and it is not so "slenderly based" as V. Taylor *ad loc.* contends. Mark has used *opsesthe* twice already precisely in connection with the parousia (Mark 13:36; 14:62). And in 9:1 the verb "to see" (*idōsin*) is used with reference to the coming of the kingdom of God, a coming which is clearly identical with the parousia of the Son of man (see the previous verse, 8:38). This parousia use of the future *opsomai* is also common in the Johannine writings. In the Gospel it occurs in logia which have been re-interpreted in the sense of the Evangelist's demythologized eschatology, but which in the pre-Johannine tradition undoubtedly had a parousia reference.[35] (John 1:51; 16:16–22, also John 19:37). There are other occurrences of *opsomai* in an undemythologized parousia reference in other Johannine writings (1 John 3:2; Rev. 1:7; 22:4). According to N. Perrin, this parousia use arises from an early post-Easter *pesher* combination of Zechariah 12:10 with Daniel 7:14.[36] In fact the parousia usage of *opsomai* may even antedate Christianity, since the verb occurs in a parousia context in Testament of Zabulun 9:8 ("you shall see him in Jerusalem"). In any event, the parousia use, whatever its origin, is firmly established in primitive Christianity.

But is this the meaning of Mark 16:7? To begin with, there is nothing *a priori* impossible in the use of *opsomai* for a resurrection appearance. The same verb occurs in a Pauline resurrection passage discussed in the last chapter (1 Cor. 9:1), in the final scene in Matthew (28:17), and in the Johannine resurrection narrative (20:18; 25, 29). Matthew certainly understood Mark 16:7 to refer to the resurrection appearance (Matt. 28:7, repeated by the Risen One at v. 10), for he clearly intends it to lead up to the scene recorded in Matthew 28:16–20.[37] But the decisive argument which proves it to be, in Mark 16:7, a resurrection rather than a parousia reference is the naming of Peter as well as the disciples, a circumstance which indicates clearly that the Evangelist is alluding to the two appearances listed in 1 Corinthians 15:5. If Mark 16:7 were pointing forward to the parousia it is hard to see why Peter should be singled out for special mention. But if it points to resurrection appearances, the reason for the mention of Peter is obvious. There is also a further relevant consideration. We should like to suggest that the silence of the women, which, as we have seen, was in the tradition an expression of the biblical reaction to angelophany, has been re-interpreted by the Evangelist in connection with this special theory of the messianic secret.[38] For, as the crucial secrecy passage in Mark 9:9 indicates, it is not until the resurrection that the secret is fully lifted, and then it is to be proclaimed by the disciples. This is why the women may not proclaim it. Hence Mark would see no contradiction between the angel's charge in verse 7 and the silence of the women in verse 8. The charge to the women was simply a device to point forward to the final unveiling of the messianic secret in the two resurrection appearances, to Peter and to the disciples.[39]

The ending of Mark's Gospel

This interpretation of the Evangelist's intention in 16:7–8 will be even more plausible if he intended to end his work at verse 8 and not to narrate the appearances. Here we touch upon the highly controverted problem of the end of Mark. No one today would question the evidence that the earliest and best textual tradition of Mark concludes at verse 8, and that the various endings in later manuscripts, including the canonical ending (Ps.–Mark 16:9–20), are subsequent attempts to make good the apparent deficiency. There are three types of explanation as to how the abrupt ending at 16:8 arose.[40]

1. Accidental premature conclusion: the author was, against his intention, prevented from finishing his work—e.g., he died, whether in a persecution or from other causes. This suggestion is inevitably speculative. 2. The mutilation hypothesis: the author did fulfill the ostensible intention of verse 7 and did continue to narrate appearances in Galilee to Peter and to the Twelve, but the ending was removed. It would be generally agreed that

this mutilation took place very early, before Mark reached Matthew and Luke. This explanation may take two sub-forms: accidental or deliberate mutilation. According to the accidental multilation hypothesis the last page of the original autograph was accidentally destroyed very soon after the original writing. According to the deliberate mutilation hypothesis, the end was intentionally removed. Why? Perhaps because the early Christian community, with its developing conceptions of the resurrection appearances (they were now being conceived in more physical terms),[41] could no longer accept the more primitive "spiritual" account in Mark. This theory has recently been championed by H. Grass.[42] 3. The deliberate conclusion hypothesis: according to this, Mark intended to conclude his Gospel at 16:8, and to add no further concluding appearance stories, despite the angelic announcement of verse 7. An initial obstacle to this hypothesis is the notoriously abrupt ending, far more abrupt in the Greek than in the English, since it concludes with the conjunction *gar* ("for"), which normally occurs at second place in a Greek sentence: *ephobounto gar*, "for they were afraid." While examples of sentences ending in *gar* can be produced,[43] no one has as yet come up with a *gar* at the end of a *book*.

In view of Bauer's evidence (see last footnote) there would now seem to be no reason why a work of *Kleinliteratur* of the type that Mark's Gospel represents should not have concluded thus. That difficulty out of the way, the question arises why Mark should have chosen to conclude at this point. Here several different types of explanation have been advanced. Particularly interesting, if not altogether convincing, are the following: 1. The pre-Marcan passion narrative had concluded not with an empty tomb, but with "spiritual" appearances in Galilee. Having introduced the empty tomb, which rests on a materialistic interpretation of the resurrection, Mark was unable to reconcile the two conceptions, and therefore contented himself by pointing (v.7) to what he was unable to relate.

This interpretation breaks down because of its highly questionable assumption that the empty tomb is incompatible with a "spiritual" conception of the appearances. Far from being incompatible, a resurrection from the grave followed by "spiritual" appearances "from heaven" is, as we have seen, exactly what the apocalyptic conceptions of earliest Christianity require. In any case, Matthew saw no difficulty over this, because he retains the empty tomb pericope, but appends an appearance in Galilee "spiritually" conceived. 2. According to an explanation apparently first advanced by E. Meyer and much favored by advocates of the deliberate conclusion hypothesis, Mark deliberately closed his Gospel at verse 8 because, although he was aware of resurrection narratives, as he indicates by verse 7, he wished the resurrection appearances to remain a mystery. Such a desire would arise from Mark's peculiar theology of revelation.[44]

Now it is of course true that the concept of "mysterious revelation" is fundamental to the Marcan theology. We have already suggested that Mark re-interpreted the silence of the women in verse 8 precisely in this direction. But that Mark deliberately should have suppressed appearance stories, if such were known to him and to his church (verse 7), demands a procedure which is extremely difficult to imagine.[45]

All these hypotheses assume that Mark had appearance stories at his disposal (whether he went on to narrate them or deliberately chose to omit them). It is this assumption that ought to be questioned. As we have already seen, the earliest church did not narrate resurrection appearances, but proclaimed the resurrection. Paul adds to this proclamation a list of appearances, which he has compiled from separate items of information. The practice of adding lists of appearances to the resurrection proclamation seems later to have been adopted in other circles outside of the Pauline tradition. It is found in an archaic survival at Luke 24:34 ("The Lord has risen indeed [literally, "been raised"], and has appeared to Simon"). It is suggested in the kerygmatic speeches of Acts (2:32b; 3:15c; 11:40f; 13:31). But there is nothing to indicate at the time of the origin of these primitive formulae that appearance *stories* were actually in circulation, any more than Paul himself ever *narrated* his own call on the Damascus road. The empty tomb pericope in Mark seems to reflect a similar stage in the tradition. The resurrection is proclaimed (verse 6) and to it is appended an allusion to the first two appearances by title: those to Peter and to the disciples (verse 7). In other words, this verse is a reference not to appearance *narratives*, but to an appearance *list* like the one in 1 Corinthians 15:5. Conformably with the development inaugurated by Paul and imitated elsewhere, Mark reinforces the proclamation of the resurrection by listing certain appearances. He adopts his own peculiar method of doing this. Already in pre-Marcan tradition the proclamation of the resurrection was achieved by the device of giving the role to the angel in the empty tomb pericope. Mark simply extends the angel's function by making him allude further to the list of appearances. This further reference was vital to Mark's structure. Mark 9:9 had pointed forward to the resurrection as the *terminus ad quem* for the preservation of the messianic secret. Mark must indicate that this *terminus ad quem* has now been reached. He could not narrate the final unveiling of the secret if no appearance narratives were as yet available for the purpose. So the angel simply points forward to the unveiling. In the light of Mark 9:9, Mark 16:7 points forward not only to the appearances to the disciples (and especially to Peter) but also to the publication of the messianic secret and the inauguration of the mission. Mark thus achieves in a highly oblique manner what the later Evangelists achieve more directly through the missionary charges which they put into the mouth of the Risen One.

This results in an important modification of the earlier tradition as recorded in 1 Corinthians 15:5. There, as we saw, the first two (Peter and the Twelve)—and in a rather different way the third (the +500)—appearances have church-founding significance. Only the later appearances (James, to all the apostles, and to Paul) have mission-inaugurating significance. Mark has suppressed the church-founding aspect of the appearances and transferred the mission-inaugurating aspect to the first two appearances. This will have far-reaching consequences for the subsequent development of the resurrection narratives.

Why has Mark done this? For the Gentile churches, the original foundation of the church has become a matter of past history (a view particularly developed by Luke). Mark is not concerned with past history but rather with present proclamation. What has ongoing, contemporary relevance is not the original foundation of the church, but the extension of the church through the apostolic mission. In Mark, already the Twelve are on the way to acquiring the status of "apostles" (i.e., missionaries) after the resurrection (16:7, fulfilling 9:9). As we shall see this perspective is developed by the later Evangelists, and in particular is systematized by Luke.

We must now pose the question, how much does Mark add to our understanding of the *earliest* tradition of the Easter events? In some ways he confirms the earliest tradition preserved by Paul in 1 Corinthians 15. The resurrection itself was *proclaimed* as God's eschatological act (verse 6: note the passive *ēgerthē* and compare with Paul's *egēgertai*), not narrated; resurrection appearances also are *listed*, not narrated either. Over and above 1 Corinthians 15, Mark gives a specific location for the first two appearances: they occurred in Galilee (14:28; 16:7). Is this authentic information derived from the earliest tradition, which can therefore be used to supplement 1 Corinthians 15 (Grass), or is this Marcan theology (Hoskyns, Evans, Marxsen)? It is true, as we have seen, that the two verses, Mark 14:28 and 16:7, are redactional. It is also true, that the references to Galilee invariably occur in the Marcan redaction[46] and play an important role in the Marcan theology. But we must beware of concluding that everything in the Marcan redaction is Marcan composition *de novo*. Where we can study Mark's redactional procedures, e.g., in 3:6–11 and 6:53–56, we find him drawing on material already existing in the pre-Marcan pericopes. No one would deny that the earthly ministry of Jesus transpired largely in Galilee, despite the fact that the word Galilee never occurs in the body of the pericopes, but always and only in the Marcan redaction. In the case of the *pre*-Easter ministry, Mark has certainly not invented the Galilean location, but has taken it from the tradition and given it theological significance, as the place of mysterious revelation. Now in constructing the redactional verse 16:7, Mark has drawn from tradition to the extent of mentioning appearances to the disciples and to Peter. It would therefore seem to be unjustified skepticism to suppose that the Galilean location does not come likewise from the tradition, but was introduced by the Evangelist for the first time. The Matthean Great Commission is still located in Galilee (Matt. 28:16), despite the location of the first appearance to the women in Jerusalem (28:9–10). The Johannine appendix locates its post-resurrection scenes in Galilee. The tradition of appearances in Galilee survives as late as the apocryphal *Gospel of Peter*. But for the strength of it, Mark might very well have transferred the appearance to Jerusalem, since that is what the exigencies of the empty tomb story would naturally require. Instead, he contents himself with a slight adjustment of the earlier tradition, according to which the disciples fled at the arrest to Galilee (14:27,50, see above, ch. 1). The disciples now wait in Jerusalem to receive the angel's message from the women. In doing so, Mark re-motivates the journey of the disciples to Galilee. It is no longer a flight, but an orderly journey to see the Lord at his express pre-resurrection command (14:28) reiterated by the angel at the tomb (16:7). Mark's procedure in joining the empty tomb narrative to Galilean appearances shows how strong for him the Galilee tradition was. So we can with full confidence, despite the recent arguments of W. Marxsen, follow Grass in supplementing 1 Corinthians 15 by Mark's information to the extent of locating the two primary appearances in Galilee.

Much more difficult to decide is the question whether the women or Mary Magdalene really discovered the tomb empty. Our investigations have shown at least that, contrary to widespread critical opinion, the empty tomb narrative with its angelophany rests on presuppositions which are not late Hellenistic and materialistic, but early Palestinian and apocalyptic. As such it is fully compatible with the kerygma of the resurrection as summarized in 1 Corinthians 15:4. Thus there is no reason why the pericope of the empty tomb should not be early and Palestinian in origin. A traditio-critical analysis enabled us to remove the angelophany and its accompanying features, and to reconstruct a basic nucleus out of which the pericope with its angelophany was apparently constructed (see above, pp. 53ff.). Beyond that the historian cannot go. We could only surmise that the basic nucleus was derived from a report given by Mary Magdalene to the disciples. But if our surmise is correct, an important consequence follows. The disciples received Mary's report not as the origin and cause of their Easter faith, but as a vehicle for the proclamation of the Easter faith which they already held as a result of the appearances. It is as such that the Christian historian and the community of faith can accept the report of the empty tomb today.

CHAPTER FOUR

The Resurrection Narratives in Matthew

The deception of the high priests (Matt. 28:11–15)

[62]Next day, that is, after the day of Preparation, the chief priests and the Pharisees gathered before Pilate [63]and said, "Sir, we remember how that impostor said, while he was still alive, 'After three days I will rise again.' [64]Therefore order the sepulchre to be made secure until the third day, lest his disciples go and steal him away, and tell the people, 'He has risen from the dead,' and the last fraud will be worse than the first." [65]Pilate said to them, "You have a guard of soldiers; go, make it as secure as you can." [66]So they went and made the sepulchre secure by sealing the stone and setting a guard.

(Matt. 27:62–66)

[11]While they were going, behold, some of the guards went into the city and told the chief priests all that had taken place. [12]And

when they had assembled with the elders and taken counsel, they gave a sum of money to the soldiers [13]and said, "Tell people, 'His disciples came by night and stole him away while we were asleep.' [14]And if this comes to the governor's ears, we will satisfy him and keep you out of trouble." [15]So they took the money and did as they were directed; and this story has been spread among the Jews to this day.

(Matt. 28:11–15)

In order to appreciate the alterations which Matthew has made to Mark's story of the empty tomb it is necessary first to examine Matthew 27:62–66, the story of the guard at the tomb, which Matthew has added to the Marcan narrative of the burial.

There are some surprising features in this story. The opening phrase is curiously worded, in a way that obscures the fact that the "next day," the day after the Preparation, was actually the sabbath! The chief priests and Pharisees[1] sought an interview with Pilate (v.62), obtained permission for a guard, sealed the tomb and placed the guard—all on the sabbath. Since Jeremias'[2] researches into the exceptions permitted to the sabbath law we should perhaps not attach too much weight to these apparent breaches of the sabbath, but our suspicions at least are aroused.

In the next verse (v.63) the Jewish authorities refer to Jesus as "that impostor" (*planos*). This must refer to the "first deception" (v.64), namely, the alleged claim of Jesus to be the Messiah. Already therefore, since Jesus historically speaking probably did not *claim* to be "the Messiah,"[3] but was *proclaimed* as such by the Christian community only after his resurrection, verse 63 presupposes the post-Easter kerygma as well as the Jewish reaction to it.

Later in the same verse, the leaders of the Sanhedrin quote the resurrection part of the passion predictions, not the Matthean ("on the third day") but partly in the Marcan ("after three days") and partly in a form which is neither Marcan nor Matthean but which employs the middle voice, *egeiromai*, for "I will rise," i.e., "I will raise myself" instead of *anastēsomai* (Mark), *egerthēsomai* (Matthew). Since there is every reason to suppose that predictions of his own resurrection are post-Easter additions to the Jesus tradition, this is another indication of the post-Easter origin of the perciope.

Again, the request that the grave might remain sealed "until the third day" reflects not only the early Christian kerygma of 1 Corinthians 15:4 that Jesus was raised on the "third day," but also the later identification of the third day with the day of discovery of the empty tomb, as in Mark. The words which the authorities fear will be reported by the disciples to the people, "he has been raised from the dead," is precisely the formulation of the earliest post-Easter kerygma. The "first" fraud (v.64), as we have seen, was Jesus' claim to be Messiah, the "last" was the Christian community's kerygma of the resurrection of Jesus from the dead. The rise of the Jewish polemic is of considerable importance, for it shows that "resurrection" to the Jewish mind naturally suggested resurrection *from the grave*. It was to the Christian kerygma that Christ "had been raised from the dead" that they replied by the allegation that the empty tomb was a fraud. It never occurred to them, apparently, to separate the concept of resurrection from the concept of the empty tomb. This has an important bearing on the interpretation of the earliest Christian kerygma, quite apart from the ultimate origin of the Marcan pericope of the empty tomb.

Note finally that the whole story presupposes the later form of the burial tradition as found in Mark. If the Sanhedrin had disposed of Jesus as a last hostile act, as in the presumably earlier tradition of Acts 13:29, such a request to Pilate would not have been necessary.

Thus the story presupposes many earlier stages in the history of the tradition:

1. The earliest resurrection kerygma of the resurrection of Jesus from the dead on the third day.
2. The story of the burial and empty tomb in its Marcan form.
3. The Jewish polemic against that story.

Bultmann has designated Matthew 27:62–66 an "apologetic legend." We cannot but agree.

The angels at the tomb (Matt. 28:2-4)

[2]And behold, there was a great earthquake; for an angel of the Lord descended from heaven and came and rolled back the stone, and sat upon it. [3]His appearance was like lightning, and his raiment white as snow. [4]And for fear of him the guards trembled and became like dead men.

Further legendary material of a similar kind is carried over into Matthew's retelling of the Marcan story of the empty tomb. In verse 4 the guards at the tomb (*hoi tērountes*), alarmed by the earthquake and the descent of the angel,[4] "trembled and became like dead men" (28:4). But some (*tines*, v.11) of them apparently recovered quickly enough to report what had happened, not to Pilate, however, but to the high priest. Whereupon a meeting of the Sanhedrin was summoned (v.12), as a result of which the guards were bribed to say that the disciples had stolen the body. The Sanhedrin also offered to square matters with the Roman prefect should the story come to his ears (v.14). This, we are told, is how the slander of the disciples' stealing of the body gained currency. And the slander has been current among the Jews down to the time when Matthew was written (v.15).

In addition to these apologetic elements Matthew has inserted certain accompanying miraculous phenomena. There is an earthquake. An angel descends from heaven, rolls away the stone and sits on it. This is the nearest that the canonical Gospels ever come to narrating the actual resurrection. The final action, the angel's sitting on the tomb, is an anticlimax, and a puzzling one at that. Did the Risen One come out of the tomb before the stone was rolled away, as Mark apparently thought, so that the stone was rolled away to let the women see that the grave was empty? Or did Matthew conceive the resurrection in such highly physical terms (unlike the pre-Pauline formula, Paul himself, and Mark) that the opening of the grave was necessary for the egress of the Risen One, as in the *Gospel of Peter*? Are the women supposed to have seen all this happen, as verse

1 suggests, or did it happen before they reached the tomb, as perhaps verse 5 suggests? These obscurities in the course of events suggest to Grass[5] that Matthew has selected certain features of an already current legend, and rejected others that were not suited to his purpose. This, Grass thinks, is the same legend which underlies the *Gospel of Peter* 9:35ff. It may have contained an actual description of the resurrection, at which angels assisted.[6] Matthew takes up certain features of the legend omitting, however, the actual description of the resurrection, and reducing the function of the angel to that which he serves in Mark—simply that of proclaiming the resurrection to the women.

In the *Gospel of Peter* the women play no part in the resurrection legend. The resurrection takes place at night, before the women arrive on the scene. If Grass's analysis is correct, then Matthew will have combined two stories, Mark 16:1–8 and a legend of the actual resurrection. Hence the obscurities. In combining the two stories, Matthew has transferred the earthquake and the descent of the angel to the early morning (v.2; in the *Gospel of Peter* these events take place at night), and made it coincide with the arrival of the women, which he took from Mark.

The women at the tomb (Matt. 28:1,5–8)

[1]Now after the sabbath, toward the dawn of the first day of the week, Mary Magdalene and the other Mary went to see the sepulchre.

[5]But the angel said to the women, "Do not be afraid; for I know that you seek Jesus who was crucified. [6]He is not here; for he has risen, as he said. Come, see the place where he lay. [7]Then go quickly and tell his disciples that he has risen from the dead, and behold, he is going before you to Galilee; there you will see him. Lo, I have told you." [8]So they departed quickly from the tomb with fear and great joy, and ran to tell his disciples.

Here Matthew follows Mark, with only minor alterations. He reduces the number of the women at the grave to two only, omitting Salome so as to remove the Marcan discrepancy between the names of the women at the burial and those of the women at the tomb. He changes the motive of the women's visit. In Mark they come to complete the burial rites ("so that they might go and anoint him," Mark 16:1). In Matthew they simply come "to see the sepulchre" (Matt. 28:1). Evidently Matthew has felt the difficulty inherent in Mark's account, according to which Joseph of Arimathea had apparently already completed the burial rites. Conservative scholars who otherwise accept the priority of Mark, prefer the Matthean account as more historical.[7] But if our analysis of the Marcan tradition is correct, and also our conclusion that there was an earlier form of the burial tradition in which the burial was presented as a hasty act of Jesus' enemies, the Marcan account, as we have seen, may here be original, while the Matthean alteration will represent an adjustment to the later accretions to the burial story, i.e., to the Marcan or pre-Marcan addition of Joseph of Arimathea's friendly gesture, and to Matthew's own additions of the sealing of the tomb and the placing of the guard. So we assign the words "to see the sepulchre" to Matthean redaction.

Matthew removes "and Peter" from the angel's charge to the women (v.7). Unlike Mark, Matthew intends the charge to lead up to an actual narrative, which will take the form of a single, omnibus appearance to all of the disciples. He therefore sees no point in singling out Peter for special mention, as Mark, reflecting the earliest tradition of the two primary appearances to Peter and to the Twelve, had done. This, incidentally, proves that Matthew's copy of Mark ended with the words "for they were afraid" (Mark 16:7). The tradition accessible to Matthew knew nothing of the primary appearance to Peter.[8]

There is a small but significant alteration at the end of verse 7. In Mark 16:7 the angel refers back to Jesus' prediction that he would go before the disciples into Galilee (Mark 14:28) "as he told you." Matthew removes the cross reference (although he had already reproduced the prediction of Mark 14:28 at 26:32), and substitutes the words: "Lo, I have told you" (28:7). The reasons for this change are obscure, and various explanations have been offered.[9] It is noticeable that Matthew makes the

Risen One repeat the angel's charge almost *verbatim* in his appearance to the women in verse 10. It looks therefore as though Matthew has canceled Mark's cross reference to the earlier prediction in order to prepare the way for the repetition of the charge by the Risen One in verse 10, reinforcing the angel's injunction. The result is to rivet firmly together the angelophany, the Christophany to the women, and the final appearance to the disciples.

The next change introduced by Matthew into his Marcan *Vorlage* is the removal of the statement about the silence and fear of the women with which Mark had closed his Gospel (Mark 16:8), and the substitution of the statement that the women hurried away in excitement to fulfill the command: "So they departed quickly from the tomb with fear and joy, and ran to tell his disciples" (verse 8). Matthew has little interest in the Marcan theology of the messianic secret, and has often toned it down and modified it (for instance, his omission of Mark 9:10 at Matt. 17:9). He does not share Mark's desire to point mysteriously to the appearances to Peter and to the Twelve as the final unveiling of the secret, but wishes rather to lead straight from the empty tomb narrative into the final appearance. Hence the women cannot remain silent: they must somehow link up with the disciples so that the disciples may proceed to Galilee for the Great Commission.

The appearance to the women (Matt. 28:9–10)

⁹And behold, Jesus met them and said, "Hail!" And they came up and took hold of his feet and worshiped him. ¹⁰Then Jesus said to them, "Do not be afraid; go and tell my brethren to go to Galilee, and there they will see me."

The intention of the women to carry out the angel's command to report to the disciples is interrupted en route by an appearance of the Risen One. He greets them; they react by "touching his feet" and worshiping him, whereupon Jesus simply repeats the angel's charge.

That this appearance is a Matthean insertion into the Marcan

Vorlage is obvious. Less obvious is its source. Is it a free composition of the Evangelist, or is it an earlier piece of the tradition? In favor of its pre-Matthean character we may cite, first, the fact that it dislocates the flow of the narrative: from the word of the angel we were given the impression that Jesus would appear next in Galilee to the disciples, not in Jerusalem to the women.[10] Second, the tradition of the appearance to Mary Magdalene in John 20:11–18 looks like an independent development of the same story, not as though it is derived directly from Matthew.[11] Third, the conception of the resurrection is materialized (v.9), contrary to 28:6 and 16–20. On the other hand, the charge of Jesus to the women simply repeats that of the angel, and incidentally rules out the interpretation of "he is going before you" in the sense of "walking ahead of," as far as Matthew's understanding of Mark's *proagein* is concerned (see above, p. 58). The conclusion, to which these seemingly contradictory facts appear to lead us, is that there existed a tradition prior to Matthew containing the narrative of the Christophany to the women (located in Jerusalem), and that Matthew has appended to his own Christophany the words of Jesus in verse 10, which he himself has composed on the model of the angel's words in verse 7. Only so could Matthew integrate into his narrative the Christophany to the women which his special tradition included.

What is the origin of the Christophany to the women? Its absence from 1 Corinthians 15:5–7 and from Mark makes it unlikely that it is an early tradition.[12] One can only conclude that the earlier tradition of the angelophany to the women had been later converted into a Christophany. In Luke 24:22 the women are said to have reported to the disciples that they had seen only "a vision of angels," another indication that the Christophany to the women is a later development. The earlier tradition of primary Christophanies in Galilee is beginning to react upon the originally quite separate story of the empty tomb with which only the women were originally associated (Mark 16:1f.). Matthew's addition of 28:9–10 is an enhancement of the tendency already discernible in Mark's addition of 16:7 to the pre-Marcan tradition, viz., a desire to link up the empty tomb and the appearance traditions.

The significance of the Christophany to the women in the history of the tradition is considerable: 1. It is the first symptom of a tendency which culminates in the relocation of the primary appearances to the disciples in Jerusalem in Luke 24 and John 20.[13] 2. The Christophany of Matthew 28:11–17 is the first instance we have of a materialization of the appearances. This materialization seems to originate here, not from any antidocetic motive such as we find in the later tradition (see especially Luke 24:13), but from the exigencies of narration. So long as the appearances were merely listed (1 Cor. 15:5f.; Mark 16:7), their spiritual character could be preserved intact. But they could be narrated as external events only by modeling them on the stories of encounters with Jesus during his earthly ministry. It is particularly significant that it is precisely those later traits in the narrative tradition of the earthly Jesus' ministry which represent him as a "divine man" (*theios anēr*) and are taken into the resurrection narratives. Thus the women "touch" his feet (cf. Mark 5:22) and they "worship" him (cf. Mark 5:6). This is the strongest argument against the primitive character of the appearance *narratives*. It also has an important bearing, as we shall see, on the question whether in certain instances what were originally resurrection stories have been retrojected into the earthly ministry or vice versa.

The great commission (Matt. 28:16–20)

[16]Now the eleven disciples went to Galilee, to the mountain to which Jesus had directed them. [17]And when they saw him they worshiped him; but some doubted. [18]And Jesus came and said to them, "All authority_ in heaven and on earth has been given to me. [19]Go therefore and make disciples of all nations, baptizing them in the name of the Father and of the Son and of the Holy Spirit, [20]teaching them to observe all that I have commanded you; and lo, I am with you always, to the close of the age."

Matthew concludes with a single appearance to the "eleven disciples." This is the first occasion we have met with anything approaching an actual narrative of this or of any other appearance, save that to the women in the foregoing passage, which, as we have seen, was probably developed out of an angelophany. What is the previous history of this pericope? It is clear that the narrative is heavily impregnated with Matthean style and vocabulary.[14]

Is the whole passage therefore a Matthean composition? Let us explore some of the other features of this passage.

First, it is stated that the recipients of the appearance were the "eleven" disciples. The number "eleven" is clearly a pedantic correction of 1 Corinthians 15:5, where the "official" number of Twelve is given. But this does not necessarily prove that Matthew also is reproducing a narrative tradition of which 1 Corinthians 15:5 is a summary. The idea of an appearance culminating in the Great Commission is more likely to be Matthew's own editorial inference from Mark 16:7: "Go and tell his disciples, you will see him in *Galilee*." Matthew inferred that Mark was leading up to an appearance to the disciples with a command to evangelize, and having recorded both the defection and the suicide of Judas (Matt. 27:3–10), he knew that there were only eleven of them. There is also another factor which prevents us from identifying this appearance directly with that of 1 Corinthians 15:5. The appearance to the Twelve in 1 Corinthians 15:5 was a "church-founding" appearance, whereas the appearance in Matthew 28:16–20 is a mission-inaugurating one. The history of the tradition runs from 1 Corinthians 15:5 through Mark 16:7 to Matthew 28:16, not from the source of Matthew 28:16 to 1 Corinthians 15:5. Matthew's location of the appearance in Galilee is already suggested by Mark 16:7, and need not imply that Matthew had before him a pre-Matthean *narrative* of an appearance in Galilee, any more than the number "eleven" does. The reference to the "mountain" (v.16a) as the scene of the appearance is a little puzzling. The Evangelist states in this verse that Jesus had already directed them to a mountain. This is evidently a cross-reference to 28:10, and perhaps also to 26:32, but neither passage mentions a mountain. Are we therefore to conclude from this ostensible discrepancy that Matthew found the mountain already in his tradition? This solution is particularly attractive to those who think that the story of the Transfiguration on the mountain (!) is a transposed resurrection narrative (see below, pp. 165f.). But at least it is possible that Matthew knew of a list of appearances which, unlike Paul's list, located the primary appearances *on a mountain* in Galilee. On the other hand, we know that Matthew attaches particular theological significance to the mountain as a place of revelation. The location of the Great Sermon on the mountain (5:1), as opposed to the plain in Luke, is part of Matthew's Mosaic typology: the new law, like the old one on Sinai, is delivered on a mountain. It would in any case be hazardous to conclude that Matthew had before him a *narrative* of an appearance on a mountain, for the narrative elements are minimal. The notice that "some doubted" is a trait which occurs in several of the later resurrection traditions (Luke 24:11,15,25,37f.,41; John 20:25 [Thomas]; Ps.-Mark 16:11,13,14). In the apocryphal Gospels this element has been accentuated rather than deleted,[15] and it serves apologetic interest by providing the occasion for demonstrating the physical reality of the Lord's body. But the apologetic interest is entirely absent from Matthew 28:17, where the doubting is not followed up by any demonstration. Accordingly, we find it difficult to agree with Grass[16] when he says that the doubt motif is already in Matthew the creation of later apologetic, or with G. Barth,[17] who quotes O. Michel[18] to the effect that it is motivated by "the problem of the later church, which seeks new certainty about the Risen One beyond the Easter appearance, since the appearance belongs to the tradition and to an event of the past." The presence of *kata tas graphas* in the earliest resurrection tradition (1 Cor. 15:4) indicates that already the earliest preaching had to wrestle with the problem of doubt—for the faith of the community quite as much as for the apologetic directed toward the unbelieving Jews whom they sought to win for the kerygma. Accordingly we may conclude that the phrase "some doubted" in Matt. 28:17 comes from early tradition.[19] Since there is no evidence prior to Matthew's Gospel for the existence of appearance *narratives*, we surmise too that a reference to doubts may have occurred in some lists of appearances, a view which will be strengthened when we come to analyze the material in Pseudo-Mark 16:9–20. If we can carry the motif of doubt back to early tradition, can we carry it back further to the actual history? Recall for a moment that Peter was the first who received a resurrection appearance. When he re-assembled the Twelve for the second appearance, he must have reported his own resurrection appearance to them (cf. Luke 24:34). What is more natural than that they should first have doubted his assertion, and that their doubt was not finally dissipated until they themselves received a visio-auditory self-manifestation of the Risen One? This may explain the "eleven." Matthew, having lost the appearance to Peter, has also lost the original context of the doubt and placed it *within* the narrative of the second appearance, rather than *between* the first and second appearances.

Our analysis thus far points to the conclusion that the setting for the Great Commission is a Matthean composition, but that Matthew has composed it from earlier lists of appearances. In this construction there is a complete absense of any *theios anēr* (divine man) traits,[20] and of the "epiphany style" that characterizes the later appearance narratives. Verses 16–17 therefore will have been composed by Matthew from earlier materials to serve as a setting for the Great Commission. It is not a materialistic narrative, but a statement from an appearance list.

To this Great Commission we now turn. It falls into three parts:

Verse 18: the declaration of authority.

Verses 19–20a: the missionary charge.

Verse 20b: the promise of the abiding presence.

THE DECLARATION OF AUTHORITY

There are parallels to each of these three parts elsewhere in the Jesus tradition. The declaration of authority is paralleled in the cry of jubilation (Matt. 11:27Q), and in John 3:35:

MATT. 28:18	MATT. 11:27	JOHN 3:35
All authority (exousia) has been given (edothē) to me in heaven and on earth *(epi tēs gēs).*	*All* things have been *delivered to me (paredothē)* by my Father.	(The Father) has given all things *into* his hand.

The source of this picture of the delivery of all authority to the Son by the Father is Daniel 7:14, where it is stated of the "one like a son of man" that to him "was *given* (LXX *edothē*) *dominion* (LXX, B text: *exousia*) and glory and a kingdom, that *all* peoples (B text: *panta ta ethnē tēs gēs*) . . . should serve him; his *dominion* (LXX *exousia*) is an everlasting dominion." The original context of this saying makes it clear that in Christian usage it must have first been applied to Jesus as the exalted Son of man, a Christology which we would assign to the Hellenistic-Jewish stratum.[21] This is supported by the use of the LXX text in all three passages.

Its solemn character, rhythm and subject matter (a basic kerygmatic assertion, viz., the enthronement of the Risen One) give it a hymn-like character celebrating the enthronement of Jesus as Son of man. In Matthew 28:18 this hymn-like fragment is still presented as a word of the exalted One. Matthew, unlike Luke, has no consecutive scheme of resurrection appearances and ascension. As in the early lists and in Mark, Matthew's appearance to the eleven is a Christophany of the resurrected and ascended One. In Matthew 28:18 the actual title Son of man has disappeared. In the other two passages (Matt. 11:27, John 3:35) the Son of man title has been replaced by that of "Son" with an emphasis on the Father-Son relationship, a theme which duly appears later in our present context (Matt. 28:19). The Son of man Christology has in each case been developed into a Father-Son Christology.[22]

THE MISSIONARY CHARGE

The missionary command is paralleled by Pseudo-Mark 16:15, which, it will be argued later, is not directly modeled on Matthew 28:19, but represents an independent tradition. There are other missionary charges in the synoptic tradition (Mark 6:7–13 parr.; Luke 10:1–16 par. Q). It is sometimes suggested that even the very notion of the disciples' going out on missions during the earthly ministry is a retrojection of the post-resurrection missions into the lifetime of Jesus. This theory has been successfully refuted by F. Hahn,[23] and to his arguments we would add one further consideration. Since there are no narratives of post-resurrection missionary charges in the earlier parts of the New Testament (Paul and Mark), it would seem more probable that the theory should be reversed. When the later tradition eventually came to narrate missionary charges of the risen Lord it modeled these charges on the already existing charges of the earthly Jesus. A comparison of Matthew 28:19 with 10:5 suggests just this. In any case the perspective of Matthew 28:19 is palpably late. Not only does it presuppose the Hellenistic and Pauline extension of the mission to the Gentiles (v.19a). It goes even further than Paul by supressing all reference to the evangelization of Israel in a manner which is characteristic of Matthean theology.[24]

The command to evangelize is given a characteristically Matthean twist in the word *mathēteusate*—"make disciples of" (cf. Matt. 13:52; 27:57; elsewhere in the New Testament only at Acts 14:21). Strictly speaking this is not evangelistic preaching (contrast Luke 24:47–8; Acts 1:8; Ps.-Mark 16:15). One suspects (see below p. 157) that the pre-Matthean tradition of the charge, like Pseudo-Mark 16:15, read: "preach the gospel," and that Matthew has substituted his own word, "make disciples." Disciple making is spelled out as involving two phases: baptism and teaching.

The command to baptize

The narrative of Acts dates the beginning of the practice of baptism by the Christian community from the day of Pentecost (Acts 2:38). Older critics questioned its early origin. Lake and Jackson pointed out that Acts 3 (which in many ways seems to enshrine earlier material than chapter 2) makes no reference to baptisms after Peter's speech at the portico,[25] and advanced the thesis that baptism did not originate until the emergence of Hellenistic Christianity, perhaps under the influence of the mystery religions. On this view, Acts 2:38 will have read back a later practice into the earliest, Aramaic-speaking community. This thesis now seems to have been generally abandoned, even by quite radical critics. For instance, R. Bultmann[26] notes that according to Paul (Rom. 6:3; 1 Cor. 12:13) *all* Christians were baptized. The difference between the earliest, Aramaic-speaking community and the later Hellenistic community was one not of initiatory rite or absence thereof, but of the theological understanding of the rite. In the Palestinian community baptism was understood eschatologically, as a proleptic participation in the eschatological kingdom of God through the forgiveness of sins and the gift of the Spirit. Both rite and interpretation were ultimately derived from John's baptism, modified according to the change of eschatological perspective resulting from the Easter event. When the Christian mission was taken to the Hellenistic world, ideas from the mystery, religions were taken up and the primitive eschatological understanding of baptism was re-interpreted for the Hellenistic converts. This is the background of Romans 6:3ff. (cf. Col. 3:3). Baptism is understood in the Gentile mission as a participation in Christ's death and resurrection, an understanding which Paul in Romans 6:3ff. basically accepts, yet corrects by an insistence on the "not-yet" aspect. We participate already in the death of Christ, but our participation in his resurrection is only proleptic, and conditional upon implementation of the ethical imperative. Even if this critical reconstruction of the development of baptismal theology contains certain features which we might be disposed to criticize, there is no reason today to question the statement of Acts 2:38, that baptism was practiced from the very beginning of the Christian mission in its Palestinian, Aramaic-speaking stage. It might, however, be pertinently asked whether in fact Peter and the Twelve received Christian baptism. There is no record of it. Some at least of the original disciples had received Johannine baptism, if the tradition of the Fourth Gospel, which states that they had been formerly disciples of the Baptist (John 1:35ff.), is acceptable.

Their Christian baptism was the fulfillment of Johannine baptism through their direct witness of the Christ event, culminating in the Easter Christophanies and in the reception of the Spirit. For all others, participation in the Christ event requires hearing of the kerygma, directly or derivatively, from the first witnesses, together with baptism which, whatever other theological understandings may have gathered around it in the course of later development, meant basically proleptic translation into eschatological existence through the Christ event.

Now baptism had not been practiced by the earthly Jesus, at least after he began his own distinctive ministry.[27] The practice was however revived by the earliest Christian preachers in the immediate post-Easter period. What then could be more natural than that they should have understood that the call to witness to the Christ event involved also a charge to baptize? In other words, in practicing baptism, could they not have believed themselves to be carrying out the command of the Risen One, as much a command of his as the command to establish the eschatological community or to recruit new adherents by the proclamation of the good news? There are indications that the association of the command to baptize with the word of the Risen One in the appearances was neither a pecularity of the pre-Matthean tradition, nor a Matthean invention. It is found also in Pseudo-Mark 16:16, which we shall argue, is independent of Matthew (see below). It is also implied in Luke 24:47, which represents the Risen One as charging the disciples to proclaim the "forgiveness of sins." This is baptismal language, which goes back to John the Baptist himself, and which was taken up again in early Christian usage. The language of the charge in John 20:23 (see below) is equally baptismal. Therefore it may be claimed that although the appearance narratives did not take shape until the later stages in the growth of the synoptic tradition, they nevertheless reflect an understanding of Christian baptismal practice which was already current in the apostolic age: the command to baptize was implicitly involved in the Risen One's appointment of apostles to proclaim the gospel.[28]

As Paul, the traditional materials in Acts, and perhaps also Mark[29] show, baptism in the apostolic age was performed "in the name of Jesus." Certainly the early community's experience of the gospel had triadic implications: in faith the believer is brought by the Spirit to a knowledge of the eschatological presence of God in Jesus.[30] Paul summarizes these implications in rudimentary triadic groupings:

1 Corinthians 12:4–6, Spirit . . . Lord . . . God
2 Corinthians 13:14, Lord Jesus Christ . . . God . . . Holy Spirit
Galatians 4:6 God . . . Spirit . . . Son
Romans 5:5–6, God . . . Spirit . . . Christ.

But he has no clear triadic formula as such. In the article mentioned in the last footnote, I have developed a suggestion of E. Lohmeyer that the triadic formula "Father, Son and Holy Spirit" was shaped from an earlier triadic formula found in apocalyptic writings and in apocalyptic contexts in the New Testament. This apocalyptic triad consisted of:

the angels
the elect One
the Lord of Spirits.

In early Christian usage (Mark 8:38; cf. Luke 12:8f; 1 Thess. 3:13; 5:21) it is modified thus:

the Son of Man
the Father
the angels.

With the development of the Father-Son Christology[31] this evolves into

the Father
the Son
the angels.

Then finally, the angels (who also figure in the apocalyptic literature as "spirits," e.g., Rev. 1:4) are replaced by the "Holy Spirit." Thus we arrive at the triadic formula first attested in Matthew 28:19 and a little later in *Didache* 7, by which time it is firmly established in liturgical practice.

Some have argued that the triadic formula is a later interpolation into the Matthean text,[32] and indeed there is some slight textual evidence to support this claim.[33] Wherever Eusebius of Caesarea cites Matthew 28:19 in writings prior to the Council of Nicea (325), he cites it in the form "in *my* name." But we find the same variation in Justin (*Dial.* 39.2, contrasted with *Apol.* 61:3), and there is ample evidence for the existence of the longer text in the pre-Nicene manuscript tradition. And, too, the evidence of *Didache* shows that the triadic formula was already used liturgically by the early second century. It looks as though there were two forms of the baptismal formula current in the second century: the monadic ("in the name of Jesus") and the triadic. But were there two variant forms of the text of Matthew? It is significant that we have no manuscript (as opposed to patristic) evidence of any other reading than the triadic one. Two alternative explanations might be given for the variations in the patristic quotations: either the monadic form reflects continuing liturgical practices in some parts of the church; or (what amounts to much the same thing) an earlier, pre-Matthean monadic form of the tradition, which Matthew edited to produce the triadic form in the canonical text of verses 16–20, continued to exist side by side until the Council of Nicea.

The instruction to converts

The second aspect of "disciple-making" is "teaching them to observe all that I have commanded you." The fact that this is mentioned *after* the command to baptize suggests that the instruction envisaged here is not pre-baptismal catechesis but post-baptismal instruction. In any case, "it is open to question whether there was pre-baptismal basic instruction at this early stage."[34] But even if such instruction was post- rather than pre-baptismal, the practice of giving instruction to converts is widely attested during the apostolic age.[35] And if C. H. Dodd is correct (last footnote), as he surely must be, in supposing that Jesus tradition was used in such catechetical instruction, what is more natural than that the church should have come to believe that its catechetical practice was literally enjoined by the risen Lord? This conviction, however, only comes to expression in this passage of Matthew. Other canonical appearance stories include the charge to preach the gospel rather than to teach. There can be no doubt that we have here a special theological interest of Matthew. He conceives the Gospel he has written as the new Torah, and has deliberately phrased this verse so as to allude to it as such. "All [things] that I have commanded you" will then refer back to Matthew's five discourses. Compare especially "all these sayings" in Matthew 26:1 with the expression "all [things]" in the present verse.

THE ABIDING PRESENCE

This verse is closely paralleled by the logion recorded as a saying of the earthly Jesus in Matthew 18:20, "where two or three are gathered in my name, there am I in the midst of them." There is no exact parallel to these sayings elsewhere in the gospel tradition, but there is a saying of Jesus among the agrapha which, if J. Jeremias' interpretation of it is correct, is akin to them:

> Lift up the stone
> and there you will find me
> cleave the wood
> and I am there.[36]

There is also a similar rabbinic saying about the presence of the Shekinah in *Pirqe Aboth* 3:2.[37] The three sayings (Matt. 18:20; 28:20b and the agraphon) appear to be derived from a common original which was circulated as a saying of the exalted Lord,[38] and originated as an utterance of a Christian prophet who modeled it on Jewish beliefs about the Shekinah.

But which is the original form of the saying, Matthew 18:20 or 28:20b? Two features of 18:20 look more primitive. First, the context for which the promise is given, viz., the gathering together of the faithful in the name of Christ, is, as we have seen, closely parallel to the rabbinic assertions about the Shekinah (see above), and gives the saying a specific *Sitz im Leben* in the Christian community—namely, the Christian assembly for worship. Second, the phrase "in the midst of" (*en meso*) has a Semitic flavor (*b'thôkh*) and actually occurs in the Shekinah saying in *Pirqe Aboth* (see above), while on the other hand[39] Matthew seems deliberately to intend the promise of Emmanuel, "God with us" (Matt. 1:23), to be fulfilled in the promise of the abiding presence of Christ, given in 28:20b. Thus the phrase "with you" will be a redactional modification of the more Semitic "in the midst of you." On the other hand there are features in Matthew 28:20b that look more primitive: 1. The saying is here placed in the mouth of the Exalted One, not of the earthly Jesus. 2. The eschatological reference ("to the close of the age") is typically Matthean, and therefore probably redactional. But at the same time it preserves an eschatological emphasis (parousia perspective) which is rooted in the earlier tradition. The saying in its original form was, we conclude, a creation of Christian prophecy, circulated as a logion of the Exalted Christ, declaring the presence of the Exalted One in the assemblies of the faithful, and assuring them of the continuation of his presence until finally the Exalted One would come again at the parousia.

THE FUSION OF THE THREE LOGIA

One further problem remains to be discussed. As we have seen, the Great Commission is a combination of the three sayings: the declaration of authority, the missionary charge, and the promise of the abiding presence. All three elements, though subjected to Matthean editorial revision, go back to pre-Matthean tradition. Was Matthew the first to combine them, or had the combination already been effected in pre-Matthean tradition? Lohmeyer championed the view that the combination was pre-Matthean, on the ground that (allowing for the omission of the threefold name) the saying falls into poetic form[40] in a recognized Aramaic rhythm:

To me was given all power
in heaven and on earth
Therefore go, make disciples of all nations
in my name
And teach them to *observe* all
that I have *commanded* you
And lo, I am *with you* all the day
until the end of the world-time

But Lohmeyer fails to note the large number of Mattheanisms (italicized above), which these verses contain. We prefer therefore to follow O. Michel[41] and assign the combination of these three separate logia to the Evangelist himself.

The final scene in Matthew's Gospel adds only one fresh point to our knowledge of the resurrection appearances as they actually occurred, viz., that some of the disciples doubted. He has taken from the earliest tradition (via Mark) the second appearance to the Twelve in Galilee, and by drawing out the implications of Mark 16:7 (see above, pp. 67f.) has re-interpreted this appearance, not as the founding of the eschatological community, but as the inauguration of the mission. He has thus transferred to the second appearance the basic significance of the fourth appearance, that to "all apostles." But for this re-interpretation, Mark 16:7, as we have seen, had already prepared the way. Matthew has then (probably) located his scene on a mountain for theological reasons, and used it as a carrier for the Great Commission. This Commission he has composed by editing and combining three separate logia which he has received from the tradition.

But there is, strictly speaking, no narrative of an appearance in Matthew 28:16–20. The participle *idontes* (v.17), like the Marcan *opsesthe*, simply reflects the primitive listing of the appearance under the rubric *ōphthē*. Nothing is said of the form in which the Lord appeared, nothing is said of his disappearance in the end. There are no *theios anēr* traits. The scene is an artificial theologoumenon, constructed on the basis of the primitive statement that the disciples "saw" the Lord. Matthew has no *narrative* of this appearance at his disposal, presumably because at this time no such narrative existed.

The Great Commission itself then is a combination (made by the Evangelist) of three separate logia, the declaration of authority, the command to evangelize and the promise of the abiding presence. Of these, the command to evangelize is the one most certainly rooted in the Easter tradition, for it gives verbal expression to the meaning of the appearance to "all the apostles." The declaration of authority is an "I-saying," constructed from the use of Daniel 7:14 as a *testimonium* and expressing the Hellenistic-Jewish community's faith in the resurrection as the exaltation of Jesus as Son of man. The promise of the abiding presence was originally a prophetic word, circulated as a saying of the exalted Christ. It reflects the faith in the presence of the Exalted One in the Christian assembly as an anticipation of his final coming as expressed in the invocation *"Marana tha."*

The inclusion of the command to baptize in the missionary charge is pre-Matthean and widespread in the tradition (Ps.-Mark 16:16; Luke 24; John 20), and therefore comparatively early. It has a certain historical justification, since the earliest community practiced baptism, so far as we can tell, from the very beginning of the Christian mission, and believed that the practice had the authority of the risen Lord behind it.

In combining the three logia, Matthew has rephrased them in accordance with his own theological interests, emphasizing especially the teaching aspect of the church's mission and the instructions of the earthly Jesus, as the new Torah. But the concept is not entirely novel. Matthew has given explicit expression to a conviction which implicitly lay behind the gathering of the logia of the earthly Jesus which we know as Q. The very existence of this collection of dominical sayings rested upon the Easter faith that the resurrection had vindicated the authority of the word of the earthly Jesus, an authority which had been radically called into question by the event of the cross.[42]

The tendency to put post-Easter theology into a resurrection appearance was implict from the very beginning. For the entire post-Easter kerygma of the community sprang from the impact of the Easter events. But until there were appearance narratives —and not just lists of appearances—there was no opportunity to develop this tendency. By pointing forward to appearances within the framework of a continuous narrative Mark had opened up the possibility of such a development. Matthew took the hint and developed 28:16–20 from the suggestion of Mark 16:7. But the development of an actual narrative in Matthew is minimal (28:17) and amounts to little more than a repetition of the statement in the original list, that the disciples "saw" the Risen One.

CHAPTER FIVE

The Resurrection Narrative in Luke–Acts

The empty tomb (Luke 24:1–11)

¹But on the first day of the week, at early dawn, they went to the tomb, taking the spices which they had prepared. ²And they found the stone rolled away from the tomb, ³but when they went in they did not find the body. ⁴While they were perplexed about this, behold, two men stood by them in dazzling apparel; ⁵and as they were frightened and bowed their faces to the ground, the men said to them, "Why do you seek the living among the dead? ⁶Remember how he told you, while he was still in Galilee, ⁷that the Son of man must be delivered into the hands of sinful men, and be crucified, and on the third day rise." ⁸And they remembered his words, ⁹and returning from the tomb they told all this to the eleven and to all the rest. ¹⁰Now it was Mary Magdalene and Joanna and Mary the mother of James and the other women with them who told this to the

apostles; [11]but these words seemed to them an idle tale, and they did not believe them.

In recording the story of the discovery of the empty tomb Luke has either introduced considerable changes into his Marcan *Vorlage*, or else has followed (as seems to be the case throughout the passion narrative) an independent tradition, though always with an eye on Mark as well.

We will ignore the passages where Luke is clearly following Mark and concentrate on those which show substantial variations.

Luke lists the women not at the beginning of the pericope (as Mark), but at the end (v.10). Luke's list of women differs somewhat from all three of Mark's lists. Mary Magdalene remains, as in all four Gospels; Joanna, who has already been introduced in the special Lucan material at 8:3, comes second, and the third place is occupied by "Mary of James" (she is second in Mark); then come "the other women with them," which again recalls the "many others" of the special Lucan material at 8:3. Of those mentioned in the earlier passage, only Susanna does not reappear at the tomb. From this it would seem that Luke has combined two distinct traditions of the discovery of the tomb. He prefers to follow his special material in placing the list of women at the end rather than at the beginning. He takes Joanna from his special material, Mary of James from Mark, and the ever-present Magdalene (who also figures in the special material at Luke 8:2) from both sources.

Luke agrees with Mark against Matthew that the women came to complete the burial rites, but he does not mention the spices since he had already stated (23:56) that the women bought and prepared the spices immediately after the burial on Good Friday just before the beginning of the sabbath at sundown. The variations, whether Lucan redactions or—as we are inclined to think—derived from his special material, look like attempts to relieve some of the difficulties in the Marcan version. Why was the burial not completed on the Friday? Answer: the women (who in 23:55–56 seem to be in close cooperation with Joseph of Arimathea, not just looking on from afar) tried to complete the burial on Friday evening, but were overtaken by the sabbath before they could reach the grave. Consequently, they were obliged to wait, devoutly keeping the sabbath according to the commandment (23:56b) until the first opportunity on the Sunday morning. This does not look like an older and more reliable version of the facts but an attempt to wrestle with the difficulties of the Marcan version.

In Luke the women are not concerned as in Mark about the opening of the sepulchre (presumably because of their close cooperation in this version with Joseph of Arimathea). The motif of perplexity is reserved until a slightly later stage in the narrative (v.4), as we shall see in a moment. As in Mark, the women find the stone rolled away, but in Luke they enter on their own initiative and discover for themselves that the tomb is empty. In Mark, it will be remembered, they noticed that the stone was rolled away before they were intercepted by the angel and invited to inspect the empty tomb. In Luke it is when they have discovered for themselves first that the tomb is empty that their perplexity begins. At this moment *two* men in dazzling apparel appear, i.e., angels (cf. Acts 1:10). They have no need, as in Mark, to point out first the empty tomb, so they go straight on to proclaim the resurrection. All these variations in detail suggest that Luke prefers an alternative version to Mark. This probability is enhanced when we note the parallel between this story and the ascension story which the same author will record in Acts 1:10. There again, there are *two* angels, who serve the same function of interpreting an event after it has occurred. It is also worth noting that in the *Gospel of Peter* 9:36ff., two angels assist in the (highly legendary) description of the resurrection itself. Now the ascension scene of Acts, as we shall see later, has been constructed partly out of parousia imagery, and this apocalyptic scenery may be the source of the tradition about the angels and their role at the tomb as elsewhere. Their presence underlines the eschatological significance of the event which is being witnessed. Such is the kerygmatic truth expressed in the palpably legendary feature. Why two angels? In an interesting passage in his *History of the Synoptic Tradition*[1] R. Bultmann shows that pairs of figures are exceedingly common in folklore and also in the Bible. There can be no doubt that this predilection for pairs has operated here. There is a further difference between Luke and Mark in the opening address of the angel to the women:

MARK 16:6	LUKE 24:5
You seek Jesus of Nazareth, who was crucified.	Why do you seek the living among the dead?

The Lucan variation (which apparently comes from Luke's special material) contains within it already the implied announcement of the resurrection. According to the Alexandrian and Koiné texts, the angel continues, "He is not here, but has risen" (RSV margin), which (apart from a variation in word order) is exactly what follows that part of Mark 16:6 quoted above. But these words are omitted in Codex Bezae and in the old Latin texts, and are probably due to assimilation of the Lucan text to Mark-Matthew.

In the rest of the angels' address to the women, Luke evidently has Mark before him, but has completely re-written the Marcan text:

MARK 16:7	LUKE 24:6–8
Go, tell his disciples and Peter that he is going before you to *Galilee*; there you will see him, as he told you.	Remember how he told you, while he was still in *Galilee*, that the Son of man must be delivered into the hands of sinful men, and be crucified, and on the third day rise. And they remembered his words.

Luke's changes are clearly motivated by his editorial requirements. He is going to give us a series of appearances in or around *Jerusalem*. Therefore he cannot, as Mark does, point forward to appearances in *Galilee*. Nor could he refer back, as Mark had done, to the prediction of Jesus at the last supper that after his resurrection he would go before his disciples into Galilee (Mark 14:28). Luke had omitted that prediction, doubtless for the same reason, namely, because he intended to record appearances in Jerusalem rather than in Galilee. Therefore he had to substitute another cross-reference compatible with his intention, and found what he wanted in the Marcan passion predictions. None of these predictions corresponds exactly with the cross-reference. Luke 9:22 is a passion-resurrection prediction delivered in Galilee, but there were no women present on that occasion. Luke 9:44 is a passion prediction delivered in Galilee with women present, but unlike its Marcan parallel it does not mention the resurrection. Finally, the prediction in Luke 18:32–33 is made not in Galilee but on the way to Jerusalem. These considerations have led A. J. B. Higgins[2] to argue that in the cross-reference Luke is following an independent, non-Marcan passion prediction.

If we could be sure of this, it would lead to the important consequence that passion-resurrection predictions are not peculiar to Mark or to passages where other Evangelists are following Mark. However, with one exception, every word or phrase in Luke 24:7 can be paralleled either from Mark or from Luke's editing of Mark.[3]

The one word not found in the earlier predictions in Mark or Luke is *staurōthēnai* ("be crucified"). The Marcan and Lucan predictions elsewhere use the word *apoktanthēnai* ("be killed"). *Staurōthēnai* is the verb that Matthew uses in passion predictions at Matthew 20:19 and 26:2, the former in an alteration of Mark, the later in a free composition of a Son of man passion prediction modeled on Mark. Now this later instance is significant, for it shows that later writers, when they were not directly following Mark, tend to prefer *staurōthēnai*, "to crucify." This is a good Hellenistic word, while *apoktanthēnai*, "to be killed," comes from the martyrological language of Palestine. We conclude therefore that Luke 24:7 is the Evangelist's own composition.

We can see why Luke would have wanted to remove the Marcan form of the angelic message, which directed the disciples to Galilee for appearances there. But why should he have adopted this particular device, a résumé of the earlier passion predictions? The answer to this question seems to lie in the use of the word *dei* ("must"). This word plays a major role in the Lucan theology. According to W. Grundmann[4] it occurs more frequently in Luke (forty-one times) than in any other New Testament writer. He uses it especially in the context of the suffering of Jesus as the necessary pathway to his messianic glory.[5] This word "must," as Grundmann goes on to observe, denotes the plan of God in salvation history as enunciated in the Old Testament scriptures. It is a theme which is stressed no less than three times in the Lucan resurrection narratives (Luke 24:7,26,44–46). In the first two passages the theme is expressed by the used of *dei* ("must"), in the third by an equivalent phrase, "written . . . in the law of Moses" etc. The two terms, "must" and "the scriptures," are brought together in verses 26–27: "was it not necessary (*edei*) . . . all the scriptures." This concept plays a central role in the Lucan theology. Luke has rightly been called the theologian of salvation history. For him there are two major periods in this salvation history: the age of promise and the age of fulfillment. And it is the Christ event which has decisively inaugurated the age of fulfillment. In this sense, Christ is the mid-point of time.[6]

Luke is thus using the resurrection narratives as a vehicle for the explication of his own theology. But this theology is not entirely his own invention: it is an adaption of the earliest Easter tradition, that Christ both died and rose again "in accordance with the scriptures" (1 Cor. 15:3–4).

Luke, like Matthew, has felt it necessary to alter the ending of the Marcan pericope of the empty tomb:

MARK 16:8	LUKE 24:9
And they went out and fled from the tomb; for trembling and astonishment had come upon them; and they said nothing to any one, for they were afraid.	And returning from the tomb they told all this to the eleven and to all the rest.

The reaction of the women to the angelophany (which, we suggested, Mark had re-interpreted in terms of his theology of the messianic secret) is of no use to Luke. Like Matthew, he finds it necessary for the women to convey the angelic message, so as to lead into the further material which he has added to his Marcan *Vorlage*.

Matthew and Luke achieve the very same end of making the women report back to the disciples, though in different terminology. Matthew emphasizes the joy and haste with which they returned to the disciples, while Luke simply has them return, with no reference to their joy or haste, and speaks of their meeting with the "eleven and the rest" (*tois loipois*). This is a favorite Lucan way of referring to a larger group than those immediately specified (cf. Luke 8:10;19:9,11;24:10; Acts 2:37; 5:13;17:9;27:44), and suggests that this verse as a whole is a Lucan composition. But both later Evangelists use the same verb for "told": Matthew *appangeilai*, Luke *appēngeilan*. From this we might conclude either that Luke is following Matthew (as some would hold that he did) or that both Matthew and Luke are following the lost ending of Mark. But there is no compelling need for either of these conclusions. The use of the same verb *appangellein* may be purely coincidental. The tendency today is to require a much higher percentage of verbal agreement than a single word in order to establish literary relationship.

The list of the women in verse 10 has already been discussed. The use of the term "apostles" for the disciples prior to their post-resurrection commission is characteristic of Luke (cf. also 17:5;22:14). The earliest tradition applied the term *apostolos* to the recipients of the fifth resurrection appearance (1 Cor. 15:7).[7] Mark had used it in a purely functional sense when the disciples returned from their mission during Jesus' earthly life (Mark 6:30). For Luke, however, an apostle is a witness to the whole series of saving events from the baptism of Jesus by John until the ascension (Acts 1:22). The use of "apostles" in 24:10 may therefore be assigned to the redaction. It is an expression of Lucan theology.

In verse 11 the motif of doubt is introduced: "these words [sc. the women's report of the empty tomb] seemed to them an idle tale, and they did not believe them" (cf. v.22a). This occurrence of the doubt motif does not serve an apologetic function, as other, later occurrences of it do (cf. Matt. 28:17), but is intended to preserve the independence of the apostolic witness:

apostles cannot come to faith as a result of the testimony of third parties. They must see and believe for themselves in order that they can provide first-hand witness.

The empty tomb: Peter (Luke 24:12)

This brings us to verse 12 (RSV margin), which occurs in most texts but is omitted by manuscripts of the "Western" type. Since the question of its authenticity depends on its relation to a similar text in John 20:6ff., we set out the two verses side by side:

<table>
<tr><td>

LUKE 24:12 (WESTERN TEXT)
But Peter rose and ran (*edramen*) to the tomb (*mnēmeion*); stooping and looking in (*parakupsas*), he saw (*blepei*) the linen cloths lying (*ta othonia keimena*) by themselves; and he went home, (*apēlthen pros heauton*) wondering at what had happened.[8]

</td><td>

JOHN 20:3–10
Peter then came out with the other disciple, and they went toward the tomb (*mnēmeion*). They both ran (*etrechon*), but the other disciple outran (*proedramen*) Peter and reached the tomb first; and stooping to look in (*parakupsas*), he saw (*blepei*) the linen cloths lying (*keimena ta othonia*). . . . Then the disciples went back to their homes (*apēlthon pros heautous*).

</td></tr>
</table>

There are obviously some striking verbal similarities between the two passages, a fact which prompts the conclusion that Luke 24:12 is a later interpolation summarizing the story in John and largely echoing its language. Yet there are notable differences. The percentage of verbal parallels is about the same as those in other Johannine passages which used to be thought to be directly dependent on the synoptics, but for which P. Gardner-Smith argued the use of common oral tradition, rather than direct literary relationship. Moreover, the introduction of the "other disciple" in John looks like the redaction of an earlier tradition, a tradition which is perhaps better preserved in Luke 24:12 than in John. It looks as though Luke 24:12 is not dependent on John, but represents an earlier version of the tradition in John. But is it part of the original text of Luke? Note that Luke 24:24 gives a cross-reference to this story: "some of those who were with us went to the tomb, and found it just as the women had said; but him they did not see." This permits the conclusion that the Evangelist, and not only a later redactor, knew the story of a visit by the disciples to the tomb, and enhances the possibility that verse 12 belongs to the original text of Luke A.R.C. Leaney has gone further.[9] Starting from a later passage in the Lucan resurrection material which is also found only in the Western textual tradition, and which is usually dismissed as an interpolation, namely, verse 40: "And when he had said this, he showed them his hands and feet." Leaney argues that this cannot be derived from John, since John has "side"[10] in place of "feet." From this Leaney goes on to reconstruct a common source underlying Luke 24:12, 30–40 and John 20:3–10, 19–22, narrating two events: Peter at the tomb; the appearance in the upper room. The first episode Leaney reconstructs as follows:

> But Peter got up and ran to the tomb, and stooped down and saw the bandages lying by themselves; and he went away wondering what had happened, for he did not yet know the scripture that he must rise from the dead.

Leaney's view is attractive, though we should probably assign the last clause about Peter's ignorance of the scripture to the Johannine redaction (it is not alluded to in Luke 24:12), and that for two reasons. First, the motif of the disciples' preliminary misunderstanding of the scripture is a common Johannine theme (John 2:22; 12:16; 14:26). Now it is arguable that the first two Johannine passages just cited come from the Evangelist's narrative source. The two events referred to, namely, the cleansing of the Temple and the triumphal entry, must have originally belonged together (though in the reverse order). It is most likely that the Johannine redaction has separated them, placing the cleansing at the beginning of the Gospel for programmatic reasons. On these grounds we may also assign John 20:9 to the same pre-Johannine source. But it seems most unlikely that this verse was already present in the tradition as Luke received it, for then it is inconceivable that Luke, with the interest in the fulfillment of scripture that colors his resurrection narratives, should have omitted it.[11]

If Leaney is right—and his thesis is plausible—then the tradition behind both Luke and John contained a story of the discovery of the empty tomb by certain disciples including Peter. This was followed by an appearance to the eleven in the upper room. These two traditions apparently grew out of and replaced the pre-Pauline tradition of the first appearance to Peter and the second to the Twelve, probably in Galilee. But even if, with von Campenhausen, we remain unconvinced that Luke 24:12 was in the original text, we still have verse 24 as sufficient testimony to the existence of a tradition of the visit of disciples to the sepulchre, a tradition which was known to Luke independently of John.

This tradition can hardly have independent source value. Rather it is the result of the coalescence of the appearance and the empty tomb traditions, or to put it another way, the combination of the Galilean and Jerusalem traditions. Peter and the other disciples, who in the earliest tradition had received appearances in Galileee, must now become witnesses of the empty tomb in Jerusalem. The element of historical truth behind this shift is that Peter and the disciples are the primary witnesses of the resurrection. The change marks a shift of emphasis to the empty tomb as the primary cause of the Easter faith, a tendency even more marked in John 20.

The Emmaus story (Luke 24:13–35)

[13]That very day two of them were going to a village named Emmaus, about seven miles from Jerusalem, [14]and talking with each other about all these things that had happened. [15]While they were talking and discussing together, Jesus himself drew near and went with them. [16]But their eyes were kept from recognizing him. [17]And he said to them, "What is this conversation which you are holding with

each other as you walk?" And they stood still, looking sad. [18]Then one of them, named Cleopas answered him, "Are you the only visitor to Jerusalem who does not know the things that have happened there in these days?" [19]And he said to them, "What things?" And they said to him, "Concerning Jesus of Nazareth, who was a prophet mighty in deed and word before God and all the people, [20]and how our chief priests and rulers delivered him up to be condemned to death, and crucified him. [21]But we had hoped that he was the one to redeem Israel. Yes, and besides all this, it is now the third day since this happened. [22]Moreover, some women of our company amazed us. They were at the tomb early in the morning [23]and did not find his body; and they came back saying that they had even seen a vision of angels, who said that he was alive. [24]Some of those who were with us went to the tomb, and found it just as the women had said; but him they did not see." [25]And he said to them, "O foolish men, and slow of heart to believe all that the prophets have spoken! [26]Was it not necessary that the Christ should suffer these things and enter into his glory?" [27]And beginning with Moses and all the prophets, he interpreted to them in all the scriptures the things concerning himself.

[28]So they drew near to the village to which they were going. He appeared to be going further, [29]but they constrained him, saying, "Stay with us, for it is toward evening and the day is now far spent." So he went in to stay with them. [30]When he was at table with them, he took the bread and blessed, and broke it, and gave it to them. [31]And their eyes were opened and they recognized him; and he vanished out of their sight. [32]They said to each other, "Did not our hearts burn within us while he talked to us on the road, while he opened to us the scriptures?" [33]And they rose that same hour and returned to Jerusalem; and they found the eleven gathered together and those who were with them, [34]who said, "The Lord has risen indeed, and has appeared to Simon!" [35]Then they told what had happened on the road, and how he was known to them in the breaking of the bread.

It is universally agreed that the Emmaus story is a gem of literary art. To submit it to traditio-historical analysis seems irreverent, for any analysis will fail to capture its true spirit. Nevertheless, if we are to pursue the same methods which have served us thus far, we must dare to lay the impious hands of criticism even upon this beautiful story. Just because Luke has already had a hand in its composition, it is necessary to distinguish between his contribution and the earlier levels of tradition it enshrines.

First, it is clear that the cross-reference to the visits to the empty tomb (24:22–24) belongs to a stage when the empty tomb, Emmaus and upper room stories were combined. If the reader skips from 21a (which expresses the disillusionment of the Emmaus disciples) to verse 25 (which reproaches them for their slowness of heart to believe the predictions of the prophets), a smooth sequence of thought will be noted. This cross-reference takes the form of a flashback to the visit of the women at the tomb, their discovery that it was empty, the ensuing angelophany, and the subsequent confirmation of their report by the disciples.

Similarly, verses 33–35 serve as a connecting link between the Emmaus story and the upper room appearance, and contain a flashback to the primary appearance to Simon not otherwise related. This flashback stands in contradiction to the general tenor of the Emmaus story, which seems to regard the appearance to Cleopas and his companion as the first of the appearances, for the earlier flashback contains no reference to appearances.

The dialogue material with which the narrative is interspersed (14–15a; 17–21a; 25–27) appears on the grounds of form to be a later addition. But whether these elements are pre-Lucan[12] or Lucan redaction[13] is disputed.

Now an examination of this passage indicates that there are several disparate elements in the material. Verses 19d–20 are reminiscent of the kerygmatic speeches in Acts 2:22–23; 10:37–39. In all three of these kerygmatic formulae (which we regard as essentially pre-Lucan) a statement regarding his teaching and mighty works precedes the reference to his final rejection and condemnation to death. Luke 24:19d–20 appears to consist of pre-formed kerygmatic materials inserted by the Evangelist into his narrative source.

The poignant saying in verse 21, "we had hoped that he was the one to redeem Israel," as has often been pointed out,[14] appears to recapture precisely the actual historical mood of the disciples between Good Friday and the Easter revelations, and therefore to belong to the original pre-Lucan narrative. Verses

25–27, on the other hand, are typical expressions of Lucan theology: Christ's suffering as the pathway to glory, and the prophecy of the suffering-glory pattern in the scriptures (see above p. 99).

The earliest form of the Emmaus story must accordingly have been something like this: The Risen One appears as a traveler incognito, encounters the disciples, and manifests his identity to them in the course of a meal, after which he vanishes.[15]

Similar stories of the entertainment of supernatural beings unaware occur in folklore, both biblical and profane. A reference to such stories occures in an exhortation in Hebrews 13:2, "Do not neglect to show hospitality to strangers, for thereby some have entertained angels unawares." One need only recall the stories of Abraham and Lot in Genesis 18:1–8 and 19:1–3 respectively, or, in classical literature, the beautiful legend of Philemon and Baucis in Ovid's *Metamorphoses*, to see the influence of a popular motif in the Emmaus narrative. The story looks like the product of the story-telling proclivities of the community. But it is not early if, as we have argued, the resurrection appearances were at first listed rather than narrated. There are grounds for thinking that Luke drew his special material from Syrian tradition.[16] The connection between the special Lucan resurrection narratives and those of the Fourth Gospel, which we have already had occasion to note, points to the same provenance. It was here, in circles which loved to tell stories and which operated with a *theios anēr* (divine man) interpretation of the earthly Jesus, that the late resurrection narratives may well have originated. In them the Risen One is portrayed on the one hand precisely as if he were still the earthly Jesus: he walks with his disciples, he accepts an invitation to supper in their home, and he breaks the bread before them as he had done during his earthly ministry. All these data are reproduced from the tradition of the earthly Jesus in the Gospels. Yet on the other hand he is a mysterious "divine man," who appears and disappears at will. Behind this portrait there is also authentic Christian experience: the Risen One made himself known to the disciples in the breaking of the bread. In this motif there is enshrined a generation or more of Christian eucharistic worship (cf. the primitive liturgical acclamation, *Marana tha*) and behind it further the earliest understanding of the resurrection appearances as revelatory encounters (see above, p. 33).

Some have endeavored to extract a kernel of factual information which would anchor the Emmaus tradition firmly in history, namely, from the place name Emmaus and from the proper name Cleopas.

First, Emmaus. It is stated to be sixty stadia from Jerusalem, i.e., some seven miles. Three different identifications have been proposed for the village. Traditionally it was identified with an Emmaus known in Maccabean times (1 Macc. 3:40, etc). However, this is 120 stadia from Jerusalem, twice the distance of the Emmaus in Luke 24.[17]

The medieval Franciscans identified Emmaus with a place called El-Kubebe, but this seems to be purely conjectural. A third possibility is the military colony of Vespasian called Ammaous (Josephus, *Bell. Jud.* VII, 6,6), known today as Kaloniye. True, the standard text of Josephus gives the distance of this place as only thirty stadia from Jerusalem, though there is a manuscript of Josephus which reads "sixty," the same distance as the Emmaus of Luke 24.

Of the three possibilities the last looks most likely. But was the name originally part of the story, or was it added later? It is impossible to say.

Next, the name Cleopas (his companion is unnamed). Cleopas has been frequently indentified with the Clopas of John 19:25. But identification, though tempting, is uncertain. According to Bauer (BAG, s.v.), Clopas is probably the Semitic QLOPA, while Cleopas is an abbreviation of the Hellenistic name Kleopatros. Yet even this is not conclusive, for Jews often took a similar-sounding Greek name in addition to their Semitic name. The companion has provided a happy hunting ground for legendary identification in later tradition, in the church fathers, apocryphal gospels, and manuscript tradition,[18] and the following have been proposed: Nathanael, Luke himself, Simon (not Peter) or Simeon, and Amaon (possibly a corruption of Simeon).

Of these, Nathanael was an obvious candidate for minor roles in the passion-resurrection narrative (cf. John 21:2), for he was a near-disciple but not originally accounted as one of the Twelve. The identification with the Evangelist himself was also obvious, especially given the anonymous way in which he apparently refers to himself in the we-sections of Acts. The name of Simon or Simeon is more interesting. There is a tradition that Clopas was the brother of Joseph, the father of Jesus, and that he became the second Bishop of Jerusalem. Of course the lynchpin of this tradition is the identification of Cleopas with Clopas, which, as we have seen, is not at all certain. In short, we cannot get very far with the proper names as a means of establishing a historical nucleus for the Emmaus story. More pertinent is the question how this appearance is related to the early list of appearances in 1 Corinthians 15. Since Luke is not creating this masterpiece *de novo*, we have obviously here a Judean (as opposed to a Galilean) appearance. In an earlier chapter we were led to the conclusion that the first appearances (Cephas and the Twelve) were best located in Galilee. The next three (the +500, James and all the apostles) were more likely associated with Jerusalem; we can rule out an identification with the first two of these (the appearance to the +500 took place on a single occasion, while that to James was an appearance to a single individual). This leaves us with the appearance to "all the apostles." It is not absolutely necessary (see above) to suppose that this was a single appearance. Could the Emmaus appearance have been one of the appearances to "all the apostles"? If Cleopas is rightly identified with Clopas, then this appearance would be associated closely with the appearance to James who was his brother. He could therefore be one of the original Jerusalem missionary apostles (as opposed to the Twelve) and one of the Aramaic-speaking group. Such a view would substantiate our earlier thesis that the appearances to James and to all the apostles are in some way connected. On the other hand, if Cleopas is a purely Greek name quite distinct from Clopas, then we could regard him as one of the Greek-speaking apostles, i.e., as a member of the Hellenistic Jewish Christian mission emanating from Jerusalem. Either of these identifications provides the most likely link with the earliest tradition; that it is completely independent of them is hardly conceivable,[19] unless we are to suppose that the pre-Pauline list is not exhaustive or that the Emmaus story has no basis in history.

If, however, we accept one or other of these identifications, it will mean that the call to mission, which was originally associated with this story, has been worn away in the course of transmission, so that Luke was able to use it as a repository for his post-resurrection kerygmatic theology. The Emmaus story leaves us with problems which are incapable of solution.

One final feature in the pre-Lucan tradition of the Emmaus story calls for comment. That is the location of the appearance in the context of a eucharistic meal. This motif occurs in other Easter traditions: Luke 24:41–42; Acts 1:4 (where "staying" may also be translated "eating"); Acts 10:41; John 21:9–14. Some scholars, e.g., O. Cullmann,[20] regard this as an important piece of historical information: the resurrection appearances occurred in a eucharistic context, and in them the earliest church found the fulfillment of the Lord's promise at the last supper of restored table fellowship with his disciples in the kingdom of God. On the other hand, H. Grass[21] rejects this thesis on the ground that the meal motif serves so many different purposes in the tradition. But this consideration could point equally to varying applications of an original tradition. There is no apparent reason why the eucharistic meal should not have provided the occasion for some at least of the resurrection appearances, more probably those which occurred to groups rather than those to single individuals. When the Christian community began to *narrate* appearances, it may have modeled its narrations on the meals which Jesus celebrated with his disciples during his earthly ministry (e.g., *he* pronounces the blessing). Next, it developed these eucharistic appearances in the interest of apologetic (the risen Lord is made to eat in front of the disciples as a demonstration of the physical reality of his risen manifestation). The eucharistic setting for group appearances in that case would antedate the *narration* of appearances in meal contexts and belong to the primitive *statements* of appearances. Note that the reference to the meal in Acts 1:4 occurs in a summary statement rather than in an appearance narrative.

There are three main theological motifs in the dialogue material of the Emmaus story: 1. Jesus as a prophet; 2. a summary of the passion tradition; and 3. a scriptural proof of the suffering-glory pattern. Each of these topics must be examined in turn.

1. Jesus as prophet (v.19b). This means Jesus is the eschatological prophet like unto Moses (Acts 2:22, 36, 38). Under this rubric the words and deeds of Jesus are included (Acts 2:22; 10:38, in the latter passage the deeds only). The deeds of Jesus (his healings and other mighty works) are properly part of the eschatological-prophet Christology, not of the Messiah-Son of David Christology. This shows that the miracle tradition in the Gospels antedates the *theios anēr* (divine man) Christology, though of course the miracle narratives have also passed through the *theios anēr* stratum and have been modified by it.[22] Luke is here drawing on Palestinian kerygmatic material.

2. Jesus as the one who was "to redeem Israel" (v.21a). It could be that this refers to the disappointment of messianic hopes in the Davidic or Zealot (nationalist-political) mistaken sense, hopes which Jesus raised in the course of his ministry. This would certainly be the case if the formulation, and not merely the general mood, accurately reflects the feeling of Jesus' followers after his crucifixion (cf. Bornkamm). But it could equally reflect the more positive hope associated with the Mosaic-eschatological prophet. Given the designation of Jesus as prophet, introduced a few verses earlier (v.19), we incline to see in the formulation an expression of the post-Easter eschatological-prophet Christology, albeit of the very earliest period. As such it may well be a genuine reflection of the historical situation after the first Easter. The word redeem (*lutrousthai*) is full of Old Testament associations, recalling the deliverance from Egypt and entry into the promised land, as also the return from the exile. In this case 19b and 21a will belong to the same stratum of tradition, that of a Mosaic eschatological-prophet Christology (cf. also Acts 3:12–14 and 7:2–53).

The passion formula (v.20) reflects the language of the Marcan predictions: note especially the verb deliver (*paredōken*), which belongs to the earliest interpretation of the passion (the passion as the Jews' No and the resurrection as God's Yes). On the other hand, we find the same substitution of the verb crucify (*estaurōsan*) for the usual *apokteinein* as in the Lucan adaptation of the angelic charge to the women (v.7). This alteration is a sign of Lucan editing.

    3. The fulfillment of scripture. This is stressed no less than three times in the dialogue, and must be regarded as the principal motif of the story as edited by Luke:

> all that the prophets have spoken (v.25)
> was it not necessary? (*edei*, see above, p. 99) (v.26)
> Moses and all the prophets . . . all the scriptures (v.27).

The expressions are very similar to those we find in verses 44–46. The motif is of course traditional and goes back, as we have already observed, to the primitive formula "in accordance with the scriptures" in 1 Corinthians 15:3–4 and to earliest passion-resurrection apologetic. But Luke has given it his own special nuance in the concept that suffering is the pathway to messianic glory.

    The word for suffer (*pathein*) appears to be a Hellenistic term, for which surprisingly there is no exact Hebrew or Aramaic equivalent. We find the same pattern of suffering and glory in 1 Peter 1:11b, which suggests that this theological emphasis is not a Lucan invention, but a commonplace of Hellenistic Christian theology. It corresponds to the two-stage Christology of Hellenistic Jewish Christianity.[23]

    Luke is trying here to build a bridge between the earthly ministry and its continuation in the kerygma. He interprets the whole earthly ministry as the eschatological act of God (the title Christos, the fulfillment of the scriptures) and lays down (through the mouth of the Risen One) the terms of its proclamation for the Book of Acts.

    Verses 33–35 form an appendix to the story, serving as a connecting link between the Emmaus pericope and the Jerusalem appearance which is to follow. Is it Lucan or pre-Lucan? As it stands it contains a cross-reference to the Emmaus story in its present Lucan form, for it alludes to the dialogue which the Evangelist had composed. If the two stories were brought together before Luke, as we think quite possible, then Luke himself will have added the reference to the conversation (*ta en te hodō, kai,* v. 35).[24] Verse 34, "who said, 'The Lord has risen indeed, and has appeared to Simon,'" interrupts the flow of the narrative. Its effect is to take the wind out of the sails of the Emmaus disciples. It is a surprising reference to the primary appearance to Peter, which nowhere else in Luke is either narrated or even mentioned. Verse 34 is almost certainly an insertion of the Evangelist.

But did Luke himself compose it? The title *Kurios* is certainly characteristic of his style. But the rest of the wording reproduces almost *verbatim* 1 Corinthians 15:5:

LUKE 24:34	1 COR. 15:4–5A
(he) has risen (*egerthē*) indeed,	he was raised (*egēgertai*) . . .
and (he) has appeared to Simon	and that he appeared to Cephas.

We suggested in chapter 1 that Paul was the first to combine the kerygmatic statement of the resurrection with a list of appearances. The two traditions have now completely coalesced: there is now no intervening *hoti* (that). There are abundant indications of this coalescence of the resurrection and appearances in the kerygmatic speeches in Acts (Acts 2, 3, 10, 13). So it is here. Luke 24:34 is a valuable testimony to the primary appearance to Peter, confirming 1 Corinthians 15:5 and Mark 16:7 and also indicating that Luke knew no *narrative* of that appearance, only the statement of it in a list.[25]

Why then has Luke inserted this allusion to the primary appearance to Peter? Evidently because he does not agree with the impression created by his source that the Emmaus appearance was the primary one: he wishes to correct it on this (for him) decisive point. Why? Because Peter will stand out later in Acts as the leader of the earliest Christian community (Acts 1–12). Already in Luke 22:32 Luke recorded Jesus' prediction of Peter's temporary defection and his restoration to a position of leadership over his brethren. He must therefore allude to the primary appearance in order to bridge the gap between the earthly ministry and the history of the early community, between the first and second volume of his historical work. To ask why Luke did not include a narrative of an appearance to Peter is beside the point, once we are prepared to face the probability that not such narrative ever existed.

The Emmaus story is thus a unique compendium of Easter traditions, the product of a considerable process of development. It may contain a basic nucleus of historical fact, if it can be identified with one of the appearances included among the appearances "to all the apostles" and especially if the name Clopas warrants some connection with James. A primitive *statement* of such an appearance, if it is historical, was later thrown into the form of a *narrative* with the kind of legendary elements one might expect in such an environment as Syria—still fairly Semitic in outlook, but with overtones of the *theios anēr* (divine man) Christology. This stage contributes such elements as: Jesus as the Risen One traveling as an earthly figure yet mysteriously incognito, the earthly form of the conversation, the meal (though, as we have seen, this may belong to earlier and perhaps even historical tradition), the recognition.

Originally an isolated unit, this story was, probably prior to Luke, incorporated into a series of resurrection narratives (the empty tomb in a non-Marcan version, with an angelophany to the women, and with the visit of the disciples including Peter to the grave). At this stage a cross-reference was provided within the story to the preceding and ensuing pericope.

Lastly, there comes the Lucan redaction. Drawing upon other traditional materials (the synoptic predictions, Palestinian and Hellenistic forms of the Christological kerygma, the primitive motif of the resurrection "in accordance with the scriptures") and adding the corrective reference to the first appearance to Peter, Luke refabricates this story not only into a gem of narrative art, but also into a bridge between the first and second volumes of his historical work.

The appearance to the eleven and others
(Luke 24:36–39,41–49)

[36]As they were saying this, Jesus himself stood among them. [37]But they were startled and frightened, and supposed that they saw a spirit. [38]And he said to them, "Why are you troubled, and why do questionings arise in your hearts? [39]See my hands and my feet, that it is I myself; handle me, and see; for a spirit has not flesh and bones as you see that I have." . . . [41]And while they still disbelieved for joy, and wondered, he said to them, "Have you anything here to eat?" [42]They gave him a piece of broiled fish, [43]and he took it and ate before them.

[44]Then he said to them, "These are my words which I spoke to you, while I was still with you, that everything written about me in the law of Moses and the prophets and the psalms must be fulfilled." [45]Then he opened their minds to understand the scriptures, [46]and said to them, "Thus it is written, that the Christ should suffer and on the third day rise from the dead, [47]and that repentance and forgiveness of sins should be preached in his name to all nations, beginning from Jerusalem. [48]You are witnesses of these things. [49]And behold, I send the promise of my Father upon you; but stay in the city, until you are clothed with power from on high."

This narrative falls into two halves. Verses 36–43 provide a demonstration of the resurrection, while verses 44–49 contain a further compendium of kerygmatic-christological instruction. The Jerusalem location of the appearance is not indicated in the narrative part of the pericope, but only in the connecting link with the Emmaus story (v.33) and in the instruction (v.47). This, together with the mention of fish (v.42), suggests that as a separate pericope this appearance was originally located in Galilee. In that case, it would have been a narration of the second appearance to the Twelve in 1 Corinthians 15:5, which the pre-Lucan link, like Matthew 28:16, has pedantically corrected to eleven. But already in the pre-Lucan tradition (since we have assigned the connecting link, vv.33–35, to the pre-Lucan stratum), the appearance will have been transferred to Jerusalem. At the same time its character has been altered. It is no longer, as in 1 Corinthians 15:5, a church-founding appearance, but a mission-inaugurating one—the same shift which was already prepared for by Mark 16:7 (see above, pp. 67f.) and made explicit in Matthew 28:16–20.

But the character of this appearance has undergone a double alteration. First, it has received a highly apologetic coloring not merely absent from 1 Corinthians 15:5, but quite contrary to it. The motif of doubt (*dialogismoi* and *apistountōn*, v.41, see above, p. 81) has been redirected to provide the occasion for a massively physical demonstration. The Risen One invites his disciples to touch him so that they can see for themselves that he is not a "spirit" or "ghost," but a figure of flesh and blood. This new interpretation of the mode of the resurrection (resuscitation of the earthly body) is quite contrary to the apocalyptic framework of the earliest kerygma of 1 Corinthians 15:5, to Paul's concept of the *pneumatikon sōma* (see esp. 1 Cor. 15:35ff.) and to the presentation in Mark 16:1–8 and in Matthew 28:16–20. But it was made inevitable by the development of appearance narratives. We have already had an example of materialization in Matthew 28:9 which, however, is contrary to the general tenor of the Matthean presentation. For appearances could be narrated only by borrowing the traits of the earthly Jesus—he must walk, talk, eat, etc., as he had done in his earthly life. These features, at first conceived quite naïvely (as in the Emmaus story) are now drawn out and emphasized in the interests of apologetic. The demonstration is threefold: they are invited not only to touch and to see, but also to watch the Risen One eating fish.[26] The story presumes, though it does not expressly state, that the demonstration was successful and the disciples were convinced. One suspects that the pre-Lucan form of the story reached its climax in a statement to that effect. Luke is not prepared to jettison the demonstration, for it enables him once more to link his two volumes together—the exalted Christ who presides over his church in Acts is identical with the earthly Jesus of the Gospel. But he does not wish to over-emphasize it either. He therefore removes the climax, and substitutes the christological-kerygmatic discourse in verses 44–49.

We agree with Bultmann[27] that this discourse is Lucan redaction though, like the Emmaus story, it takes up traditional kerygmatic themes and motifs which are paralleled elsewhere in Luke-Acts. The discourse makes two major points: 1. During the earthly ministry (note once more Luke's concern to link the earthly and the post-resurrection phases of Christ's work) the earthly Jesus had told them how the scriptures (comprehensively defined as "Moses, the prophets, and the psalms") had predicted his fate. Thus the scripture fulfillment is carried back into the period of the earthly Jesus (cf. e.g., Luke 4:18–21). This teaching, however, was apparently not grasped at the time, for: 2. it is now necessary for Jesus to "open" once more the scriptures, whose import, as in 24:26, is that the suffering of the Messiah is the pathway to glory.

First, the theme of scriptural fulfillment. The historical Jesus, as a critical reconstruction of his message indicates, did not explicitly proclaim a theology of scriptural fulfillment in his own message and mission. But his proclamation that the kingdom of God had drawn near in his person and work indirectly implied it. The post-resurrection church, with its apologetic needs, sought to demonstrate that the whole Christ event, and in particular his death and resurrection, had taken place "in accordance with the scriptures"—an explicit insight which it reached as a result of the impact of the Easter experiences. It therefore discovered and used *testimonia* texts as an apologetic armory for its kerygma. These testimonia were later read back into the Jesus tradition. But the constant emphasis throughout the Gospels, especially the Fourth Gospel, that the disciples did not understand the words of the earthly Jesus and that these became clear only after the resurrection preserved the earlier perspective. Luke is here trying to reconcile the earlier tradition, according to which it was the resurrection which opened the eyes of the community to the theme of scriptural fulfillment, with the later tradition which placed these themes on the lips of the earthly Jesus.

Verse 46 (as we have already had occasion to observe) is close in formulation to verse 26:

24:26	24:46
Was it not necessary that the Christ should suffer these things and enter into his glory?	Thus it is written, that the Christ should suffer and on the third day rise from the dead.

"It is necessary" is equivalent in meaning to "it is written" (cf. above, p. 99). The same christological title (*ho Christos*) is used, and the same verb for suffer (*pathein*). Only the resurrection statement is different. Both formulae have points of contact with, yet differences from, the Marcan passion predictions.[28]

Although the material in this kerygmatic summary comes from pre-Lucan traditions, the Evangelist uses it to express his own distinctive theology, specifically to connect the two phases of the second period of salvation history—the ministry of Jesus and the kerygma of the church, the Gospel and the Acts.

In verse 47, Luke further inserts a missionary command. As we have already suggested, this is a transferral of the theme which originally belonged with the appearance "to all the apostles" to what was originally the church-founding appearance to the Twelve (eleven). The beginnings of this shift we have traced back to Mark's Galilee symbolism in 16:7. Matthew and Luke have taken up Mark's suggestion in two different ways. Matthew combines the Great Commission with the appearance to the eleven in Galilee, while Luke appends the missionary command to the christological-kerygmatic instruction in the same appearance, now shifted to Jerusalem. Thus Luke makes the mission, like the original saving events, part of the fulfillment of the scripture ("*that . . .* and *that,*" vv.46–47). We have already discussed the historical basis for this shift to mission in connection with Matthew 28:16–20 (see above, pp. 83f.). Certain features which the Lucan form of the charge has in common with other forms (the baptismal reference in "repentance and forgiveness of sins," "in his name," cf. Matt. 28:19; Ps.-Mark 16:15–16) and the universality of the command ("to all nations" *verbatim* at

Mark 13:10; Matt. 28:19; also cf. Ps.-Mark 16:15) suggest that Luke has derived this charge from earlier tradition. As we have already observed, its universalistic form is a development of salvation-historical perspective which already presupposes the Pauline interpretation. But the words "beginning from Jerusalem" must surely be Lucan redaction. Here we have in outline the pattern of Acts. Jerusalem will be the center from which the Christian mission will go forth, and to which at every stage the mission is subordinated. This is a point in which Luke differs from Mark and Matthew, for whom the mission was to go forth from Galilee. If we are right in locating the appearance(s) to "all the apostles" in Jerusalem, it will mean that Luke is in one way closer to history,[29] although his concern is with salvation history rather than with historical fact.

In verse 48 the Risen One addresses the eleven directly: "You are witnesses of these things." Here "those who were with them" are forgotten (v.33). The apostles in Luke's understanding are precisely witnesses (see Acts 1:8, 22)—"witnesses of these things," viz., of the ministry, death and resurrection of Jesus, which the Risen One has interpreted as the eschatological fulfillment of Old Testament prophecy.

Finally, in verse 49 the Risen One promises to send the Spirit to equip the disciples for the mission. The verb used for sending the Spirit (*exapostellō*) is identical with that used for the sending of the Spirit in Galatians 4:6. But there the subject is God, here it is the Risen One. In John 15:26 it is stated that the Son sends (*pempei*) the Spirit. But the context in which the verb is used in Luke 24:49 suggests that the pre-Lucan tradition spoke not of the sending of the Spirit, but of the sending forth of the apostles (*apostolos* and *exapostellō* are akin). In the missionary charges of the earthly ministry the conferral of the Spirit or of authority (*exousia*) takes place simultaneously with the sending forth of the missionaries (Matt. 10:16 Q: Mark 6:7; Luke 9:2). Similarly, in the post-resurrection charge of John 20:21 the conferral of the Spirit on the disciples by the Risen One takes place simultaneously with their sending. If the pre-Lucan tradition combined the sending and the conferral of the

Spirit in the same way, then it is the Evangelist who has separated the two events to conform with his schematization: resurrection—appearances—ascension—Pentecost.

Our analysis of the history of the tradition in Luke 24:36–49 has led us to the following conclusions. The historical kernel of tradition behind the pericope is a conflation of the originally distinct appearances to the Twelve and to all the apostles, a conflation which has transformed the appearance to the eleven from a church-founding into a mission-inaugurating one. Here Luke has achieved substantially the same result as Matthew, though in a rather different way. The endowment of the Spirit to equip the apostles for their mission is a motif which we have not encountered in the resurrection narratives so far but, like the command to baptize, it is one of the theological implications of the resurrection encounters which were present from the earliest days of the community. For this community understood that it had received the Spirit as the outcome of the Christ event (Rom. 8:11).

While Luke develops his own distinctive understanding of salvation history by means of the reference to the fulfillment of scripture, the germ of this development lies in the formula "in accordance with the scriptures," which had been attached to both the passion and the resurrection in the earliest kerygma. This understanding was also the result of the impact of the Easter experiences, and to that extent Luke is true to history.

From the pre-Lucan tradition come the following elements: kerygmatic formulae (Palestinian and Hellenistic) covering the earthly life, passion, and resurrection of Christ; the reading back of the fulfillment of scripture explicitly into the preaching of the earthly Jesus, the repentance-baptismal motif, the universalization of the mission.

The Evangelist himself integrated the resurrection narratives into his scheme of salvation-history. In this scheme, the resurrection becomes the bridge between "all that Jesus began to do and teach" (Acts 1:1), i.e., the earthly ministry, conceived as the eschatological fulfillment of scripture, and the continuation of this action by the Risen and Exalted One in the universal mission of the Christian community. It should be particularly noted that only in the Lucan resurrection narratives is the mission of the church brought under the rubric of scripture fulfillment,[30] a point which underlines both the continuity and the difference between the two successive phases of salvation history, Jesus' earthly ministry (Luke) and the church (Acts).

Luke certainly did not invent the Jerusalem location of the appearances. Matthew 28:9–10 had already located the appearance to the women at Jerusalem (cf. John 20:11f.). But this was a development of the earlier angelophany at the tomb and is a sideline in the tradition. The pre-Lucan tradition had an appearance in the environs of Jerusalem (Emmaus) and, when this tradition was combined with the appearance to the eleven, the effect was to transfer the two primary appearances (those to "Simon" and to the eleven) to Jerusalem as well. If the appearance(s) to "all the apostles" (as opposed to the Twelve) took place in or around Jerusalem, this procedure had at least some historical justification. Luke, however, as we have already had occasion to note, is concerned not with history, but with salvation history. He shows this by inserting the phrase "beginning from Jerusalem" at verse 46. For Jerusalem is the place where salvation history is fulfilled and from which the proclamation of that salvation history goes out to the ends of the earth.[31]

The departure of Jesus (Luke 24:50–53)

[50]Then he led them out as far as Bethany, and lifting up his hands he blessed them. [51]While he blessed them, he parted from them. [52]And they returned to Jerusalem with great joy, [53]and were continually in the temple blessing God.

The major problem in this pericope is whether or not it includes an allusion to the ascension. The majority of early manuscripts read in verse 51 "he parted from them." But a few early manuscripts (the original reading of Sinaiticus, plus Western texts such as Bezae, the Italian Old Latin and the Sinaitic Syriac) add: "and was carried up into heaven" (RSV margin). Earlier scholars[32] sought to eliminate the ascension both from this passage and from Acts 1:1–11, arguing that both passages were interpolations into the text of Luke-Acts. (Reasons for this will be discussed further when we come to examine Acts 1:1–5). An intermediate view, championed by K. Lake,[33] H. Sahlin,[34] A. N. Wilder,[35] and especially P. Menoud,[36] would eliminate Luke 24:50–53 and Acts 1:1–5 as later interpolations. The last named offers several reasons for this omission. Luke 24:50–53 is composed allegedly on the basis of Acts 1:6–14. The phrase "lifting up his hands" is *hapax legomenon* not only in Luke but in the whole of the New Testament, whereas it becomes common in the Church Fathers after the second century. The "great joy" of verse 52 is entirely unmotivated in its present context, but explicable from Acts 1:9–11, where the disciples have just been assured that Jesus "will come in the same way." A slight variation on this thesis appears in Conzelmann, *op. cit.*, who thinks that Luke 24:50–53 and (unspecified) parts of Acts 1:1–11 are interpolations.

Most of these writers start out from the assumption that Luke-Acts was originally a single volume, and that when it was split into two, Luke 24:50–53 was composed as the conclusion of the Gospel and Acts 1:1–5 as the beginning of Acts.

Against these views P. A. van Stampvoort[37] has argued for the authenticity of both Luke 24:50–53 and Acts 1:1–5 (as well as 6–11). The final pericope of the Gospel, the departure of Jesus, is carefully composed in such a way as to make it integral to the structure of Luke-Acts. The Gospel begins and ends at the temple. It is in the context of the temple that the church originates and it is from the temple that the church goes out into its mission in the world. The Gospel also begins and ends with a priestly act: in Luke 1, Zecharias, the pious representative of the priesthood of the old covenant, performs his priestly liturgy in the temple. In Luke 24, the messianic priest lifts up his hands to impart the highly-priestly blessing.[38] It is this blessing that produced the allegedly unmotivated joy (cf. Sir. 50:20–24). Van Stampvoort also pleads for originality of the words "worshiped him" (RSV margin), found in Vaticanus and Sinaiticus (cf. Sir. 50:21) but omitted in other Western textual traditions. The blessing, significantly, takes place *outside* the temple, because the temple has now been superseded. And the actual report of the ascension ("and was carried up into heaven"), found in Vaticanus and Alexandrinus and other ancient manuscripts, though omitted by the Western textual tradition, is authentic since its omission is more easily explained than its insertion. (So, too, many other critics.) The palpable discrepancy between the Gospel's report of an ascension on Easter Day or the day following and the story of the ascension in Acts 1, which dates that event at the end of the forty days, is hardly due to a redactor. Moreover, the ascension is integral to the succession of events: led—blessed—parted—carried up—returned—were praising.

Van Stampvoort calls particular attention to the tense of "was carried up" (*anephereto*, imperfect, literally "was being carried up"). "It is a picturesque imperfect, describing his being carried up into heaven as a movement which took some time." This prepares the way for the mention of the cloud in Acts 1.

Thus, van Stampvoort concludes, Luke 24:50–53 is Luke's first presentation of the ascension. It serves as the conclusion of the Gospel, it looks backward to the finished work of Christ which the Gospel has related, and it culminates in blessing and worship. On the discrepancy of date he concludes that we are not meant to press either the suggestion of Luke 24 that the ascension took place on Easter Day or the day after, or the statement about the forty days in Acts 1. The latter is to be taken symbolically, not as a precise date. Not all of van Stampvoort's arguments and interpretations are convincing, but we concede that the report of the ascension in 51b is textually Lucan and integral to the narrative. It is hardly likely that a later redactor would have interpolated 51b in such a way as to create a discrepancy with Acts 1. It is, moreover, worth noting that the word used for the ascension in verse 51b "was carried up" (*anephereto*) does not appear in Acts 1 which uses two different words: "was taken up" (*anelēmphthē* 1:2, cf. 11) and "was elevated" (*epērthē*, 1:9).[39]

Is then Luke 24:50–53 as a whole redactional, or is it based on earlier tradition? Bultmann inclines to the opinion that it is traditional.[40] Yet he also recognizes it as a literary product. Since it is a literary product and integral to the structure of Luke-Acts, we think that Luke has deliberately composed this closing scene. But the central statement ("and was carried up into heaven") may well be based on a primitive kerygmatic formula, belonging to the Palestinian-Aramaic christological stratum. According to this Christology the resurrection of Jesus was at the same time his assumption (rather than his exaltation) into heaven.[41] Both its form (concise kerygmatic statement rather than narrative) and its content (an assumption into heaven) indicate its primitive character. In the original conception, it must be remembered, resurrection and assumption from the grave were hardly distinguishable. Luke has thus (*contra* the presupposition of 1 Cor. 15:3–7; Mark 16:6–7; Matt. 28:16–20) separated assumption from resurrection, making it a distinct event subsequent to the appearances. The idea of a final appearance was already implicit in the earliest tradition, at least in the way reproduced by Paul (especially "last of all," 1 Cor. 15:8). With the progressive materialization of the appearances, it was becoming increasingly difficult to conceive of them as appearances from heaven. They are thus transformed into appearances of a resuscitated earthly figure, conceived in terms of the divine-man Christology, and concluded by an ascension as a distinct event.

The forty days' appearances (Acts 1:1–5)

[1]In the first book, O Theophilus, I have dealt with all that Jesus began to do and teach, [2]until the day when he was taken up, after he had given commandment through the Holy Spirit to the apostles whom he had chosen. [3]To them he presented himself alive after his passion by many proofs, appearing to them during forty days, and speaking of the kingdom of God. [4]And while staying with them he charged them not to depart from Jerusalem, but to wait for the promise of the Father, which, he said, "you heard from me, [5]for John baptized with water, but before many days you shall be baptized with the Holy Spirit."

After a brief introduction linking the second part of Luke's historical work to the first (1:1), there follows a circumstantial

account of the forty days' companionship between the Risen One
and his disciples (1:2–5).

Ever since E. Meyer's analysis of this pericope (see above,
p. 121, n. 32), critics have been acutely aware of the many problems which it poses. We have already discussed the discrepancies
between Luke 24 and Acts 1. We now turn to the discrepancies
within the second passage. The opening sentence starts out with
the Greek particle *men*, meaning "on the one hand," but there
is no *de*, "on the other hand," to complement it. Instead of following the usual style of contemporary historiography, which
calls for the résumé of the contents of volume I to be followed
by a statement of the contents of volume II, the second volume
leads into a flashback of the pre-ascension period already covered
in Luke 24. Verse 2b is particularly rough in the Greek. What
does the statement mean that the Risen One gave his charge
to the disciples "through the Holy Spirit"? The allusion to the
ascension in verse 2 curiously anticipates the narrative of verses
9–11. Even van Stampvoort boggles at this, and proposes to
interpret *anelēmphthē* as a reference to Jesus' elevation on the
cross (cf. Luke 9:51).[42]

And what conception underlies the notion of his "appearing
to them during forty days" (v.3)? Does it mean that he appeared
repeatedly, or does it mean that his presence with them was
continuous? The latter is favored by Grass,[43] on the ground that
it corresponds with Luke's materialization of the appearances:
where would Jesus go before the ascension? The former view
would presuppose the earlier, more spiritual conception of the
appearances as appearances from heaven, and is favored by
P. Menoud in his second article (p. 213, n. 37) on the
ground that the word "during" (*dia* with the genitive) indicates
"time within which." "Time how long" would require an accusa-
tive of duration. Also the "many proofs" points to a purality of
appearances. I think P. Menoud is the more convincing. The
difficulties Grass raises are the consequence of Luke's failure to
adjust the earlier ascension tradition (see below) to his own
theology. The earlier perspective of repeated appearances is
still discernible in Acts 13:31, "for many days" (*epi pleious*

hēmeras). Luke's retention of this earlier perspective fits ill
with his articulated scheme, but it is unlikely to be Lucan redaction or a later interpolation since it reflects a more primitive
conception.

Yet another discrepancy has been discerned between verse 3
and verse 6. If the Risen One has exhaustively covered the
subject of the kingdom of God in verse 3, why are the disciples
still perplexed about it in verse 6? This can be answered from
Luke's theological concern. Verse 3 emphasizes that the kingdom
is to be the content of the apostles' preaching, as it is throughout
Acts,[44] while verse 6 deals with the sub-apostolic problem of the
delayed parousia. Both verses are Lucan redaction and Lucan
theology.

There has been much discussion of the meaning of the word
sunalizomenos in verse 4, translated "staying" (RSV). Literally
this means "taking salt with." Many years ago H. J. Cadbury suggested that it should be corrected to *sunaulizomenos*, which
would mean "staying with." But that would imply a continuous
residence on earth of the Exalted One. Most recent commentators prefer to take it literally and as a reference, like Luke
24:42–43 and Acts 10:41, to the eucharistic setting of the appearances (see below).

Another curious feature of these verses is the repetition of
the promise of the Spirit (4f. and 8). Some have suggested that
one or other of these passages is an interpolation by a later
redactor. But again the duplication of the promise of the Spirit
should be seen as an expression of Lucan theology. The first
promise is stated in terms of the Baptist's saying (Matt. 3:11Q),
repeated by Peter in Acts 11:16. Luke attaches considerable
significance to the double fulfillment of this promise, first at
Pentecost for Israel, then second in the Cornelius episode, which
has sometimes been called the Pentecost of the Gentiles. In
verses 4 and 8 Luke deliberately combines two different aspects
of the Spirit's work: first, the pentecostal endowment with the
Spirit which created the distinctive inner life of the community
and, second, the Spirit as the impelling inner force behind the
outward mission of the community, first to Israel and then to the

Gentiles. The first promise of the Spirit is linked to the teaching of the kingdom of God by verse 4, which is a deliberate cross-reference to Luke 24:50–52.

Despite the stylistic unevenness and discrepancies in this passage, the content of verses 2–5 is integral to the structure of Luke-Acts, and therefore must be accepted as part of the genuine text. And precisely because of this, these verses must be the composition of the author. But they contain older materials. This is obviously the case with verse 5 which echoes a saying of John the Baptist. But verses 2–4 also contain concise allusions to Easter events which we have already encountered in other traditions:

> assumption (*anelēmphthē*, v.2).
> appearances to apostles (*hois parestēsen heauton zōnta*),
>   conceived as revelatory encounters.
> eucharistic meal (*sunalizomenos*).
> conferral of the Spirit (v.4, cf. v.2).

The author has arranged these kerygmatic facts in conformity with his own articulated scheme (resurrection—appearances—ascension—Pentecost). The confusion will be due to the fact that the rearrangement is incomplete. While the assumption precedes the appearances (v.3), as it would have done in a primitive formula, it also follows them (v.2). Then there are two references to the Spirit, the confused reference to the instructions given by the Risen One "through the Holy Spirit" in verse 2 and the directive to wait for the Spirit at Pentecost in verse 4. They are perhaps more intelligible as re-arrangements of an original tradition which spoke of the Risen One's equipping the apostles with the Spirit for their mission.

What of the absence of any résumé of the contents of the ensuing volume? To answer this question we have to look also at the second part of the pericope (through v.8). Verses 5–8 aptly summarize the course of events in Acts—a period of waiting for the Spirit, Pentecost, and missionary expansion from Jerusalem to Rome. Luke departs from the normal procedure of the historian because he is not a normal historian. The contents of the second volume are announced not by the author himself but by the Risen One. Acts contains not merely history but salvation history.

The final charge and the ascension (Acts 1:6–11)

⁶So when they had come together, they asked him, "Lord, will you at this time restore the kingdom to Israel?" ⁷He said to them, "It is not for you to know times or seasons which the Father has fixed by his own authority. ⁸But you shall receive power when the Holy Spirit has come upon you; and you shall be my witnesses in Jerusalem and in all Judea and Samaria and to the end of the earth." ⁹And when he had said this, as they were looking on, he was lifted up, and a cloud took him out of their sight. ¹⁰And while they were gazing into heaven as he went, behold, two men stood by them in white robes, ¹¹and said, "Men of Galilee, why do you stand looking into heaven? This Jesus, who was taken up from you into heaven, will come in the same way as you saw him go into heaven."

Verse 6 marks a fresh beginning. At the close of the forty days the disciples gather with Jesus for a final meeting. Thus Luke introduces the ascension narrative (vv.9–11). But he prefaces the ascension story with a further discussion about the kingdom of God, specifically about its delay. Since this expresses a typical concern of sub-apostolic Christianity it is surely redactional. The missionary charge in verse 8 is to be seen precisely in the context of the delay in the parousia. World-wide mission is a kind of substitute for the delayed parousia. This, too, is Lucan theology.

The endowment with the Spirit (v.8) to empower the world-wide witness of the apostolic community is already announced in Luke 24:48–49, while the missionary program (Jerusalem, Judea, Samaria and to the ends of the earth) sets out the pattern of the ensuing Book of Acts. All of verses 6–8 may therefore be safely assigned to the Evangelist's redaction.

The narrative of the ascension proper comprises verses 9–11. It is the third reference to that event in Luke-Acts (see Luke

24:51; Acts 1:2). Luke 24:51 locates the ascension at Bethany, while verse 12, after the conclusion of the ascension narrative, locates it at the Mount of Olives. But there is no real contradiction, since the Mount of Olives was en route to Bethany.

The narrative is highly realistic. Jesus is "taken up" *epērthē* (literally: elevated). A cloud receives him out of sight. The disciples are left gazing up to heaven. Two angels appear with an interpretive function (v.10), as in the Lucan version of the empty tomb story, and deliver instruction about the parousia (v.11). The imagery is derived from Old Testament and apocalyptic sources. The "elevation" of Jesus to heaven is reminiscent of the assumption of Elijah in 2 Kings 2:11, "And Elijah *went up* (LXX *anelēmphthē*, cf. Acts 1:2) by a whirlwind into heaven." The cloud is reminiscent of the parousia scene in Daniel 7:13f. and occurs also in Mark 13:26; 14:62; 1 Thessalonians 4:16 and Revelation 1:7. The ascension narrative is often regarded as the author's free composition.[45] But, as we have already pointed out in our discussion of Luke 24:51b, the ascension is conceived in more primitive terms than we should expect in such a late document as Luke-Acts. We have here the same primitive conception as in Acts 3:21, namely, that of an assumption rather than an exaltation. The Risen One is taken up into heaven and waits there inactively until his return at the parousia. He is not, as in Acts 2:36, exalted to an active reign as Kurios or Christos. As Hahn commented:[46]

Acts 1:9–11 has to be mentioned here; the exaltation plays no sort of role in this story of the ascension, the outlook is exclusively toward the return of Jesus, and the idea of the Son of man coming then on the clouds of heaven has probably been the pattern here. We cannot without more ado define this narrative as a Lukan composition as Haenchen . . . does; that with all its marks of Luke's pen there is here an early tradition may not be disputed.

But if the ascension story belonged to a more primitive stratum, its location—at the end of the appearances and forty days after the resurrection—will be a later modification. Originally the ascension must have been conceived as coinciding with the resurrection from the grave and prior to the appearances. Traces of this earlier perspective (which incidentally supports the thesis that the ascension story is pre-Lucan) survive in the *Epistle of Barnabas* 15:9 (though *Barnabas* itself, like Luke, inserts the appearances between the resurrection and ascension):

Wherefore also we keep the eighth day for rejoicing, in the which also Jesus rose from the dead, and having been manifested ascended into the heavens.

Even clearer is the statement of the *Gospel of Peter* 13:57, where the angel at the tomb announces to Mary Magdalene on Easter morning: "He has risen and is gone thither whence he was sent."[47]

The history of the tradition of Acts 1:9–11 may be reconstructed thus: First, there was a very primitive kerygmatic affirmation, alternative to the statement that the Christ was raised on the third day, that he was assumed into heaven (cf. Luke 24:51b). At this stage the appearances would be located after the assumption, as in the *Gospel of Peter*. The appearances were appearances of the Resurrected and already Assumed One. There are traces of this conception in the narratives of the conversion of Paul in the Book of Acts.

Next, this brief kerygmatic assertion was expanded into a narrative, using Elijah typology and apocalyptic imagery (cloud, angels). The ascension now becomes an event witnessed by the disciples in process, and the angels assume the role of *angeli interpretes* as in the empty tomb pericope. This stage of the tradition appears to be contemporary with the special Lucan tradition of the discovery of the empty tomb by the disciples (Luke 24:12, 24). The effect of this need for witnesses to the ascension was to reverse the order of the ascension and the appearances. The order now becomes resurrection—appearances —ascension. This has happened in the *Epistle of Barnabas* 15:9.

Finally, Luke has incorporated the ascension narrative into his introduction of the second volume of his historical work. The ascension now becomes a farewell scene with a promise of the Spirit at Pentecost and a charge to universal mission as a substitute for the delayed parousia.

Leaving aside the Great Commission scene, which Matthew

has artificially constructed and in which the narrative elements
are extremely tenuous, it is in Luke that we first encounter
fully fledged *narratives* of resurrection appearances. These com-
prise: the Emmaus story, the appearance in the upper room,
and a farewell scene with a brief statement of the ascension.
These three narratives are prefixed by the story of the disciples'
discovery of the empty tomb. They are all located in or near
Jerusalem. They conceive the appearances as Christophanies of
a resurrected but not yet ascended Lord, and they relate them
as prolongations of his earthly presence, though in the somewhat
magnified terms of the *theios anēr* (divine man). These stories
are not the creation of Luke (for he edits them in accordance
with his own theology). They perhaps developed somewhere in
Syria (where Luke came from) during the period between the
completion of Mark's Gospel (67–70) and Luke's own writing
(85–90). Their massive conception of the appearances of the
Risen One was apologetically motivated and intended to answer
the doubt of second-generation Christians and to provide a
demonstration of the reality of the Risen One. Luke takes these
stories into his work, but develops them in a different direction.

The appearances of the Risen One become occasions when
he reveals the whole plan of salvation history as understood in
the sub-apostolic age (fulfillment of scripture in universal mission). In developing the sub-apostolic theology, however, Luke
does, *mutatis mutandis*, come closer again to the import of the
original Easter tradition of 1 Corinthians 15:5ff. for the appearances signalized the foundation of the church and the inauguration of the mission. Despite the legendary features, which have
accumulated in the stories Luke had at his disposal, he has in
a very real sense re-christianized them for his day.

The Johannine Resurrection Narratives (John 20)

THE MODERN CRITIC FINDS it difficult to accept the traditional view of the Fourth Gospel in its finished form as the work of the Beloved Disciple and therefore as direct, eye-witness testimony to the events that it records. The resurrection narratives in John 20 are the product of a long process of transmission, not an eye-witness testimony. The current trend is to recognize the independence of John over against the Synoptics. Accordingly, we shall not look for literary relationship between John and the other Gospels, but for the Evangelist's use of traditional material at a certain stage of its development. This traditional material to some extent overlaps with that of the Synoptics and to some extent is independent of them. It seems probable that John had a narrative source comprising at least a continuous account of the passion and resurrection, and that the narratives in chapter 20 are derived from this source. At the same time they will have received some editorial touches from the Evangelist.[1]

This narrative has some affinities with the special Lucan traditions, both in broad outline and in specific detail. There is the same location of the appearances in Jerusalem, and the same physical conception of the body of the Risen One, the same massive demonstration of its reality. In John 20:20 the Risen One displays his wounds, while in verses 25ff. he invites Thomas to touch him. As in Luke-Acts, the resurrection and ascension are separate events, though this distinction is conceived somewhat differently. In both traditions the giving of the Spirit is associated with the Easter events, though again there is a difference. In Luke, the Spirit is promised by the Risen One and given after the ascension at Pentecost whereas, in John, the Spirit is personally bestowed by the Risen One on Easter Day. It is clear that there is some connection between the Johannine and special Lucan traditions. But there is not enough similarity to prove direct literary dependence, even allowing for considerable editorial activity on John's part. For the differences between them are differences of detail in the narrative, and are not for the most part characteristic expressions of Johannine theology. We conclude that Luke and John have independently received divergent forms of the same basic tradition.

The burial (John 19:31–42)

In order to put John's empty tomb narrative in its proper perspective, we should first glance at the burial story, as we did when dealing with the earlier Evangelists. Some of its features have already been noted (see above, pp. 54f.).

According to John the burial was fully completed by Joseph, assisted by Nicodemus,[2] before the beginning of the Passover feast on Good Friday evening. We are told that the grave was a new one. This is not necessarily a genuine piece of historical information but part of the upgrading of the burial from the final hostile act of Jesus' enemies into an act of devotion. There is no mention of any women as eye witnesses to the burial (contrast the Synoptics), although there were women at the crucifixion scene as in Mark and its parallels, to wit, the mother of Jesus and his mother's sister, Mary of Clopas, and Mary Magdalene. It is possible that the Johannine passion assumes that these women, except the mother of Jesus who had gone home with the Beloved Disciple (v.27), were present through the burial. If so this would explain how Mary Magdalene was able to make straight for the tomb on Easter morning.

The events at the tomb (John 20:1–18)

[1]Now on the first day of the week Mary Magdalene came to the tomb early, while it was still dark, and saw that the stone had been taken away from the tomb. [2]So she ran, and went to Simon Peter and the other disciple, the one whom Jesus loved, and said to them, "They have taken the Lord out of the tomb, and we do not know where they have laid him." [3]Peter then came out with the other disciple, and they went toward the tomb. [4]They both ran, but the other disciple outran Peter and reached the tomb first; [5]and stooping to look in, he saw the linen cloths lying there, but he did not go in. [6]Then Simon Peter came, following him, and he went into the tomb; he saw the linen cloths lying, [7]and the napkin, which had been on his head, not lying with the linen cloths but rolled up in a place by itself. [8]Then the other disciple, who reached the tomb first, also went in, and he saw and believed; [9]for as yet they did not know the scripture, that he must rise from the dead. [10]Then the disciples went back to their homes.

[11]But Mary stood weeping outside the tomb, and as she wept she stooped to look into the tomb; [12]and she saw two angels in white, sitting where the body of Jesus had lain, one at the head and one at the feet. [13]They said to her, "Woman, why are you weeping?" She said to them, "Because they have taken away my Lord, and I do not know where they have laid him." [14]Saying this, she turned round and saw Jesus standing, but she did not know that it was Jesus. [15]Jesus said to her, "Woman, why are you weeping? Whom do you seek?" Supposing him to be the gardener, she said to him, "Sir, if you have

carried him away, tell me where you have laid him, and I will take him away." [16]Jesus said to her, "Mary." She turned and said to him in Hebrew, "Rabboni!" (which means Teacher). [17]Jesus said to her, "Do not hold me, for I have not yet ascended to the Father; but go to my brethren and say to them, I am ascending to my Father and your Father, to my God and your God." [18]Mary Magdalene went and said to the disciples, "I have seen the Lord"; and she told them that he had said these things to her.

An analysis of this passage suggests a combination of two different traditions. Mary Magdalene visits the tomb (v.1) but then goes back to inform the disciples, not reappearing until verse 11, when she is again present at the tomb. Verses 3–10 are devoted entirely to the discovery of the empty tomb by the two disciples, which at once duplicates and transcends Mary's discovery of it. Mary's announcement of her discovery is repeated to the angels in verse 13 almost *verbatim* from verse 2 where the same announcement is made to the two disciples. The only difference is that verse 2 has the plural "we do not know" while verse 13 has the singular "I do not know." This suggests that the Mary Magdalene tradition originally skipped from verse 1 to verse 11, thus giving a continuous account of her discovery of the empty tomb, the angelophany and the Christophany. The verses 3–10 were then originally an *alternative* version of the discovery. This alternative version has been inserted into the first version, with verse 2 composed to join together the two versions by taking Mary's lament to the angels and duplicating it for the disciples. Does the plural form in verse 2 reflect a tradition of more than one woman at the sepulchre?[3] Or is it, as Grass calls it, an "unauthentic plural," common in antique speech?[4] It is difficult to decide. If we think that the original tradition mentioned only Mary Magdalene, we should have to opt for Grass's view (see above, p. 56).

According to the editorial link in verse 2, Mary herself inferred that the tomb was empty, not needing the angel to point it out to her as in Mark. She does not, however, "believe"—a consequence reserved to the Beloved Disciple in verse 8. Yet, according to the original continuation of the narrative (v.11), she did stoop and look in. Mary's failure to understand is thus a characteristically Johannine foil for the Beloved Disciple's faith.

PETER AND THE BELOVED DISCIPLE

The earliest available version of the disciples' visit to the tomb is briefly summarized in Luke 24:24, where the reason for it was to check on the women's report of the empty tomb. This story apparently developed in two divergent ways. In Luke 24:12 (assuming the authenticity of the non-Western text) it becomes a visit to the tomb by Peter alone, and in John 20:3–10 a visit by Peter and the Beloved Disciple.[5]

Underlying the Johannine version is an earlier version whose primary intention was apologetic. Peter sees the grave cloths arranged in an orderly way, suggesting not the theft of the body (cf. Matt. 27:64; 28:13–15 for a different answer) but the miraculous passage of the body through the gravecloths, leaving them collapsed and lying as they were. This apologetic motif further developed in the *Gospel of the Hebrews*, where the Risen One hands the linen cloth to the servant of the high priest.[6] Its apologetic and legendary character is obvious.

The race between Peter and the Beloved Disciple introduces a theme which will be developed later in the Johannine appendix. This role of the Beloved Disciple represents a distinctively Johannine development, and the whole episode of the race must be regarded as editorial. The race is described curiously. The Beloved Disciple gets to the tomb first, but does not go in. Peter arrives a little later, looks in but does not enter, and observes the details of the situation; then the Beloved Disciple enters and "believes." This looks like a tentative correction or at least a qualification of the primitive view (here transferred, as in Luke 24:12, from Galilee to Jerusalem, and from the Christophanies to the empty tomb) that *Peter* was the primary witness of the resurrection. John does not dare to displace this tradition altogether, but modifies it to the extent of giving the Beloved Disciple—and therefore the specific Johannine witness—some degree of priority: he was the first to arrive at the tomb, but not the first to believe.

This transference of the rise of Easter faith from the Christophanies to the empty tomb tomb represents the most advanced development of the Easter narratives in the New Testament. Even the Lucan narratives had left the appearances as the primary vehicles of revelation (cf. the long discourses about the interpretation of the Old Testament scriptures placed on the lips of the Risen One). The faith of the Beloved Disciple does not lead to any special consequences: he does not even go and tell the other disciples, and when they assemble, in verses 19ff., there is no reference to the fact that one of their number had already come to believe in the resurrection. The whole story is thus short-circuited, a further indication of the redactional character of the race between Peter and the Beloved Disciple. Nor is there any link betwen this episode and the continuation of the story of Mary Magdalene, a further indication that the traditions of the two visits, those of Mary and of the disciples, are each of separate origin.[7]

THE APPEARANCE TO MARY MAGDALENE

Verse 11 resumes the pericope which had been interrupted at verse 2. Mary now inspects the tomb. She is not directed to the empty tomb as an answer to the enigma of the stone's removal, as in the synoptic versions; the removal of the stone itself directs her to the tomb which, as she discovers, no longer contains the body. Instead, she *now* sees two angels (duplicated as in the Lucan tradition). There was no mention of the angels when the disciples were earlier at the tomb, yet another indication of the separate origin of the two pericopes. Mary repeats the complaint of verse 2b (where it was addressed to the disciples)to the angels. Probably, when the Mary pericope stood alone, this was the first and only utterance of the complaint. The angels, however, are not given a chance to reply, for the Christophany at once supervenes. We may surmise that in the earlier form, before the Christophany was introduced into the tradition, the angels answered Mary's complaint as in Mark 16:6, i.e., that in the original version the angels served the function of *angeli interpretes*. But by the addition of the Christophany they have become superfluous relics. This again would support our thesis that the Christophanies at or near the tomb have been developed later out of the earlier angelophanies. In *Epistula Apostolorum* 9 the Christophany has entirely replaced the angelophany. This shows the direction of the development.

A similar development had already taken place in Matthew 28:9–10 (see above), but there is insufficient verbal parallel to justify a hypothesis of direct literary dependence. Rather, there is a common tradition behind both the Johannine and Matthean versions.

In verse 15 Jesus repeats the angel's question to Mary, "Women, why are you weeping?"; the hand which introduced this Christophany evidently borrowed this question from the angelophany. The gardener motif is intriguing. A later Jewish legend relates that a gardener named Judah had actually removed the body. It was this account which gave rise to the Easter faith, but Judah was able to disprove it. Von Campenhausen[8] believes that the Jewish legend of the removal of the body by the gardener was prior to the Johannine account, and that the latter is intended as an apologetic answer to the legend. Since according to 19:41 the tomb was in a garden, it would hardly require a Jewish legend to suggest to the Evangelist that the stranger was a gardener. We conclude therefore, that the Johannine account, like Matthew 28:13–15, is a reflex of the Jewish charge that the disciples stole the body, and that the legend of Judah is a later reflex of the Johannine account.

Next follows the recognition scene (v.16). Although this is a late story, it nevertheless reflects the earliest tradition that the resurrection appearances were revelatory encounters (Gal. 1:16), not ordinary physical experiences.

The meaning of the famous phrase "do not touch me" (*noli me tangere*) is much disputed. Does the Greek mean "do not start something you are not yet doing" or "do not continue what you are already doing"? The use of the present imperative in the Greek (*haptou*) suggests the latter: "stop clinging to me" (so BAG s.v.; cf. the references given there). If the pre-Johannine tradition had contained the point found in the Matthean version, that the women "took hold of his feet" (Matt. 28:9), then "stop clinging to me" makes good sense.

The reason given for this prohibition is: "for I have not yet ascended to the Father." The Greek verb for ascend (*anabaino*, literally, go up), does not occur in the Lucan ascension stories, but is characteristically Johannine.[9] The "Father" language is also strongly (though not, of course, uniquely) Johannine. All in all it seems likely that the whole verse, at least in its present form, is Johannine redaction. We would suggest that it is a re-writing for the purpose of the Christophany of a tradition similar to that of the angel's charge to the women in Mark and Matthew. The parallels are set out below:

MATT. 28:7	MATT. 28:10
Go (*poreutheisai*) quickly and tell his disciples	Go (*hupagete*) and tell my brethren

MARK 16:7	JOHN 20:17
Go (*hupagete*), tell his disciples	Go (*poreuou*) to my brethren and say to them

The unusual address, brethren, in the Matthean and Johannine Christophanies suggests that there is some connection (though not necessarily a literary one) between the two versions. John however has reinterpreted the charge. He has no place (unlike the author of chapter 21) for any Galilean appearance,[10] and has re-worded the charge to express his *katabasis-anabasis* Christology. Here we have the clue to the interpretation of this much controverted verse. John has inherited an Easter story in which, like Matthew 28:9–10, the Risen One is represented in the somewhat crude terms of a *theios anēr* Christology. This Christology he seeks to correct in terms of his own *katabasis-anabasis* Christology. Mary would like to cling to Jesus as a *theios anēr*—just as he was in his earthly ministry. But she and the brethren must learn that adherence to the *theios anēr* is an adherence to Jesus as a figure of the past. They can only know him henceforth as the One who, having descended, is now the Ascended One. Thus, while John uses traditions which go further than anything else in the canonical Gospels to enhance the purely legendary features of the appearances, he nevertheless decisively corrects them in accordance with the theology which expresses, *mutatis mutandis,* the theological concerns of the earliest kerygma. Only in the apocryphal legends do we have pure legend, uncorrected by kerygmatic theology.

The appearances to the disciples (John 20:19–23)

[19]On the evening of that day, the first day of the week, the doors being shut where the disciples were, for fear of the Jews, Jesus came and stood among them and said to them, "Peace be with you." [20]When he had said this, he showed them his hands and his side. Then the disciples were glad when they saw the Lord. [21]Jesus said to them again, "Peace be with you. As the Father has sent me, even so I send you." [22]And when he had said this, he breathed on them, and said to them, "Receive the Holy Spirit. [23]If you forgive the sins of any, they are forgiven; if you retain the sins of any, they are retained."

In its pre-Johannine, uncorrected form, verse 17, like its synoptic parallel (Mark 16:7 par.), had, we concluded, prepared the way for the Christophany to the disciples. From this we conclude further that John 20:19–23 was already connected with the Mary Magdalene story in the pre-Johannine tradition. The connection is further expressed by the temporal note, "on . . . that day" (v.19). As in the Lucan tradition, with which the pre-Johannine tradition is related (not, we hold, by direct dependence, but by dependence on a common oral tradition), the original Galilean appearance to the Twelve has been conflated with the Jerusalem appearance(s) to "all the apostles"—so that the appearance both is located in Jerusalem and acquires a mission-inaugurating rather than a church-founding significance. There are a number of parallels in detail between the Lucan and the Johannine version of the appearance. In both cases there is a physical demonstration (John 20:20/Luke 24:39–40); John, as we have already had occasion to observe (above, p. 102) has altered the original "feet" to "side" to conform with the piercing of the side of the Crucified One (John 19:34).

JOHN 20:19	LUKE 24:36
Jesus . . . stood among them	Jesus himself stood among them[11]

JOHN 20:20	LUKE 24:40
When he had said this, he showed them his hands and his side.	And when he had said this, he showed them his hands and his feet.[12]

Other more general parallels in content include: 1. The apostolic commission. This commission is worded differently, but in both cases is rooted in the appearance to "all the apostles" in the earliest tradition. 2. The gift of the Spirit. In Luke (who has separated the outpouring of the Spirit from the Christophanies and made it a separate event at Pentecost) this takes the form of a promise for the future, while in John the Spirit is imparted during the Christophany by means of insufflation (v.22). John is likely to be more original in holding together the two events of Christophany to the apostles and the giving of the Spirit.[13]

In the Johannine version it seems at first sight that the missionary element is soft-pedaled. It mentions only the "sending" of the disciples, and contains no charge as to the kerygma they are to proclaim. Instead, according to usual interpretation, the emphasis is on the administration of church discipline (v.23):

> If you forgive the sins of any,
>   they are forgiven;
> If you retain the sins of any,
>   they are retained.

This disciplinary charge is frequently compared with the Matthean charge of the earthly Jesus (Matt. 18:18):

> Whatever you bind on earth
>   shall be bound in heaven,
> and whatever you loose on earth
>   shall be loosed in heaven.

(cf. also the charge to Peter in Matt. 16:19 which is identical in wording except that the pronouns are in the singular).

Now it is clear from the context in which Matthew has placed the saying (Matt. 18:18 occurs in the community discourse, a collection of disciplinary rules for the community) that he intends "binding" and "loosing" in a disciplinary sense. They are the equivalents of the rabbinic terms *asar* and *sera'*.[14] But if this is how Matthew understands the saying, it is not certain that the Johannine version has the same meaning. On the one hand it is clear from the occurrence of the binding-loosing saying in the Matthean form of the Petrine confession, that the original context of the saying was post-resurrection as in John.[15] On the other hand, the Johannine language ("remit" rather than "loose") suggests a connection with baptism, as in Luke 24:47. From this we conclude that the remission and retention in John 20:23 refer primarily not to disciplinary binding and loosing but to the granting or withholding of baptism on acceptance or rejection of the kerygma. This saying has a number of primitive features: 1. It is in the form of a *Satz heiligen Rechtes*.[16] 2. It has the form of antithetical parallelism. 3. It contains a reverential passive: the activity of God is thrown into a passive voice:

> Whose sins you remit (now, on earth)
>> God will remit (at the last judgment)
> Whose sins you retain (now, on earth)
>> God will retain (at the last judgment).

Despite its primitive character it is impossible to assign it with certainty to the earthly Jesus. Its Easter location in John and the Easter associations of the "Thou art Peter" pericope both militate against its being so. Rather, this logion should be taken as a word of primitive Christian prophecy,[17] circulated in the earliest Aramaic community as a saying of the Risen and Exalted One. Indeed, this may be the most primitive form of the command to baptize.

One element in the Lucan version of this appearance which is absent from John is the element of doubt. The demonstration which John preserves (v.20) is left unmotivated, and suggests

that this element was present in the earlier form of the tradition, as in Luke.[18] Its removal here is probably due to the
elaboration of the same motif in the ensuing Thomas pericope.
Whether it was John or the pre-Johannine tradition that removed
it must depend on our view of the Thomas story.

Doubting Thomas (John 20:24–29)

[24]Now Thomas, one of the twelve, called the Twin, was not with
them when Jesus came. [25]So the other disciples told him, "We have
seen the Lord." But he said to them, "Unless I see in his hands the
print of the nails, and place my finger in the mark of the nails, and
place my hand in his side, I will not believe."

[26]Eight days later, his disciples were again in the house, and
Thomas was with them. The doors were shut, but Jesus came and
stood among them, and said, "Peace be with you." [27]Then he said to
Thomas, "Put your finger here, and see my hands; and put out your
hand, and place it in my side; do not be faithless, but believing."
[28]Thomas answered him, "My Lord and My God!" [29]Jesus said to him,
"Have you believed because you have seen me? Blessed are those
who have not seen and yet believe."

Recent criticism seems to be generally agreed that the Thomas
story is not a free creation of the Evangelist.[19] There is a tendency in the narrative traditions used by John to give a more
definite role to Thomas. In the synoptic Gospels he appears only
as a name in lists of the Twelve. In John he becomes the vehicle
of misunderstanding and doubt (11:16;14:5). In the later apocryphal literature there is a whole cycle of Thomas writings (cf.
the recently discovered *Gospel of Thomas*). The trend of the
development suggests that John's assignment of a more precise
role for Thomas marks the beginnings of the Thomas legend.
The role of misunderstanding and doubt in the synoptic tradition
is assigned in the main to Peter.

The Thomas story cannot originally have been connected with
the appearance to the eleven which precedes it, for his absence
is not mentioned in the body of the earlier pericope but only in

the connecting link (vv.24–26). As an independent pericope the Christophany to Thomas begins at verse 26b ("The doors were shut"). But a glance will show that despite the originally independent origin, it was modeled on the preceding pericope. This is indicated by the repetition of the introduction:

VERSE 19	VERSE 26
the doors being shut . . . Jesus came and stood among them, and said . . . "Peace be with you."	the doors were shut, (but) Jesus came and stood among them, and said, "Peace be with you."

It is further indicated by the demonstration in verse 27, where the invitation to see Jesus' *hands* and to put his hand into Jesus' *side* recalls the exhibition of the hands and side in verse 20. But the confession of Thomas (v.28), "My Lord and my God!" is new. Since this confession is integral to the pericope, it must already have been part of the pre-Johannine tradition. But perhaps the Evangelist himself has assimilated it to his Christology by the addition of "my God." The earlier strata of the New Testament never designate Jesus unequivocally as God.[20]

The practice begins in the later writings of the New Testament (e.g., Heb. 1:7ff.; Tit. 2:13, where, however, see RSV margin), in John, and then much more frequently in the second century. The Fourth Gospel brings the pre-existent, earthly (and now resurrected) Son into the closest possible relationship with God:

> The Word was God (John 1:1)
> making himself equal with God (5:18)
> before Abraham was, I AM (8:58)
> I and the Father are one (10:30)
> you, being a man, make yourself God (10:33)
> he who sees me sees him who sent me (12:45)
> he who has seen me has seen the Father (14:9)
> even as we are one (17:11).

But—except for the statement in the first verse of the Gospel, which refers to the pre-existent Logos and which is phrased in such a way (without the definite article before *theos*) as to suggest that the Logos partakes of the being of God without being actually himself God—without qualification, these earlier

references stop just short of calling the Son "God." The point
of such language is not ontological. It is that in Jesus there
occurs an encounter with the eschatological presence of God
directly at work. In calling the Resurrected One "God," Thomas
is not making a metaphysical statement, but a confession of
faith that in Jesus he has encountered the eschatological presence
of God at work.[21]

At the same time, this confession integrates the Easter narratives into the Johannine scheme. They are not, as Bultmann
has argued,[22] a meaningless appendage, a mere concession to
tradition. Curiously enough, the Thomas story indicates precisely
the opposite. Bultmann's interpretation of the incident may be
true of the pre-Johannine tradition, in which presumably the
climax was Thomas' act in touching the Risen One. As the story
now stands, however, this demonstration is lacking, and instead
we have Thomas' confession, "My Lord and my God." Throughout the Gospel Jesus has revealed himself as the eschatological
presence of God, but this revelation has been misconstrued, even
by his friends, and finally they were scattered (John 16:31f.).
The Easter stories play an essential role both in reassembling
Jesus' "own" and in finally establishing them in the faith in
the eschatological presence of God in Jesus. The Johannine discourses, which proclaim the presence of this eschatological revelation, are consciously written from the other side of the Easter
event, and it requires the Easter self-disclosure of the Risen One
to validate the revelation of the discourses, as the Beloved
Disciple perceived when he "believed" at the empty tomb and
when Thomas makes his confession, "My Lord and my God."

It is much debated whether John implies that Thomas actually
touched the Risen One. Does "you have seen me" in verse 29
include touching as well as seeing? Most commentators think
not, though Markus Barth[23] and, as we have seen, even Bultmann
think that he did. The legendary account in the *Epistula Apostolorum* 11 explicitly says, "We touched him that we might know
whether he had risen in the flesh."[24] Similarly Ignatius, *Ep.
Smyrn.* 3:2f., states that "Peter and his company touched the
Risen One," and lays great stress on the fact that he was "in

the flesh" even after the resurrection. The context makes it clear that Ignatius has an anti-docetic slant. This slant is absent from the Gospel. Its presence is often alleged, but in the passages adduced, such as John 4:6 (Jesus' weariness and thirst), the anti-docetic motif is quite unemphasized. From this we may infer that while there may have been an anti-docetic motif in the pre-Johannine form of the Thomas legend, the Evangelist has shifted the emphasis from the physical demonstration to the christological confession.

The pronouncement of the Risen One in verse 29, "Blessed are those who have not seen and yet believe," is not meant to discredit Thomas' faith or any faith which relies upon the resurrection appearances. It is concerned rather with the problem of the generation in which John wrote. They cannot see, as the apostles did, but can nevertheless believe precisely because of the word of those who have seen. The doubt of Thomas is intended to highlight the possibilities of faith for John's readers, not to condemn him for wanting to see.

Summary (John 20:30–31)

30Now Jesus did many other signs in the presence of the disciples, which are not written in this book; 31but these are written that you may believe that Jesus is the Christ, the Son of God, and that believing you may have life in his name.

Chapter 20 closes with two verses which clearly mark the end of the book (vv.30–31). They summarize its contents, suggesting that the Evangelist has drawn upon a stock of material of which much more is available, and state the overall purpose of his writing. There is no indication in these verses that there is more to follow and, above all, no indication that any more resurrection appearances—appearances in Galilee rather than in Jerusalem—are to follow.

The Johannine Appendix (John 21)

THERE IS NOTHING in the style of John 21 to suggest a different hand. Certain themes which have already occurred in the first twenty chapters are taken up again, e.g., the rivalry between Peter and the Beloved Disciple, the image of the shepherd and the sheep, the bond of love (agapé) between the disciples and their Master. If chapter 21 is by a different author (and we incline to think that it is, since the Evangelist himself carefully prepares for material to come later by means of advance cross-references —e.g., John 11:2, a cross-reference to 12:1–8, whereas there are no such cross-references to chapter 21), the similarities are perhaps best explained as due to their membership of the same school.[25] Even if chapter 21 were substantially by the same author as the rest of the Gospel, it would be necessary to assign verse 24 at least to a later hand. We incline to the view that the whole of chapter 21 is by this later hand, and that one of its purposes (v.24) is to assign chapters 1–20 to a direct eye-witness, the Beloved Disciple. The author of chapter 21 has drawn upon traditions of an Easter appearance in Galilee which were apparently not available to the author of chapter 20. This tradition contains an appearance to seven disciples (vv.1–14), which continues in a dialogue between the Risen One and Peter (vv.15–23).

The appearance to the seven (John 21:1–14)

¹After this Jesus revealed himself again to the disciples by the Sea of Tiberias; and he revealed himself in this way. ²Simon Peter, Thomas called the Twin, Nathanael of Cana in Galilee, the sons of Zebedee, and two others of his disciples were together. ³Simon Peter said to them, "I am going fishing." They said to him, "We will go with you." They went out and got into the boat; but that night they caught nothing.

⁴Just as day was breaking, Jesus stood on the beach; yet the disciples did not know that it was Jesus.⁵ Jesus said to them, "Children, have you any fish?" They answered him, "No." ⁶He said to them, "Cast the net on the right side of the boat, and you will find some." So they cast it, and now they were not able to haul it in, for the quantity of fish. ⁷That disciple whom Jesus loved said to Peter, "It is the Lord!" When Simon Peter heard that it was the Lord, he put on his clothes, for he was stripped for work, and sprang into the sea. ⁸But the other disciples came in the boat, dragging the net full of fish, for they were not far from the land, but about a hundred yards off.

⁹When they got out on land, they saw a charcoal fire there, with fish lying on it, and bread. ¹⁰Jesus said to them, "Bring some of the fish that you have just caught." ¹¹So Simon Peter went aboard and hauled the net ashore, full of large fish, a hundred and fifty-three of them; and although there were so many, the net was not torn. ¹²Jesus said to them, "Come and have breakfast." Now none of the disciples dared ask him, "Who are you?" They knew it was the Lord. ¹³Jesus came and took the bread and gave it to them, and so with the fish. ¹⁴This was now the third time that Jesus was revealed to the disciples after he was raised from the dead.

The author of chapter 21 is at pains to link his new material backward to the appearances in chapter 20. He achieves this by the connecting phrase "after this" in verse 1, and with the note in verse 14 that this was the *third* appearance to his disciples after the resurrection. The appearance to Mary Magdalene is not counted among the appearances to disciples.

Nevertheless there is a slight discrepancy between the two chapters. In chapter 20, the disciples had already been commissioned for their apostolic work and equipped with the Spirit, but in chapter 21 we find them back again at their former occupation of fishing (v.3). This would indicate that the Galilean tradition preserved in this chapter was unconnected with the Jerusalem appearances in chapter 20, and was intended to depict the primary appearance to the disciples. A minor point is that the Gospel had not previously intimated that any of the disciples were formerly fishermen (though in ch. 6 they crossed the lake in a boat).

It is curious that the disciples are seven in number, not the usual twelve (or eleven) as elsewhere in John (6:67, 70, 71;20:24; cf. 6:13). Included among these disciples are Peter (of course) and the two sons of Zebedee, i.e., the three leading disciples of the synoptic tradition; and two who are prominent in John 1–20, Thomas, whose name is again explained (cf. John 20:24) to mean twin (Didymus), and Nathanael, whose only other occurrence is at John 1:45–49. Finally, there are two other unnamed disciples. From the continuation of the story in verses 20–23 we learn that one of these seven was the Beloved Disciple. The traditional identification of this disciple with John bar Zebedee would mean that he is to be included in verse 2 among the two sons of Zebedee mentioned there. If this tradition is neither accepted nor intended by the author of chapter 21, the Beloved Disciple must be one of the two unnamed disciples in that verse. Since Peter, James, and John figure in the similar story of the miraculous draft of fishes in Luke 5:1–11, we may conclude that the author of chapter 21 found these three names already in the existing tradition, and that he added Thomas and Nathanael in order to connect this story with the preceding chapters. Perhaps the author added the two unnamed disciples to bring the total to the holy number of seven.

These disciples are back at their old occupation. Grass observes that this gives an impression of antiquity to the story. Without going so far, we would say that this story has its ultimate source in the tradition of the two appearances to Peter and to the Twelve, and that it has preserved the original situation of the first two appearances. These appearances, as we have argued already, occurred after the disciples had scattered at the arrest of Jesus and had returned to Galilee, at least some of them reverting to their old occupation of fishing. This original tradition has been obscured by the Jerusalem tradition in Luke and John 20. But this does not mean that we have here an original *story*. As a story it has a long tradition behind it, as we shall see. The disciples return from their nocturnal fishing expedition without a catch. The Risen One is awaiting them incognito on the shore, and bids them to try again, casting their net on the right side of the boat, the side of good luck. They do so, and bring in a large and miraculous (?) catch. The Beloved Disciple recognizes the Risen One. Peter hears that it is the Lord, and proceeds toward the shore, apparently not to greet the Lord but to deal with the catch.

Then at verse 9 the story takes a new turn. Jesus has a charcoal fire burning with fish (not part of the catch) on it already. Then—curiously—he invites them to contribute some of their own catch to the meal. At this point, Simon Peter returns abroad and proceeds to haul in the net. Now we are told that the catch numbered 153. Jesus next invited them to the meal, but, again curiously, we are told that the disciples did not dare ask him who he was, despite the lifting of the incognito already in verse 7. In verse 13 a eucharistic motif is introduced. Bread is served as well as fish, and Jesus performs the eucharistic acts of taking it and giving it to them, the fish having by now become a mere appendage to the meal.

Many elements in this story are paralleled in Luke 5, as the following synopsis will show:

LUKE 5:4–11

And when (Jesus) had ceased speaking, he said to Simon, "Put out into the deep and let down your nets for a catch." And Simon answered, "Master, we toiled all night and took nothing! But at your word I will let down the nets." And when they had done this, they enclosed a great shoal of fish; and as their nets were breaking, they beckoned to their partners in the other boat to come and help them. And they came and filled both the boats so that they began to sink. But when Simon Peter saw it, he fell down at Jesus' knees, saying, "Depart from me, for I am a sinful man, O Lord." For he was astonished, and all that were with him, at the catch of fish which they had taken; and so also were James and John, sons of Zebedee, who were partners with Simon. And Jesus said to Simon, "Do not be afraid; henceforth you will be catching men." And when they had brought their boats to land, they left everything and followed him.

JOHN 21:4–13

Just as day was breaking, Jesus stood on the beach; [yet the disciples did not know that it was Jesus]. Jesus said to them, "Children, have you any fish?" They answered him, "No." He said to them, "Cast the net on the right side of the boat, and you will find some." So they cast it, and now they were not able to haul it in, for the quantity of fish. [That disciple whom Jesus loved said to Peter, "It is the Lord!" When Simon Peter heard that it was the Lord,] he put on his clothes, for he was stripped for work, and sprang into the sea. But the other disciples came in the boat, draging the net full of fish, for they were not far from the land, but about a hundred yards off.

[When they got out on land, they saw a charcoal fire there, with fish lying on it, and bread.] Jesus said to them, "Bring some of the fish that you have just caught." So Simon Peter went aboard and hauled the net ashore, full of large fish, a hundred and fifty-three of them: and although there were so many, the net was not torn. [Jesus said to them, "Come and have breakfast." Now none of the disciples dared ask him, "Who are you?" They knew it was the Lord. Jesus came and took the bread and gave it to them, and so with the fish.]

The Johannine passages in square brackets are those passages which are unparalleled in the Lucan account and which introduce entirely different motifs: the appearance of the Risen One and his presidency over a eucharistic meal with his disciples. It is hard to resist the conclusion that the author of John 21 has combined two different traditions: a miraculous catch of fish like the story in Luke 5 and a eucharistic-resurrection appearance of a type familiar to us from Luke 24. Although the latter story places the appearance at Jerusalem, its mention of fish, as we have seen, indicates that it may originally have been located in Galilee. If so, the affinities between the Lucan and Johannine stories are enhanced. From this follows the important conclusion that the Johannine eucharistic appearance represents a much older tradition.

But what of the miraculous catch of fish? Has Luke projected a resurrection story back into the earthly ministry of Jesus?[26] Or vice versa, has John converted a story of the earthly Jesus into a resurrection appearance?[27]

The strongest point in favor of the originality of the resurrection setting is the apparently unmotivated confession of sin by Peter in the Lucan version (Luke 5:8b). This would make better sense if it came after Peter's denial, and therefore in an Easter setting. In the setting of the earthly ministry it would be no more than a general reaction to the *mysterium tremendum* of the miracle. But there are considerations on the other side. If this story were originally a resurrection appearance it would be the only case of a miracle performed by the Risen One. The tendency elsewhere, as we have seen, is to construct resurrection narratives from features in the (highly miraculous) stories of the earthly Jesus as a *theios anēr*. For this reason we are now inclined to favor the view that the pre-Easter setting was original and that the story has been transformed into a resurrection appearance by combining it with the eucharistic appearance.

In both the Johannine and Lucan versions the draft of the fish symbolizes the call to mission. As such it would be intelligible as a dramatization of the dominical saying, "I will make you become fishers of men" (Mark 1:17). John has seemingly combined the eucharistic-resurrection appearance with the story of the catch, and thus transformed it into a call to mission.

The pastoral charge (John 21:15–23)

[15]When they had finished breakfast, Jesus said to Simon Peter, "Simon, Son of John, do you love me more than these?" He said to him, "Yes, Lord; you know that I love you." He said to him, "Feed my lambs." [16]A second time he said to him, "Simon, son of John, do you love me?" He said to him, "Yes, Lord, you know that I love you." He said to him, "Tend my sheep." [17]He said to him the third time, "Simon, son of John, do you love me?" Peter was grieved because he said to him the third time, "Do you love me?" And he said to him, "Lord, you know everything; you know that I love you." Jesus said to him, "Feed my sheep. [18]Truly, truly, I say to you, when you were young, you girded yourself and walked where you would; but when you are old, you will stretch out your hands, and another will gird you and carry you where you do not wish to go." [19](This he said to show by what death he was to glorify God.) And after this he said to him, "Follow me."

[20]Peter turned and saw following them the disciple whom Jesus loved, who had lain close to his breast at the supper and had said, "Lord, who is it that is going to betray you?" [21]When Peter saw him, he said to Jesus, "Lord, what about this man?" [22]Jesus said to him, "If it is my will that he remain until I come, what is that to you? Follow me!" [23]The saying spread abroad among the brethren that this disciple was not to die; yet Jesus did not say to him that he was not to die, but, "If it is my will that he remain until I come, what is that to you?"

This is not really a separate appearance but a continuation of the appearance of verses 1ff. The Risen One asks Peter three times whether he loves him. As most commentators recognize, the threefold question corresponds to Peter's threefold denial. He then receives the threefold command to feed the sheep/lambs. This is a command, not to mission, but to pastoral oversight of the community. Hence it is in slight conflict with the missionary motif implicit in the symbolism of the 153 fishes. As such it has closer affinity with the church-founding appearances to Peter and the Twelve than with the other developed appearances in Matthew, Luke and John 20, which like the original appearance to "all the apostles" emphasizes the missionary import of the appearances. The affinities of John 21:15–18 are with Matthew 16:17–19, which we have also assigned to the Easter tradition. Both are concerned with the institution of Peter by the Risen One as the foundation of the church. We may therefore venture to speculate that the pericope originally ran somewhat as follows:

> The Risen One appears to the disciples in the context of a eucharistic meal by the lake of Galilee.
>
> He institutes Peter to the office of pastoral care over the church by the threefold command, "Feed my sheep."

Of all the stories that have been examined so far, this story, late though it is, seems to be in closest touch with the primitive tradition. Its Galilean location, the meal motif (not a demonstration) and the foundation of the church under the supervision of Peter—all are features going back to Mark 16:7 and behind it to 1 Corinthians 15:5.

Appended to the story are two further features. First, there is prediction of Peter's martyrdom. One can hardly doubt that this is a *vaticinium ex eventu* reflecting Peter's execution (probably at Rome) in *ca.* A.D. 64. Possibly it even betrays knowledge of the actual mode of the martyrdom, viz., crucifixion. This is suggested by the phrase "You will stretch out your hands" (v.18) and the comment that the Risen One was predicting this was the manner of death by which he should glorify God. We are thus in the unusual position of being able to give a *terminus a quo* for this half of the story.

The second addition is the discussion of the fate of the Beloved Disciple. This must have been added by the redactor himself with the intention of identifying the Beloved Disciple with the author of the Gospel. It must therefore be dated after the composition of John 1–20. Here the Johannine school protests, not against the Petrine primacy as such, but against its exclusive assertion *vis à vis* the equal validity of the Johannine tradition. Yet the saying in which the question about the eventual fate of the Beloved Disciple is parried has a link with earlier tradition (Mark 9:1; Matt. 16:28; 1 Thess. 4:15). In the primitive church there was circulated a saying predicting that some of the disciples would still be alive at the parousia. As the original disciples died one by one, and yet the parousia did not occur, this created a problem. Perhaps the last of the disciples to die was the bearer of the Johannine tradition. He was the last surviving disciple to whom the promise of Mark 9:1 could apply. When he, too, died, the promise must somehow be re-interpreted. The Risen One had not meant that the Beloved Disciple should not die. He had merely said that such questions were irrelevant to discipleship.

The Johannine traditions add little to our historical knowledge of the Easter events though, at some places, especially in chapter 21, they are in surprisingly close contact with earlier tradition. Here they confirm the Galilean location, the eucharistic setting, and the church-founding significance of the primary appearances to Peter and the Twelve.

The Appearances in Pseudo-Mark

The "canonical" or longer ending (Mark 16:9–20)

⁹Now when he rose early on the first day of the week, he appeared first to Mary Magdalene, from whom he had cast out seven demons. ¹⁰She went and told those who had been with him, as they mourned and wept. ¹¹But when they heard that he was alive and had been seen by her, they would not believe it.

¹²After this he appeared in another form to two of them, as they were walking into the country. ¹³And they went back and told the rest, but they did not believe them.

¹⁴Afterward he appeared to the eleven themselves as they sat at table; and he upbraided them for their unbelief and hardness of heart, because they had not believed those who saw him after he had risen. ¹⁵And he said to them, "Go into all the world and preach the gospel to the whole creation. ¹⁶He who believes and is baptized will be

saved; but he who does not believe will be condemned. [17]And these signs will accompany those who believe: in my name they will cast out demons; they will speak in new tongues; [18]they will pick up serpents, and if they drink any deadly thing, it will not hurt them; they will lay their hands on the sick, and they will recover."

[19]So then the Lord Jesus, after he had spoken to them, was taken up into heaven, and sat down at the right hand of God. [20]And they went forth and preached everywhere, while the Lord worked with them and confirmed the message by the signs that attended it. Amen.

The usual view of the so-called canonical ending is that it is a colorless, artificial summary of the appearances recorded at the ends of Matthew, Luke and John. Certainly each individual allusion to an appearance has parallels in the other Gospels.[1]

The appearance to Mary Magdalene is found in John 20:11–18, supplemented with further information about Mary derived from Luke 8:2.

The report of the appearance to the two disciples in verse 12 is clearly an allusion to the Emmaus story in Luke 24:13–35.

The appearance to the eleven (vv.14–16) exhibits parallels with Luke 24:36–48, John 20:19–21 and Matthew 28:16–20, while the conferral of miraculous powers on the disciples recalls Luke 10:17–19.

Verses 19–20 are a summary statement of the ascension recalling Luke 24:51, followed by a kind of condensed Acts of the Apostles.

Some scholars, however, have recently questioned this commonly accepted view of the canonical ending. C. H. Dodd twice questions it,[2] and in support he lists the following differences between Pseudo-Mark and the resurrection narratives of the other Gospels:

1. The appearance to the eleven is stated to have occurred while the disciples were at table, a point not mentioned by Luke or John.
2. In the Emmaus story, where an appearance at table occurs, it is an appearance to *two* disciples.
3. In John 21:13 it is to *seven* disciples that the Risen One distributes bread and fish.

4. Only here does the Risen One *reproach* the eleven for their unbelief.

Later, Dodd compares the longer ending of Mark with the list in 1 Corinthians 15, a comparison which Goguel had already drawn.[3] Particularly noticeable is the series of chronological particles: "first," "after this," "later," recalling the series of chronological particles in the list of 1 Corinthians. But it also differs from that list, for the bare statements of the appearances are supplemented with materials drawn from the appearance stories of Matthew and Luke. Unlike 1 Corinthians 15, it does not name the official witnesses Peter and James, but only Mary Magdalene. This shows that the list of appearances in Pseudo-Mark serves a different function from the earlier list. For as a woman, Mary Magdalene could not be an authoritative witness. The pseudo-Marcan list serves therefore not to authenticate the resurrection kerygma (contrast 1 Cor. 15), but to prepare the way for the Great Commission which follows. This Commission is independent of the commissions in the other Gospels.[4] Finally, the brief statement of the ascension differs from that in Acts (and from Luke 24:51) in that it explicitly cites 2 Kings 2:11 and Psalm 110:1. Dodd accordingly concludes that the author of the longer ending is composing freely from tradition, supplementing it in part from the appearance stories in Matthew and Luke.[5]

We conclude therefore that the canonical ending is not merely an artificial summary of the appearance stories in the other Gospels. In form it is modeled on the earlier lists of appearances (1 Cor. 15:5ff. and Mark 16:7), but with the substitution of longer summaries of the appearances in the other Gospels, and an independent statement about the ascension. The missionary charge and the command to baptize are also independent traditions.

The Freer Logion

In the Freer Museum at Washington there is a fourth- or fifth-century manuscript containing a remarkable insertion into the canonical ending after verse 14. It reads as follows:

And they excused themselves, saying, "This age of iniquity and unbelief is under Satan, who prevents (?) the truth of God and his power (?) from being apprehended by the unclean spirits (?); therefore reveal your righteousness now," [they said to Christ]. And Christ answered them, saying, "The term of the years of Satan's authority has been fulfilled, but other terrors are at hand; even for those sinners for whose sake I was delivered to death, that they might return to the truth and sin no more, that they might inherit the spiritual and incorruptible glory of righteousness, which is in heaven" (my translation: the question marks denote places where the text is ungrammatical and its meaning uncertain).

The Freer ending is dominated by two themes: persecution and the longing for the parousia. Theologically, it exhibits a fascinating combination of apocalyptic images (the two ages, the terrors at hand and Satan's authority) with Hellenistic, perhaps even Gnostic concepts ("spiritual" and "incorruptible"). On the one hand, it perpetuates themes associated from earlier times with the resurrection appearances (the parousia, cf. Matt. 28:20b; Acts 1:6,7, and 11; and a backward reference to the passion, cf. Luke 24:20,26,46). On the other hand, there are new themes: persecution (which in the authentic Gospel tradition appears only in sayings of the earthly Jesus) and the Hellenistic-Gnostic themes. The latter point forward to the Gnostic developments of the teaching of the Risen Christ such as we find in the *Gospel of Thomas* and other Gnostic writings.

The shorter ending

After the authentic conclusion of Mark (16:8), some manuscripts[6] add a different conclusion, which reads as follows (RSV margin):

But they reported briefly to Peter and those with him all that they had been told. And after this, Jesus himself sent out by means of them, from east to west, the sacred and imperishable proclamation of eternal salvation.

Unlike the first ending, which was simply tacked on to the authentic ending of Mark, this ending has obviously been deliberately composed to fit on to the authentic conclusion. The women's silence is interpreted to mean they said nothing to anyone en route, but went straight to the disciples to deliver the angel's message. Peter is singled out for special mention in accordance with verse 7 ("Go, tell his disciples and Peter"). Without stating so explicitly, the composer seems to imply that Peter and the disciples went to Galilee as the angel had commanded and there saw the Risen One, who sent them forth with the gospel message. This mission is conceived in the universalist terms ("from east to west"), current in the second century.[7] The phraseology ("imperishable" and "eternal") has a Hellenistic ring. But the author is true to the intention of Mark (if our interpretation of "Galilee" in Mark 16:7 was correct) in interpreting the appearance of the Risen One to Peter and the disciples as the inauguration of a world-wide mission, and true, finally, to the meaning of the appearance to "all the apostles."

These various attempts to bring Mark to what seemed to later writers a more satisfactory conclusion in no way undermines our argument that Mark himself intended to conclude at 16:8. They were judging Mark by second-century standards, at a time when the appearances were not merely listed but narrated.

Transposed Resurrection Narratives?

THERE ARE in the tradition of the earthly Jesus six narratives which have been held to be resurrection appearances transposed into a pre-Easter setting.

1. The miraculous draft of fish (Luke 5:1-11)

¹While the people pressed upon him to hear the word of God, he was standing by the lake of Gennesaret. ²And he saw two boats by the lake; but the fishermen had gone out of them and were washing their nets. ³Getting into one of the boats, which was Simon's, he asked him to put out a little from the land. And he sat down and taught the people from the boat. ⁴And when he had ceased speaking, he said to Simon, "Put out into the deep and let down your nets for a catch." ⁵And Simon answered, "Master, we toiled all night and took nothing! But at your word I will let down the nets." ⁶And when

they had done this, they enclosed a great shoal of fish; and as their nets were breaking, [7]they beckoned to their partners in the other boat to come and help them. And they came and filled both the boats, so that they began to sink. [8]But when Simon Peter saw it, he fell down at Jesus' knees, saying, "Depart from me, for I am a sinful man, O Lord." [9]For he was astonished, and all that were with him, at the catch of fish which they had taken; [10]and so also were James and John, sons of Zebedee, who were partners with Simon. And Jesus said to Simon, "Do not be afraid; henceforth you will be catching men." [11]And when they had brought their boats to land, they left everything and followed him.

The strongest candidate for a transposed resurrection narrative is the miraculous draft of fish, since it occurs not only in this pre-Easter setting but also as a resurrection appearance in the Johannine appendix (21:1-14). As we saw however in our analysis of John 21, the transposition was more probably in the opposite direction. In no other appearance story does the Risen One perform a miracle, and therefore as a post-Easter scene the draft of fish is unique.

Now the resurrection appearances of the Gospels have the following features in common:[8]

A. The initial absence of the Risen One is either stated or presumed.

B. He then makes a supernatural appearance.

C. A recognition: the Risen One is identified by the recipients of the appearance as Jesus himself, or alternatively they make a confession of faith in him as the exalted Lord.

D. The delivery of an instruction or a charge by the Risen One.

Let us apply these criteria in turn to the five other pericopes which have been held to be resurrection appearances transposed into a pre-Easter setting.

2. The stilling of the storm (Mark 4:35-41)

[35]On that day, when evening had come, he said to them, "Let us go across to the other side." [36]And leaving the crowd, they took him

with them, just as he was, in the boat. And other boats were with him. [37]And a great storm of wind arose, and the waves beat into the boat, so that the boat was already filling. [38]But he was in the stern, asleep on the cushion; and they woke him and said to him, "Teacher, do you not care if we perish?" [39]And he awoke and rebuked the wind, and said to the sea, "Peace! Be still!" And the wind ceased, and there was a great calm. [40]He said to them, "Why are you afraid? Have you no faith?" [41]And they were filled with awe, and said to one another, "Who then is this, that even wind and sea obey him?"

In this story Jesus is present from the beginning: he does not appear at a later stage and consequently there is no recognition. Neither is there any instruction or charge. Thus all of the criteria for an appearance story are lacking.

3. The walking on the water (Mark 6:45–52)

[45]Immediately he made his disciples get into the boat and go before him to the other side, to Beth-saida, while he dismissed the crowd. [46]And after he had taken leave of them, he went into the hills to pray. [47]And when evening came, the boat was out on the sea, and he was alone on the land. [48]And he saw that they were distressed in rowing, for the wind was against them. And about the fourth watch of the night he came to them, walking on the sea. He meant to pass by them, [49]but when they saw him walking on the sea they thought it was a ghost, and cried out; [50]for they all saw him, and were terrified. But immediately he spoke to them and said, "Take heart, it is I; have no fear." [51]And he got into the boat with them and the wind ceased. And they were utterly astounded, [52]for they did not understand about the loaves, but their hearts were hardened.

According to Bultmann's analysis[9] this story has undergone expansion in the course of transmission through the addition of motifs from the other story of the stilling of the storm (6:50a, 51b). When we examine the residue in the light of our four criteria, we find that Jesus is certainly absent at the beginning of the story (v.47), and that he appears (*erchetai*, v.48) in a supernatural way. However, he appears not from heaven, as in the resurrection narratives, but from the land, where he had remained in solitude (v.47). If this pericope was originally a resurrection narrative, we should have to excise "and he was alone on the land" from verse 47 and probably also the first two clauses of verse 48 ("And he saw that they were distressed in rowing, for the wind was against them") which may be derived from the stilling of the storm. The supernatural character of the appearance is suggested by the reaction of the disciples who thought they were seeing a ghost (*phantasma*, cf. *pneuma* in Luke 24:49). The disciples' reaction of fear is occasionally found in the later resurrection narratives (see Luke 24:38). The self-disclosure of Jesus by means of the mysterious pronouncement, I am (so literally the Greek at v.50c, where RSV translates "It is I"), occurs also in the resurrection narratives (Luke 24:39; cf. Acts 9:5). It is the device by which the recognition is achieved.

There is, however, no instruction or charge; the story culminates in the amazement of the disciples (v.51). To this the Marcan redaction has added a comment about the disciples' misunderstanding (v.52), which is part of the messianic secret motif. If this were originally an appearance story, we should have to suppose that an original charge has been worn away in transmission. But is this likely to have happened at such an early stage? Our analysis thus far has suggested that there were no pre-Marcan resurrection narratives, and that when eventually, after Mark, the community began to feel the need of such narratives, they borrowed them from the traditions of the earthly Jesus, particularly from the miracle tradition as modified by the *theios anēr* (divine man) motif. While it is possible (if one grants that there were primitive resurrection narratives) that the walking on the water was originally a resurrection narrative, it is equally possible that it is a story of Jesus as the *theios anēr* (divine man) which has contributed motifs to the later resurrection narratives. It is impossible to give a conclusive verdict on this story, and it depends on one's general understanding of the history of the tradition. To the present writer it seems more probable that the shaping of the miracle stories in the earthly life of Jesus, especially under the influence of the divine man concept, have provided traits which were later carried over into the narration of the appearances.

4. The feeding of the multitude
(Mark 6:32–44; 8:1–10)

[32]And they went away in the boat to a lonely place by themselves. [33]Now many saw them going, and knew them, and they ran there on foot from all the towns, and got there ahead of them. [34]As he landed he saw a great throng, and he had compassion on them, because they were like sheep without a shepherd; and he began to teach them many things. [35]And when it grew late, his disciples came to him and said, "This is a lonely place, and the hour is now late; [36]send them away, to go into the country and villages round about and buy themselves something to eat." [37]But he answered them, "You give them something to eat." And they said to him, "Shall we go and buy two hundred denarii worth of bread, and give it to them to eat?" [38]And he said to them, "How many loaves have you? Go and see." And when they had found out, they said, "Five, and two fish." [39]Then he commanded them all to sit down by companies upon the green grass. [40]So they sat down in groups, by hundreds and by fifties. [41]And taking the five loaves and the two fish he looked up to heaven, and blessed, and broke the loaves, and gave them to the disciples to set before the people; and he divided the two fish among them all. [42]And they all ate and were satisfied. [43]And they took up twelve baskets full of broken pieces and of the fish. [44]And those who ate the loaves were five thousand men.

[1]In those days, when again a great crowd had gathered, and they had nothing to eat, he called his disciples to him, and said to them, [2]"I have compassion on the crowd, because they have been with me now three days, and have nothing to eat; [3]and if I send them away hungry to their homes, they will faint on the way; and some of them have come a long way." [4]And his disciples answered him, "How can one feed these men with bread here in the desert?" [5]And he asked them, "How many loaves have you?" They said, "Seven." [6]And he commanded the crowd to sit down on the ground; and he took the seven loaves, and having given thanks he broke them and gave them to his disciples to set before the people; and they set them before the crowd. [7]And they had a few small fish; and having blessed them, he commanded that these also should be set before them. [8]And they ate, and were satisfied; and they took up the broken pieces left over, seven

baskets full. ⁹And there were about four thousand people. ¹⁰And he sent them away; and immediately he got into the boat with his disciples, and went to the district of Dalmanutha.

There is no indication of an initial absence of Jesus, no appearance, no recognition and no charge or instruction. This story is a combination of a miracle framed to express the eschatological prophet Christology (cf. the similar story in 2 Kings 4:42–44), with eucharistic motifs. The eschatological prophet Christology is an interpretation specifically of the earthly Jesus,¹⁰ not of the Risen or Exalted One. The eucharistic motif is certainly paralleled in the resurrection narratives (e.g., Luke 24:30). But it is not exclusively confined to a post-resurrection setting (cf. the last supper). Thus, in this case, the arguments for an original post-Easter setting are very weak.

5. The transfiguration (Mark 9:2–8)

²And after six days Jesus took with him Peter and James and John, and led them up a high mountain apart by themselves; and he was transfigured before them, ³and his garments became glistening, intensely white, as no fuller on earth could bleach them. ⁴And there appeared to them Elijah with Moses; and they were talking to Jesus. ⁵And Peter said to Jesus, "Master, it is well that we are here; let us make three booths, one for you and one for Moses and one for Elijah." ⁶For he did not know what to say, for they were exceedingly afraid. ⁷And a cloud overshadowed them, and a voice came out of the cloud, "This is my beloved Son; listen to him." ⁸And suddenly looking around they no longer saw any one with them but Jesus only.

An original Easter setting for this story has long been advocated¹¹ by critics. The history of the tradition behind the transfiguration story is extremely complex and difficult to handle, though I have attempted to do this elsewhere.¹²

The original Christology expressed by the story was once more a Christology of the eschatological prophet and servant of Yahweh. This Christology, however, interprets the earthly Jesus, not the Risen and Exalted One. Jesus is not initially absent. He does not appear and there is no recognition. There is indeed a charge ("listen to him"), though it is a charge delivered not by the Risen One (or the earthly Jesus in the present context), but by a voice from heaven. This is a feature never otherwise found in the resurrection narratives, where it is always the Risen One, not the Father, who speaks. Despite the weight of critical opinion in favor of an original post-Easter setting, the evidence for it is on examination not very strong. This is not, of course, to deny that the Easter faith has influenced the development of the transfiguration story. If the earliest church was able to believe that the earthly Jesus was the eschatological prophet like Moses whose face shone when he came down from the mountain, and if, too, the later Hellenistic community was able to believe that the earthly Jesus was transfigured like a *theios anēr* (divine man), it was able to do so precisely because of its resurrection faith.

6. The "Thou art Peter" saying (Matt. 16:17–19)

[17]"Blessed are you, Simon Bar-Jona! For flesh and blood has not revealed this to you, but my Father who is in heaven. [18]And I tell you, you are Peter, and on this rock I will build my church, and the powers of death shall not prevail against it. [19]I will give you the keys of the Kingdom of heaven, and whatever you bind on earth shall be bound in heaven, and whatever you loose on earth shall be loosed in heaven."

We have already agreed that this saying was circulated originally as a saying of the Risen One. As such it is comparable in form to the Matthean Great Commission. We would not contend that either saying was spoken as such by the Risen One: rather, that both sayings verbalize the meaning of the respective resurrection encounters. The "Thou art Peter" saying is thus a verbalization of the primary appearance to Peter. But this verbalization is not set in the framework of an appearance: it is simply a detached saying, which as such was easily transferable to a setting in the earthly ministry. This is what has happened in Matthew's editing of Mark's story of Peter's confession.

Bultmann's thesis is somewhat different. He regards Matthew 16:17–19 not as a separate logion, but as the original conclusion of the confession of Peter which the Marcan version of the confession has suppressed. As such, he maintains, the confession of Peter was itself originally a post-Easter narrative.[13] But again, applying our criteria, we find that there is no initial absence of Jesus and no miraculous appearance. Peter's confession *could* be interpreted as a recognition, like Thomas' confession of faith in John 20:28. Moreover, Christos was originally used as a christological title precisely for the Risen and Exalted One (Acts 2:36). There is also a charge in the Marcan version. But there it is a charge to secrecy, and an example of Mark's motif of the messianic secret. This charge is followed by an instruction in the form of a passion prediction. Similar material appears in the instructions of the resurrection narratives (see esp. Luke 24:46). But in the latter passage we found such instruction explicable as a transposition of the passion predictions from the earthly ministry into the resurrection narratives. That seems to be the direction of the development, rather than vice versa. Finally, we have elsewhere offered an alternative reconstruction of the history of the tradition,[14] according to which the confession of Peter originated in an authentic historical reminiscence where, however, it was not strictly a confession of faith, but a mistaken identification of Jesus as a nationalistic revolutionary leader, which evoked from Jesus the response, "Get behind me, Satan." It is of course the impact of the resurrection faith which after Easter transformed the reminiscence into a genuine confession of faith.

We have thus disposed of the alleged transpositions of appearance stories into the tradition of the earthly ministry. In each case an alternative explanation is available. Either the transposition was in the opposite direction, or alternatively, the Easter faith has contributed to the shaping of the narrative in its context of the earthly ministry.

CHAPTER EIGHT

The Resurrection Narratives in Contemporary Faith and Proclamation

WE BEGAN this work by characterizing the difficulties which the resurrection narratives create for modern man. Many of these difficulties arise from the inconsistencies between the different versions of the Easter stories in the Gospels. It seemed hopeless to try and reconstruct what happened, and that basic uncertainty threatened to undermine the whole foundation of the Christian faith.

A study of the resurrection narratives with the modern methods of tradition and redaction criticism enables us to explain the inconsistencies and contradictions. They have nothing to do with a primary uncertainty about the resurrection faith. Rather they represent varying attempts to give that faith expression. At the very earliest stage in the tradition, the resurrection events were not related: rather, the resurrection was proclaimed.[1] "God raised

Jesus from the dead." This proclamation was couched in the language of Jewish apocalyptic, which had hoped for the day when the elect would be raised out of their graves and enter into an entirely new mode of existence. What the apocalyptic hope had anticipated has now been fulfilled in the case of a single individual, Jesus of Nazareth, whose resurrection, however, was to be decisive for the subsequent raising of the elect in the very near future. This phasing out of the apocalyptic hope represents a corrective of the earlier plan of salvation history. It also meant that Jesus' proclamation, "The kingdom of God has drawn near," had indeed begun to be fulfilled. Meanwhile, Jesus' followers have some anticipation of the kingdom of God and of the resurrection existence in their common life. They live in the Spirit-filled community, and this Spirit is the same Spirit that raised Jesus from the dead and which is now already engaged in transforming their existence (which Paul calls the "inner man"[2]) in anticipation of their total transformation at the End.[3]

This proclamation, however, could not have been self-generated, nor could it have arisen directly from Jesus' proclamation of the advent of the kingdom. If the only sequel to that proclamation was the crucifixion, then that proclamation would have been demonstrably false. Jesus had proclaimed the coming of the kingdom and it had not come. Instead, his message had ostensibly been utterly discredited by the crucifixion.

The very fact of the church's kerygma therefore requires that the historian postulate some other event over and above Good Friday, an event which is not itself the "rise of the Easter faith"[4] but the cause of the Easter faith. Yet the earliest kerygma, as we see it for instance from a traditio-critical reconstruction of 1 Corinthians 15:3ff., did not voice this presupposition: it spoke only of the death and burial and resurrection, and said nothing, e.g., of the empty tomb or of the disciples' visions.

It was, as we saw, Paul who secured the information which led him to formulate a list of appearances. Here was stated explicitly one of the presuppositions of the kerygma: the Risen One had appeared to Cephas (Peter), then to the Twelve, and after that to the +500. Next he appeared to James, then to all the apostles. It is possible that such lists had been formulated before this, particularly the series: Peter, the Twelve.[5] But we do not know for certain. Such lists, however, were in existence at the very latest by the year 35 or thereabouts, when Paul paid his visit to Jerusalem after his Damascus call.

These encounters with the Risen One were characterized as "visions,"[6] an ambiguous word which may mean subjective experiences, but also the reception of a revelation from God. The way in which Paul ranges his own Damascus road encounter in the same series as the earlier visions in the list indicates that Paul, who is the only recipient of such an experience from whom we have a first-hand report of it, understood it to be distinct from the subjective experiences he had subsequently. Thus we infer that the earlier visions were also revelatory encounters.

An analysis of the list of encounters in 1 Corinthians 15 indicated that they fall into two main groups, those concerned with the initial establishment of the eschatological community, and those concerned with the inauguration of the community's mission.

The Pauline account mentioned the burial of Jesus, but said nothing of an empty tomb. Yet the language in which Paul speaks of resurrection, derived as it was from Jewish apocalyptic, would not be wholly incongruous with such an assertion, provided the empty tomb was understood not as the resuscitation of Jesus' earthly body, but as the transformation of his whole being into the new mode of eschatological existence. The fact that Paul thus interpreted the future resurrection of the believers, the direct dependence of the believers' resurrection on the primary and constitutive resurrection of Jesus the Christ,[7] and the analogy which Paul draws between the resurrection of Jesus and the resurrection of the believers make it as clear as possible that Paul understood the resurrection of Jesus to be just such a transformation.

Even in the earliest Gospel, Mark, writing ten to fifteen years after Paul's letter to the Corinthians, still did not narrate appearances, but, like Paul, merely listed them.[8] Mark did, however, include what Paul did not even mention, namely, a narrative of the discovery of the empty tomb by some women on the Sunday morning. He used this narrative as a means to point forward to resurrection appearances in Galilee as the inauguration of the Christian mission. The empty tomb story was not the Evangelist's creation, but tradition with a long history behind it. Basic to it, we found, was an alleged factual report, the discovery of the empty tomb by the women. This alleged factual report was then used as a vehicle for the proclamation of the resurrection. This, we decided, happened at the time when the empty tomb narrative was attached to the passion narrative. Finally, there was the Evangelist's own redaction of the story, the introduction of the Galilee–mission motif. The alleged factual element must go back a considerable way in the tradition. Since the story is embedded in a theological outlook that is wholly compatible with the earliest proclamation of the resurrection, that of a transformation of the body out of the grave, we were prepared to assign this alleged fact to the very earliest period. This entitled us to speculate that the first disciples, having returned to Jerusalem after their experiences in Galilee, heard the story of the women, and welcomed it as congruous with the resurrection faith to which they had attained in Galilee. It is impossible for us at this distance to check the reliability of the women's report. The disciples were apparently not interested in it as a historical fact and so we hear nothing of their having checked it. They were interested only in using it as a vehicle for the proclamation of the resurrection. For the disciples, faith in the resurrection did not rest upon the empty tomb, but upon their revelatory encounters with the Risen One.

Actual narratives of the appearances are found only in the later Gospel strata. They are just beginning in Matthew, and one is found in a still somewhat early form in John 20:15ff. The appearances on the mountain in Galilee in Matthew 28 and by the lakeside in John 21 still depict a revelation of One risen and exalted into a transcendental mode of existence. In both cases the narratives are used as a repository of the community's understanding of the theological implications of the resurrection of Jesus: the foundation of the community in John 21[9] and the inauguration of the world-wide mission in Matthew 28. The words spoken by the Risen One are not to be taken as recordings of what was actually spoken by him, but as verbalizations of the community's understanding of the import of the resurrection. Yet even at the historical level, the experiences of the disciples were not merely visual: they involved the communication of meaning. Paul for instance understood his Damascus road encounter not merely as a wordless vision of the Risen One, but as a call to be the "apostle to the Gentiles." The use of the words Cephas (Rock), Twelve, and apostles in the earlier appearances show that they too involved communications of meaning. In the latest strata, Luke 24 and John 20,[10] the narratives have developed from revelatory encounters with the transcendent Risen One into appearances of the Risen One in the earthly form of a divine man. At this stage, traits of the more supernaturalized presentations of the earthly Jesus in the later Hellenized Gospel tradition are transferred to the resurrection narratives and, perhaps even, as in the case of the miraculous draft of fish in John 21, transposed in their entirety to a post-resurrection setting. Here apologetic motifs play a role (anti-docetism?), although the Evangelist also appears to be at some pains to tone down these supernatural features.[11] But something of the earlier sense that the Risen One appears as a transcendent being still remains.[12]

Contemporary faith

In the light of this history of the tradition, what is essential for Christian faith in the resurrection to believe today? Tradition and redaction criticism have altered our whole understanding of the goal of the Gospel narratives. They can no longer be read as direct accounts of what happened, but rather as vehicles for proclamation. Such was their original intention. To see what those intentions are we will start with the later narratives and work backward. The Christian cannot be required to believe that the Risen One literally walked on earth in an earthly form as in the Emmaus story, or that he physically ate fish as in the Lucan appearance to the disciples at Jerusalem, or that he invited physical touch as in the Thomas story. There are two reasons why this should be so. First, not only do the earlier accounts know nothing of these features, but the resurrection faith of the earliest community, conceived in apocalyptic terms as transformation into an entirely new (eschatological) mode of existence, directly contradicts it. Second, the Evangelists are here taking up popular stories, forged in the milieu of the "divine man" concept, and using them for purposes of their own. What the believer must listen to is therefore the purpose and intention of the Evangelists in using these stories. They used them not simply to relate past events (though they doubtless assumed that the reports were historically correct), but in order to assert e.g., the identity-in-transformation between the earthly and the Risen Jesus. This identity-in-transformation was already a theological concern of Paul, as witness, for instance, his constant use of the earthly name Jesus for the Risen One, whether absolutely or in composite formulae such as Christ Jesus and Christ Jesus our Lord. The resurrection does not mean that the earthly Jesus is relegated to past history but has as its consequence the extension of the word and work of the earthly Jesus into the present life of the community.[13]

The verbalizations of the Risen One, which occur both in the latest resurrection narratives (Luke 24, John 20), and in those of the intermediate period (Matt. 28:16ff. and John 21:15ff.), set before us, as already noted, the community's understanding of the original implications of the resurrection at different periods in its history. Thus the Lucan Christ first expounds the suffering and glorifying of the Messiah as the fulfillment of the Old Testament scriptures, and then as inaugurating the universal mission of the church, beginning at Jerusalem. Here the risen Christ is made to express the distinctively Lucan understanding of salvation history, an understanding which represents a sub-apostolic adjustment of the earlier church's understanding.[14] This does not mean that contemporary faith is bound to the Lucan understanding. But it does mean that Luke points us to

what for us, as for him, must be the clue to the understanding
of salvation history, namely, the centrality of the Christ event.
For Christian faith today, as for Luke, Christ is the "mid-point"
of time.

In John 20 the recognition scene between Mary Magdalene and
the Risen One conveys the important insight that Easter faith
cannot cling to the early Jesus, the Jesus of history, as a figure of
the past. This insight does not contradict the emphasis of the later
apologetic narratives that the Risen One is identical with the
earthly Jesus. Faith seeks the earthly Jesus not as a dead teacher,
but as the living Lord, whose word and work were not merely
accomplished once upon a time, but are now made ever present
in the community.

The Johannine appearance to the disciples on the evening
of Easter Day stresses the Risen One's gift of peace, the eschatological peace of victory over sin and death. Christian faith still
finds in the Risen One that peace, of which the Johannine Christ
is made to say: "Peace I leave with you; my peace I give to you;
not as the world gives do I give to you" (John 14:27) and "I
have said this to you, that in me you may have peace. In the
world you have tribulation; but be of good cheer, I have overcome the world" (John 16:33), a peace which Paul called "the
peace of God, which passes all understanding" (Phil. 4:7).
The Johannine resurrection appearance to the disciples at Jerusalem is unique in associating the Christophany with the gift
of the Spirit. It may well be that John has here preserved an
authentic insight from earlier tradition. At least this version
has more claim to being primitive than the Acts version of
Pentecost as a distinct event, and it is fully in accord with the
Pauline doctrine of the Spirit. The Spirit is precisely the outcome
of and the means to perpetuating in the community the achievement of the Christ event. As the Johannine Christ had been made
to say of the Paraklete, "He will teach you all things, and bring
to your remembrance all that I have said to you" (John 14:26)
and again, "he shall take what is mine and declare it to you"
(John 16:14). The Spirit, as Christian faith understands it, takes
the community not away from Jesus, earthly, crucified, risen,

but ever nearer to him, expounding anew in each successive situation the meaning of the once-for-all revelation in the Christ event. This is why for the Fourth Evangelist the Spirit is the gift of the risen Christ. This insight of faith is as relevant and meaningful for the life of the believing community today as it was in the Evangelist's own time.

The Johannine appearance to the disciples at Jerusalem has its own distinctive version of the inauguration of the Christian mission, with its tremendous emphasis on the role of the apostolate: "As the Father has sent me, even so I send you" (John 20:21). This mission is defined in the commission to forgive sins (v.23), which we have argued[15] probably contains an allusion to baptism. But this does not mean that baptism is a thing in itself. Forgiveness of sins is consequent solely upon the work of "the Lamb of God, who takes away the sin of the world" (John 1:29). The authority of the apostolate and of the apostolic church today rests solely on the kerygma. But the authority of the kerygma is not the dogmatic authority of an imperialistic institution exercising a worldly power dignified by supernatural claims. Like the word of the earthly Jesus (cf. Luke 12:8f.) it has no inherent authority of its own, but rests upon the Father's eschatological vindication: If you will forgive the sins of those who accept the kerygma, God will ratify this at the eschatological judgment; if you withhold forgiveness from those who reject the kerygma, God will withhold it from them at the judgment. Such is what Paul called the "folly" of the kerygma (1 Cor. 1:21). But "the foolishness of God wiser than men" (1 Cor. 1:25). The authority of the word trusts only in the hope of eschatological vindication. This is the permanent insight enshrined in the Johannine version of the missionary command.

The Thomas episode does not appear to have roots in the primitive tradition. Whether a creation of the Evangelist or of his source, it appears to be spun off as it were from the Jerusalem appearance to the eleven. It wrestles with a problem affecting the second or third generation of believers: How can they believe in the Risen One when they have not seen him? One does not, however, have to be an original eyewitness in order to believe.

There is indeed no personal prerogative in being an eyewitness. Thomas was granted the opportunity of direct eye witness not for his own sake, but in order that he might bear witness to those who had not seen. It is accidental for the disciples' own faith that they came to believe because they themselves had seen the Risen One. Equally blessed are those who have not seen and yet believed. But they can only believe because of the witness of those who have seen. The answer to the problem of the second and third generation is that it is possible to believe without seeing, but only because of the word of the first witnesses. The Fourth Gospel understands itself as an extension of that witness.[16] The same problem which affected the Johannine community affects the church today. The contemporary believer asks, how can he believe in the Risen One when he has not seen him? Would he have had an advantage if he had seen the Risen One like Peter and the Twelve and the +500 and James and all the apostles and Paul? The answer is: no, he would have no advantage. He can still believe, but only on the testimony of the first witnesses.

It is hard to discover what kerygmatic intention the Evangelist can have had in recording the miraculous draft of fish. As we have seen, this story is perhaps best taken as the projection of a miracle of the divine man type from the earthly ministry into the post-Easter period. As such it will belong to the latest stratum of the Easter narratives, like the stories in Luke 24 and John 20. No doubt the Johannine redactor associated it with the theme of mission (cf. the synoptic saying about the fishers of men) and intended the number one hundred fifty-three to have some symbolical significance in this connection, though it is impossible to be sure what that significance was. It would be far fetched therefore to try and discover contemporary meaning in this story, except by relating it to the theme of "fishers of men" in an allegorical way which few exegetes would find legitimate. The redactor uses this story to introduce the *Pasce oves* scene that follows, which because of the more primitive features it contains we classify with the appearances of the intermediate stratum.

Turning now to the appearance narratives of the intermediate stratum we find several themes in the verbalizations of Matthew 28:18-20. First, there is an emphasis on the authority of the Risen One (v.18). This theme had been prominent in the Easter faith almost from the beginning, in the two-stage Christology[17] for which at the exaltation God made Jesus Lord and Christ.[18] But Matthew gives this Christology a distinctive slant. Christ exercises his authority as *kurios*, not only by putting the cosmic powers in subjection under his feet, but as the law-giver for his community. The charge to mission is likewise given a similar slant. The mission is not—as in the (probably earlier) version of the charge[19] enshrined in Pseudo-Mark 16:15—to evangelize, but to make *disciples* and to *teach* them to observe the commandments of the Matthean Jesus. Matthew's own Gospel was meant as an example of obedience to precisely this command. In his careful re-arrangement of the teachings of Jesus in five discourses, and in the adjustment of that teaching to the concrete needs of his church, Matthew shows that he understands that teaching not as a rigid code delivered once for all but as capable of modification and adaptation to later circumstances. The Christian teacher is a scribe who "brings out of his treasure what is new and what is old" (Matt. 13:52). Hence the emphasis in the charge on the abiding presence of the Risen and Exalted One with his community (v.20). Tradition is not a dead document inherited from the past, but a living body of truth which the Risen One in his community constantly reapplies to contemporary needs.

We now come to the *Pasce oves* scene (John 21:15-19). This appears to be an attempt to express in narrative form the theological significance of the appearance to Peter as it occurs in the primitive lists. It is thus similar to the *Tu es Petrus* pericope in Matthew 16:16-18. It emphasizes, among other things, a fact which is true of all the appearances in the primitive lists, namely that appearances to identifiable personages are always acts of grace and forgiveness. Peter had denied the Lord, the eleven had forsaken him and fled, James had not believed in the Lord during his earthly life, and Paul had persecuted his followers. Office in the community rests not upon personal merit but on grace alone. Yet office also rests upon personal commitment and discipleship, upon "love" for the Lord—and the Johannine Christ had already defined "love" as the keeping of his commandments (John 14:15). Office in the church, then, is defined not in terms of intrinsic personal authority, but in terms of service: "Feed my sheep." It is a remarkable accident that the most relevant exposition of this command to Peter comes in a later New Testament epistle which, though somewhat Pauline in its affinities, is actually attributed (though hardly with any historical basis) to Peter, namely 1 Peter: "Tend the flock of God that is your charge, not by constraint but willingly, not for shameful gain but eagerly, not as domineering over those in your charge but being examples to the flock" (1 Pet. 5:2–3). All ministers in the church of Jesus Christ are in a very real sense successors of Peter, and all have received from Peter the charge which the early church believed to have been involved in the appearance of the Risen One to the first witness of the resurrection. The relevance of this for the church is not time-conditioned, though the precise implications of what is involved in "feeding the sheep" have to be spelled out anew in every age. In the time of the Fourth Gospel it meant, among other things, readiness for martyrdom, and it was probably given this particular slant in the tradition before it reached the Evangelist shortly after Peter's martyrdom at Rome in the sixties (21:18–19).

It was apparently the Johannine redactor who added the discussion about the fate of the disciple whom Jesus loved. This is clearly a matter of interest to his own community. It has some importance in the history of early Christian thought since it bears upon the delay of the parousia, but it hardly has *kerygmatic* significance, even for the redactor or his community. It is meant to correct a false understanding of the dominical saying that some of the disciples would live until the parousia (Mark 9:1).

Since the earlier strata of the New Testament have no narratives of appearances, it does not seem necessary for Christian faith to believe in the literal veracity of any of these particular accounts. But the purpose for which the Evangelists used them is clearly relevant to faith. As shaped by the Evangelists, these stories offer us insights into the theological meaning of the resurrection faith for the early communities, and thus offer possibilities of understanding of the resurrection for the believing community today.

We now come to the empty tomb narrative. This, we have argued, belongs to the primary stratum of the Gospel tradition despite its absence from Paul. In the New Testament it serves as a presupposition for the kerygma rather than as part of the kerygma itself. Is it therefore an integral part of Christian faith today? Must we believe that the women found the tomb empty, and does our faith in the resurrection stand or fall by this fact? If our argument as to the way in which the empty tomb came into the tradition is correct, it was possible for the first disciples in Galilee to come to believe in the resurrection of Jesus before they heard of the empty tomb. The disciples welcomed the women's story as congruous with the faith that they had already reached through the appearances, and then took up this story— since they had evolved no appearance narratives—as a vehicle for the proclamation of the resurrection kerygma: "He is not here, God has raised him." It is this proclamation, rather than the discovery of the empty tomb, which is essential to Christian faith. Whether the women's story was based on fact, or was the result of a mistake or illusion, is in the last resort a matter of theological indifference. The historian will never know the answer to this question. Yet the fact that the disciples welcomed the story as congruous with their faith does suggest that it has some importance for that faith. It indicates that for them the resurrection appearances were not manifestations of Christ's human spirit as having survived death, as when the medium of Endor conjured up the spirit of Samuel (1 Sam. 28:8ff.), but rather the eschatological reversal of death which was the content of apocalyptic hope. Can the empty tomb story still have this function today? It certainly still rules out the spiritistic misunderstanding of the resurrection. Yet even to such a sophisticated biblical scholar as Rudolf Bultmann, it suggests (wrongly, in our opinion) an interpretation of resurrection as a resuscitation of a corpse, rather than an eschatological transformation. Should we therefore regard the empty tomb pericope as useless to contemporary faith not on the ground that it is factually untrue but on the ground that it is misleading? Here we would plead that *abusus non tollit usum,* and that the proper thing to do is to interpret the story like the appearance stories, in accordance with the Evangelists' intention. That the intention of the Evangelists is to assert not the resuscitation of Jesus' body, but his translation into eschatological existence would seem to be quite clearly stated by the angelic proclamation, *ouk estin hōde, ēgerthē,* "he is not here, he is risen." We would therefore conclude that even for present-day faith this narrative is still relevant for Easter faith.

What must we believe about the resurrection appearances not as narratives, but as listed, e.g. in 1 Corinthians 15, and as predicted by the angel in Mark? Here again, as we have sought to make clear from the analysis of the traditions, the list was itself no part of the original Christian kerygma. From this it could be argued that while it is integral to Christian faith to believe that Christ revealed himself as risen, it is not essential to believe that he actually appeared to the people listed in this passage. This question touches once more on the debate between Barth and Bultmann over the role of the appearances in the Pauline kerygma—whether they are intended as "proofs." As we saw, Paul probably did not intend them as proofs, but rather as a substantiation of his own claim to be no less an apostle than the original witnesses.[20]

This point does not seem to be directly related to faith in the kerygma. Yet we cannot dismiss this list as entirely irrelevant to faith, and that for two reasons. First, the list, as our analysis showed, indicated that the appearances served a *two*fold function: that of founding the church, and that of inaugurating the church's mission. It is integral to Christian faith to believe that the Christian church is founded upon the Christ event and not, for instance, that it is merely a sociological phenomenon emerging within history (though on one level it is that as well). And it is integral to Christian faith to believe that the imperative of mission springs not from the natural desire of any society to propagate its ideas or to extend its membership, but from obedience to the command of its exalted Lord. Second, it is essential to Christian faith that it receive the resurrection kerygma as the testimony of accredited eyewitnesses and not as "cleverly devised myths" (2 Pet. 1:16). Resurrection faith rests upon eyewitnesses who testify not merely to their own belief, but to something which "happened" additionally to and outside of their belief: God revealed his Son to them as risen from the dead. Christian faith is not acceptance of the faith of the first disciples, but acceptance of their testimony to what God has done, namely that in Jesus ("in" here meaning both "in his case" and "through him for the believers") God has inaugurated eschatological existence. But the disciples could not be direct witnesses of this. They could not "see" Jesus enter into eschatological existence, for that is an event occurring at the border between this age and the age to come. Instead, this was revealed to them after it had happened: God raised his Son and showed him resurrected to the witnesses. But how can we conceive of the occurrence of a revelatory event? It is not an event unequivocally belonging to the eschatological future yet occurring within this world or within this time, for that is impossible: that cannot happen until the End. What can happen within this age is a certain event which is perfectly explicable as a historical event, yet is a disclosure of the transcendent and eschatological to the eye of faith. It is of this order that we are to conceive the Easter experiences. At one level they may be categorized as "visions" (*ōphthē*), explicable within the terms of the psychology of religion. Yet, "in, with and under" these experiences, explicable in this way, there is contained transcendental or eschatological disclosure. What the transcendental or eschatological reality defined in ontological categories really "is" or how it is to be described is by definition beyond our present knowledge. "What no eye has seen, nor ear heard, nor the heart of man conceived, what God has prepared for those who love him" (1 Cor. 2:9), and: "Now we see in a mirror dimly" (1 Cor. 13:12).

The transcendent or eschatological can be suggested only by way of myth (as in Jewish apocalyptic) or analogies (as in philosophy of religion). This kind of language is not literal description. All we can really say about it, as scholasticism realized, is only capable of being said in negatives. Transcendent or eschatological existence is existence which is *not* subject to sin, *not* subject to death, *not* subject to inauthenticity. The kind of existence we can describe is existence subject to these things. But through what happened in Jesus Christ there has been opened for us a future (in which we already to some extent participate through the Holy Spirit!) in which this present existence will be done away. The whole structure of Christian faith (the Christ event, kerygma, sacrament, church) depends on the presence of the eschatological in, with and under temporal events. Thus the resurrection visions are not unique in this regard.

Preaching the Easter narratives

If the resurrection narratives constitute a problem for faith, they are even more of a problem for the preacher. The individual believer can always pass over what he cannot understand and ignore what he cannot believe. But the preacher is confronted by texts which he has to expound publicly and cannot avoid the challenge of the texts as a whole. If the irreducible historical minimum behind the Easter narratives consists simply of (a) a well-based claim of certain disciples to have had visions of Jesus after his death as raised from the dead, and (b) an unverified claim of one or more women that they discovered the grave of Jesus empty on the Sunday morning after his death and burial, is that all he can preach? What message is there in the claim of the disciples which, however sincerely believed, remains a subjective claim open to possible hallucination, and the all too dubious claim of the women?

It cannot be too strongly emphasized that it is not the task of the preacher to try and establish the truth or credibility of these alleged experiences and leave it at that. Resurrection faith is not the historical faith that the women found the tomb empty and that disciples saw Jesus risen from the dead: it is faith in the risen Lord.

The various methods of criticism which have been applied to the resurrection narratives since the eighteenth century, so far from destroying the whole basis of the preacher's material, have in fact laid it bare as never before. By establishing the factual details of the narratives as later accretions to the tradition and by posing the question as to the purpose of these additions, it has laid bare the real intention of these stories as the tradition and the Evangelists have shaped them. In a word, it has exposed their kerygmatic character. It is this kerygma that the preacher has to offer to his hearers, not the factual details. For Christian faith is not believing *that* certain things happened, such as the discovery of the empty tomb or the disciples' visions. Rather, the preacher must offer faith in Jesus Christ as the saving act of God and the presence and availability of this saving act not only to those who consorted with the Lord in first-century Palestine, but to all in every place, yesterday and today and forever. Criticism then first relieves the preacher of the task of seeking to impose a historical faith on his hearers, and liberates him to invite them to a kerygmatic faith.

At the same time it liberates him from the task of seeking to establish the historicity of the alleged facts by apologetic. It is no part of Easter preaching to employ the arguments of apologetic to show, e.g., that the women did go to the right tomb and really did find it empty, that the Risen One did walk as a stranger along the road from Jerusalem to Emmaus, that he really did eat fish in the presence of his disciples, and that he really did invite Thomas to put his finger into the prints of the nails and to thrust his hand into his pierced side. For Christian faith does not necessarily either accept or reject these alleged facts. To faith they are in the last resort matters of indifference.

Nor does the preacher have to *attack* the historicity of these things (since his concern is elsewhere, with the Easter kerygma). There is no need for him to spend time in the pulpit trying to demonstrate that the women actually went to the wrong tomb, or that the story of their discovery only arose later as a legend in a Hellenistic milieu. There is no need for him to demonstrate that the appearances were in fact subjective hallucinations. For this might be putting an inauthentic skandalon before believers. At the same time it is his duty when questioned (though, I would suggest, in the context of the adult education class rather than in the context of the pulpit) to explain candidly his own critical understanding of the texts. This again may remove an inauthentic skandalon for believers who feel that the historicity of the resurrection narratives is at the same time a tax on their credulity. And preachers often do not give sufficient credit to their hearers in this regard. They are often more intelligent and better educated than the preacher and are relieved rather than shocked by critical candor. The preacher should never obtrude his critical understandings in the pulpit, though everything he says on the kerygmatic level should be *consistent* with them because it should have been worked out with the help of critical method. The pulpit is the place for proclamation, not for critical analysis of the text.

Thus the preacher will seek to grasp the "scopus" of the text, its kerygmatic intention, and having grasped that, in the terms of the Evangelists, seek to translate that kerygmatic intention for his contemporary hearers, making it an address to them, making it speak to them and claim their faith.

In the lectionaries of the Roman Catholic, Lutheran and Anglican churches, both traditional and experimental, the empty tomb narrative in one or other of its forms is the gospel pericope for Easter Day. Preachers have often criticized this provision and have wished for an appearance story. Why, they ask, should we not be able on Easter morning to see the risen Lord with the disciples, rather than the empty tomb with the women? The answer to this request is that the kerygmatic intention of this pericope is not contained in the women's discovery but, as we saw in our analysis of the tradition, in the angelic proclamation: "He has risen, he is not here" (Mark 16:6). This is the preacher's message. The women who went to the tomb in the story were thinking of Jesus as a figure of the past—as one who had been and no longer was, one whose mortal remains alone were accessible. But the message of Easter is that he is not of the past: he has overcome death and is forever our contemporary. He is not "here": not to be sought in first-century Palestine. He is risen, entered into God's future from which he may ever encounter us in our present.

Our critical analysis also showed that the women's story was accepted by the disciples because it was congruous with the belief which they had already reached on the ground of their visions in Galilee. If the historicity of the women's discovery is not essential to faith, that with which it is congruous is. God raised Jesus from the dead. This meant, in apocalyptic language, that the total being of Jesus, his concrete psychosomatic being, the whole man, was translated into eschatological existence, and thereby transformed. This is an integral part of resurrection faith and of resurrection kerygma. Bultmann dismissed the empty tomb as a legend and ignored it in his demythologizing. This was inconsistent with the intention of demythologizing which was to *interpret*, rather than *eliminate* the legendary or mythological language of the kerygma.[21] He has offered no demythologized interpretation of the empty tomb story, but simply eliminated it.[22] Our proposal is that it should be interpreted: interpreted as a sign that Jesus entered as the "pioneer of our faith" (Heb. 12:2) into that eschatological transformation of the totality of man's existence which is initiated likewise in the believers at baptism and is consummated for them at the End.

The Emmaus story is one of the traditional lections for Eastertide. Here the preacher will not emphasize the naive picture of the Risen One walking along the road as an unknown stranger, or his tarrying in the house to eat bread, but will concentrate upon the kerygmatic highpoints of the text, which are as follows:

1. "We had hoped that he was the one to redeem Israel" (Luke 24:21).
2. "Was it not necessary that the Christ should suffer these things and enter into his glory?" (v.26).
3. "He was known to them in the breaking of the bread" (v.35).
4. "The Lord has risen indeed" (v.34).

The first text presents the disappointment and disillusionment of the disciples after Good Friday. Jesus had staked his all on the coming of the kingdom of God, and he had died a criminal's death, rejected by men and seemingly by God. Only by the self-manifestation of the Risen One are this disappointment and disillusionment overcome. The self-manifestation takes place through the unfolding of the scriptures and the breaking of the bread. We cannot have a vision of the Risen One like the first disciples, but we can encounter him in his appointed means of word and sacrament. The Risen One still unfolds for us the scriptures and shows how it was necessary for him to suffer his passion and enter his glory, and he still makes himself known in the breaking of the bread as he presides over our eucharist as the invisible risen host. And so from this encounter we go forth with the confession on our lips, *anestē alēthōs,* "he is risen indeed!"

The traditional lection for the First Sunday after Easter (Low Sunday or *Quasi modo geniti*) is the Johannine story of the upper room, extending through the overcoming of Thomas' doubt. The preacher may choose either the first or the second half of the pericope. If he chooses the first half, he will not concentrate upon the appearance of the Risen One through shut doors, but rather upon his words: his repeated greeting, "Peace be with you."

If the preacher takes the second part, the overcoming of Thomas' doubts, he has here a situation particularly relevant to modern man. Thomas is defiant and lays down conditions for the overcoming of his doubts. The risen Lord does not harshly rebuke Thomas, but in a genuinely pastoral manner gently leads him on to faith. Through this gradual disclosure, Thomas is led to his tremendous confession, "My Lord and my God!" (John

20:28). His resurrection faith is not merely the acceptance of the resurrection as a "fact" but the confession of Jesus as One who is Lord and God, that is to say, as the One in whose death and resurrection God is savingly present—as the One who was and is the eschatological act of God. The concluding words of the pericope, "Blessed are those who have not seen and yet believe" (v.29b), open up the application of the text to modern man. His doubt often takes the defiant form of Thomas': he demands guarantees before he is ready to commit himself to faith. He wants to see God in tangible form, perhaps by some miracle. But to demand this would be to demand precisely what he cannot have. There was special reason why Thomas should have his doubt overcome by a direct sight of the Risen One. He had to become one of the first witnesses. We can only come to faith because of the word of these witnesses. We are challenged to believe without seeing, because Jesus revealed himself to the first witnesses. The modern doubter must honestly face up to his doubts and allow the Risen One to deal with him pastorally as he dealt with Thomas, not however, by an appearance, but by the word of the first witnesses.

The later Sundays of Eastertide are traditionally occupied by the great Johannine discourses, and it is not until Ascension Day that the preacher is faced once more with the difficulties of preaching on a resurrection narrative. Traditionally the gospel pericope of Ascension Day was the narrative of the ascension in the unauthentic ending of Mark. Most modern revisions of the lectionary have substituted the Lucan version for this (Luke 24:44–53). This is one of the most difficult occasions for the preacher, as J. Schniewind noted in his reply to Bultmann's essay on demythologizing:

"There is another incident which the present writer recalls from his student days at Marburg in 1906. On Ascension Day he went to the service of the Christenberg. Great crowds were flocking thither, attracted by the display of traditional costumes in the procession; most of them were people who had little sympathy with the Christian religion. Would the preacher, one wondered, be able to proclaim the message of 'Christ the King' in a way which the crowds would understand? Alas, we were given a naive picture of a literal ascension, such as a non-Christian would dismiss as mere myth. Even Luther poured scorn on such literalism: 'Oh, that heaven of the charlatans with its golden stool and Christ sitting at the Father's side vested in a choir cope and a golden crown, as the painters love to portray him.' "[23]

Schniewind advises the preacher on Ascension Day to ignore the literal incident and to concentrate on the proclamation of Christ as King. He "went up" does not mean a Cape Kennedy event of spatial levitation but indicates the worth and dignity which are his because of his achievement: "wherefore God highly exalted him." He is the sovereign king of the believers already and when he comes again will be sovereign over the whole created universe. He is the One to whom every knee shall bow. As such he must be proclaimed by the preacher so that his hearers may accept him as their king. Jesus left his disciples in Palestine in order that he might come to all believers at all times and in all places, in his word and in his sacrament. That is the message of Ascension Day.

We would claim then that criticism, so far from making the preacher's task in Eastertide more difficult, has in fact provided him with the tools to accomplish that task more relevantly and with more concentration than before. For criticism has recalled him to the central message of Easter, which underlies the varied detail of the stories.

APPENDIX:
THE RESURRECTION NARRATIVES
IN THE APOCRYPHAL GOSPELS

Translation from *New Testament Apocrypha*, Volume One
Editor: W. Schneemelcher

The Gospel of the Hebrews

And when the Lord had given the linen cloth to the servant of the priest, he went to James and appeared to him. For James had sworn that he would not eat bread from that hour in which he had drunk the cup of the Lord until he should see him risen from among them that sleep. And shortly thereafter the Lord said: Bring a table and bread! And immediately it is added: he took the bread, blessed it and brake it and gave it to James the Just and said to him: My brother, eat thy bread, for the Son of man is risen from among them that sleep.

(Jerome, *vir. inl.* 2)

The Gospel of Peter

8. 28. But the scribes and Pharisees and elders, being assembled together and hearing that all the people were murmuring and beating their breasts, saying, "If at his death these exceeding great signs have come to pass, behold how *righteous* he was!",— 29. were afraid and come to *Pilate*, entreating him and saying, 30. "Give us soldiers that we may watch his sepulchre *for three days, lest his disciples come and steal him away* and the *people* suppose that he *is risen from the dead,* and do us harm." 31. And Pilate gave them Petronius the centurion with soldiers to watch the sepulchre. And with them there came elders and scribes to the sepulchre. 32. And all who were there, together with the centurion and the soldiers, *rolled* thither a great stone and laid it against the entrance to the sepulchre 33. and *put* on it seven *seals*, pitched a tent and kept watch. 9. 34. Early in the morning, when the Sabbath dawned, there came a crowd from Jerusalem and the country round about to see the sepulchre that had been sealed.

35. Now in the night in which the Lord's day dawned, when the soldiers, two by two in every watch, were keeping guard, there rang out a loud *voice in heaven,* 36. and they saw the *heavens opened* and two men *come down* from there in a great brightness and drawn nigh to the sepulchre. 37. That *stone* which had been laid against the entrance to the sepulchre started of itself *to roll* and gave way to the side, and the sepulchre was opened, and both the young men entered in. 10. 38. When now those soldiers saw this, they awakened the centurion and the elders—for they also were there to assist at the watch. 39. And whilst they were relating what they had seen, they saw again three men come out from the sepulchre, and two of them sustaining the other, and a cross following them, 40. and the heads of the two reaching to heaven, but that of him who was led of them by the hand overpassing the heavens. 41. And they heard a voice out of the heavens crying, "Thou hast preached to them that sleep", 42. and from the cross there was heard the answer, "Yea." 11. 43. Those men therefore took counsel with one another

to go and report this to Pilate. 44. And whilst they were still deliberating, the heavens were again seen to open, and a man descended and entered into the sepulchre. 45. When those who were of the centurion's company saw this, they hastened by night to Pilate, abandoning the sepulchre which they were guarding, and reported everything that they had seen, being full of disquietude and saying, *"In truth* he was *the Son of God."* 46. Pilate answered and said, "I am clean *from the blood* of the Son of God, upon such a thing have you decided." 47. Then all came to him, beseeching him and urgently calling upon him to command the centurion and the soldiers to tell no one what they had seen. 48. "For *it is better* for us," they said, "to make ourselves guilty of the greatest sin before God than to fall into the hands of the people of the Jews and be stoned." 49. Pilate therefore commanded the centurion and the soldiers to say nothing.

12. 50. *Early in the morning* of the Lord's day *Mary Magdalene,* a woman disciple of the Lord—for *fear* of the *Jews,* since (they) were inflamed with wrath, she had not done at the sepulchre of the Lord what women are wont to do for those beloved of them who die—took 51. with her her women friends and came to the sepulchre where he was laid. 52. And they feared lest the Jews should see them, and said, "Although we could not weep and lament on that day when he was crucified, yet let us now do so at his sepulchre. 53. *But who will roll away for us the stone* also that is set *on the entrance to the sepulchre,* that we may go in and sit beside him and do what is due?—54. For *the stone was great,*—and we fear lest any one seee us. And if we cannot do so, let us at least put down at the entrance what we bring for a memorial of him and let us weep and lament until we have again gone home." 13. 55. So they went and found the sepulchre opened. And they came near, *stooped down* and saw there *a young man* sitting in the midst of the sepulchre, comely and *clothed with a brightly shining robe,* who said to them, 56. "Wherefore are ye come? *Whom seek ye?* Not him that *was crucified? He is risen* and gone. But if ye believe not, stoop this way and *see the place where he lay, for he is not here.* For he is risen and is gone thither whence he was sent." 57. Then the women *fled affrighted.*

14. 58. Now it was the last day of unleavened bread and many went away and repaired to their homes, since the feast was at an end. 59. But we, the twelve disciples of the Lord, wept and mourned, and each one, very grieved for what had come to pass, went to his own home. 60. But I, Simon Peter, and my brother Andrew took our nets and went to the sea. And there was with us Levi, the son of Alphaeus, whom the Lord—(had called away from the custom-house (?), cf. Mk. 2:14).

Epistula Apostolorum

(ETHIOPIC)	(COPTIC)
9. He of whom we are witnesses we know as the one crucified in the days of Pontius Pilate and of the prince Archelaus, who was crucified between two thieves and was taken down from the wood of the cross together with them, and was buried in the place called qarānejō (κρανίου), to which three women came, Sarah, Martha, and Mary Magdalene. They carried ointment to pour out	he concerning whom [we] bear witness that the Lord is he who was crucified by Pontius Pilate and Archelaus between the two thieves [and] who was buried in a place called the [place of the skull]. There went to that place [three] women: Mary, she who belonged to Martha, and Mary [Magd]-alene. They took ointment to pour

upon his body, weeping and mourning over what had happened.

And they approached the tomb and found the stone where it had been rolled away from the tomb, and they opened the door	But when they had approached the tomb they looked inside

and did not find his (*Coptic*: the) body.

10. And (*Copt.*: But) as they were mourning and weeping, the Lord appeared to them and said to them, "(*Copt.*: For whom are you weeping? Now) do not weep; I am he whom you seek. But let one of you go to your brothers and say (*Eth.*: to them), 'Come, our (*Copt.*: the) Master has risen from the dead.'"

And Mary came to us and told us. And we said to her, "What have we to do with you, O woman? He that is dead and buried, can he then live?" And we did not believe her, that our Saviour had risen from the dead.

Martha came and told it to us. We said to her, "What do you want with us, O woman? He who has died is buried, and could it be possible for him to live?" We did not believe her, that the Saviour had risen from the dead.

Then she went back to our (*Copt.*: the) Lord and said to him,

"None of them believed me concerning your resurrection." And he said to her,

that you are alive."
He said,

"Let another one of you go (*Copt.*: to them) saying this again to them."

And Sarah came and gave us the same news, and we accused her of lying. And she returned to our Lord and spoke to him as Mary had.

Mary came and told us again, and we did not believe her. She returned to the Lord and she also told it to him.

11. Then (*Eth.*: And then) the Lord said to Mary and (*Copt.*: and also) to her sisters, "Let us go to them." And he came and found us inside, veiled.

And we doubted and did not believe. He came before us like a ghost and we did not believe that it was he. But it was he. And thus he said to us, "Come, and

He called us out. But we thought it was a ghost, and we did not believe it was the Lord. Then [he said] to us, "Come,

do not be afraid. I am your teacher (*Copt.*: [master]) whom you, Peter, denied three times (*Eth.*: before the cock crowed); and now do you deny again?"

And we went to him, thinking and doubting whether it was he. And he said to us,

But we went to him, doubting in [our] hearts whether it was possibly he. Then he said to [us],

"Why do you (*Copt.:* still) doubt and (*Eth.:* why) are you not believing? (*Eth.:* believing that) I am he who spoke to you concerning my flesh, my death, and my resurrection.

And that you may know that it is I, lay your hand, Peter, (and your finger) in the nailprint of my hands; and you, Thomas, in my side; and also you, Andrew, see whether my foot steps on the ground and leaves a footprint.

That you may know that it is I, put your finger, Peter, in the nailprints of my hands; and you, Thomas, put your finger in the spear-wounds of my side; but you, Andrew, look at my feet and see if they do not touch the ground.

For it is written in the Prophet

'But a ghost, a demon, leaves no print on the ground.'"

12. But now we felt him, that he had truly risen in the flesh. And then we fell on our faces before him, asked him for pardon and entreated him because we had not believed him. Then our Lord and Saviour said to us, "Stand up and I will reveal to you what is on earth, and what is above heaven, and your resurrection that is in the kingdom of heaven, concerning which my Father has sent me, that I may take up you and those who believe in me."

'The foot of a ghost or a demon does not join to the ground.'"

But we [touched] him that we might truly know whether he [had risen] in the flesh, and we fell on our [faces] confessing our sin, that we had been [un]believing. Then the Lord our redeemer said, "Rise up, and I will reveal to you what is above heaven and what is in heaven, and your rest that is in the kingdom of heaven. For my [Father] has given me the power to take up you and those who believe in me."

Acts of Pilate

xi. *But a certain man named Joseph, a member of the council, from the town of Arimathaea,* who also was waiting *for the kingdom of God, this man went to Pilate and asked for the body of Jesus. And he took it down, and wrapped it in a clean linen cloth, and placed it in a rock-hewn tomb, in which no one had ever yet been laid* (Lk. 23:50–53).

XII. When the Jews heard that Joseph had asked for the body, they sought for him and the twelve men who said that Jesus was not born of fornication, and for Nicodemus and for many others, who had come forward before Pilate and made known his good works. But they all hid themselves, and only Nicodemus was seen by them, because he was a ruler of the Jews. And Nicodemus said to them: "How did you enter into the synagogue?" The Jews answered him: "How did you enter into the synagogue? You are an accomplice of his, and his portion shall be with you in the world to come." Nicodemus said: "Amen, amen." Likewise also Joseph came forth (from his concealment?) and said to them: "Why are you angry with me, because I asked for the body of Jesus? See, I have placed it in my new tomb, having wrapped it in clean linen, and I rolled a stone before the door of the cave. And you have not done well with the righteous one, for you did not repent of having crucified him, but also pierced him with a spear."

Then the Jews seized Joseph and commanded him to be secured until the first day of the week. They said to him: "Know that the hour forbids us to do anything against you, because the Sabbath dawns. But know also that you will not even be counted worthy of burial, but we shall give your flesh to the birds of the heaven." Joseph answered: "This word is like that of the boastful Goliath, who insulted the living God and the holy David. For God said by the prophet: *Vengeance is mine, I will repay, says the Lord* (Rom. 12:19; cf. Deut. 32:35). And now he who is uncircumcised in the flesh, but circumcised in heart, took water and washed his hands before the sun, saying: I am innocent of the blood of this righteous man. You see to it. And you answered Pilate: *His blood be on us and on our children* (Mt. 27:25). And now I fear lest the wrath of God come upon you and your children, as you said." When the Jews heard these words, they were embittered in their hearts, and laid hold on Joseph and seized him and shut him in a building without a window, and guards remained at the door. And they sealed the door of the place where Joseph was shut up.

2. And on the Sabbath the rulers of the synagogue and the priests and the Levites ordered that all should present themselves

in the synagogue on the first day of the week. And the whole multitude rose up early and took counsel in the synagogue by what death they should kill him. And when the council was in session they commanded him to be brought with great dishonour. And when they opened the door they did not find him. And all the people were astonished and filled with consternation because they found the seals undamaged, and Caiaphas had the key. And they dared no longer to lay hands on those who had spoken before Pilate on behalf of Jesus.

XIII. And while they still sat in the synagogue and marvelled because of Joseph, there came some of the guard which the Jews had asked from Pilate to guard the tomb of Jesus, lest his disciples should come and steal him. And they told the rulers of the synagogue and the priests and the Levites what had happened: how there was a great earthquake. "And we saw an angel descend from heaven, and *he rolled away the stone* from the mouth of the cave, *and sat upon it,* and he shone *like snow and like lightning.* And we were in great fear, and lay *like dead men* (Mt. 28:2–4). And we heard the voice of the angel speaking to the women who waited at the tomb: *Do not be afraid. I know that you seek Jesus who was crucified. He is not here. He has risen, as he said. Come and see the place where* the Lord *lay. And go quickly and tell his disciples that he has risen from the dead* and is in Galilee" (Mt. 28:5–7).

2. The Jews asked: "To what women did he speak?" The members of the guard answered: "We do not know who they were." The Jews said: "At what hour was it?" The members of the guard answered: "At midnight." The Jews said: "And why did you not seize the women?" The members of the guard said: "We were like dead men through fear, and gave up hope of seeing the light of day; how could we then have seized them?" The Jews said: "As the Lord lives, we do not believe you." The members of the guard said to the Jews: "So many signs you saw in that man and you did not believe; and how can you believe us? You rightly swore: As the Lord lives. For he *does* live." Again the members of the guard said: "We have heard that you shut up him who asked for the body of Jesus, and sealed the door, and

then when you opened it you did not find him. Therefore give us Joseph and we will give you Jesus." The Jews said: "Joseph has gone to his own city." And the members of the guard said to the Jews: "And Jesus has risen, as we heard from the angel, and is in Galilee." 3. And when the Jews heard these words, they feared greatly and said: "(Take heed) lest this report be heard and all incline to Jesus." And the Jews took counsel, and offered *much money and gave it to the soldiers of the guard, saying:* "Say that when you were sleeping *his disciples* came *by night* and *stole him. And if this is heard by the governor, we will persuade him and keep you out of trouble"* (Mt. 28:12–14).

XIV. Now Phineës a priest and Adas a teacher and Angaeus a Levite came from Galilee to Jerusalem, and told the rulers of the synagogue and the priests and the Levites: "We saw Jesus and his disciples sitting upon the mountain which is called Mamilch. And he said to his disciples: *Go into all the world and preach the gospel to the whole creation. He who believes and is baptized will be saved; but he who does not believe will be condemned. And these signs will accompany those who believe: in my name they will cast out demons; they will speak in new tongues; they will pick up serpents; and if they drink any deadly thing, it will not hurt them; they will lay their hands on the sick, and they will recover* (Mk. 16:15–18). And while Jesus was still speaking to his disciples, we saw him taken up into heaven."

2. Then the elders and the priests and the Levites said: "Give glory to the God of Israel, and confess before him if you indeed heard and saw what you have described." Those who told them said: "As the Lord God of our fathers Abraham, Isaac and Jacob lives, we heard these things and saw him taken up to heaven."

Notes

PREFACE

1. W. Marxsen, *The Resurrection of Jesus of Nazareth* (Philadelphia: Fortress Press, 1970), pp. 92, 95–96, 107.
2. Julius Schniewind, "A Reply to Bultmann" in *Kerygma and Myth*, ed. H. W. Bartsch (London: S.P.C.K., 1953), pp. 45–100, esp. pp. 69–80.
3. See especially Theodore J. Weeden, *Mark—Traditions in Conflict* (Philadelphia: Fortress Press, 1971, paperback 1979), and Werner H. Kelber, *The Kingdom in Mark* (Philadelphia: Fortress Press, 1974). These two works were based on doctoral theses written under James M. Robinson at Claremont and Norman Perrin at Chicago respectively. Robinson himself defends the view that the transfiguration is a retrojected resurrection story in James M. Robinson and Helmut Koester, *Trajectories through Early Christianity* (Philadelphia: Fortress Press, 1971, paperback 1979), pp. 48–49, n. 43. His reply to Dodd is that while the transfiguration story does differ from later resurrection stories it is wholly compatible with such earlier traditions as the appearances to Stephen and Paul in Acts. In neither story, however, is the earthly Jesus present from the first, and only later manifested as glorified, so Robinson has not answered Dodd on this point. Perrin's view that Mark interpreted the transfiguration as a proleptic parousia manifestation, a view I would accept, does not to my mind actually require the origin of the story in a post-resurrection appearance. See N. Perrin, *A Modern Pilgrimage in New Testament Christology* (Philadelphia: Fortress Press, 1974), pp. 115–121; *idem, The Resurrection according to Matthew, Mark, and Luke* (Philadelphia: Fortress Press, 1977).
4. Raymond E. Brown, S.S., *The Gospel according to John (xiii–xxi)*, Anchor Bible 29A (Garden City: Doubleday, 1970), pp. 1090–1092.
5. E.g., Edward L. Bode, *The First Easter Morning*, Analecta biblica 45 (Rome: Biblical Institute, 1970), pp. 159–173.
6. E.g., G. E. Ladd, *I Believe in the Resurrection of Jesus* (Grand Rapids: Eerdmans, 1975).
7. U. Wilckens, *Resurrection* (Edinburgh: St. Andrew Press, 1977).
8. J. A. T. Robinson, *The Human Face of God* (London: SCM Press, 1973), pp. 131–141; *idem, Can We Trust the New Testament?* (Grand Rapids: Eerdmans, 1977), pp. 121–124.
9. *Can We Trust?* p. 127. In August 1979 Robinson appeared on a BBC television program devoted to the shroud and seemed almost persuaded of its genuineness.

10. N. Perrin, *Rediscovering the Teaching of Jesus* (New York/Evanston: Harper & Row, 1976), p. 32. Perrin is there speaking of the sayings tradition, but the same principle applies to the narratives as well.
11. *Peter in the New Testament*, ed. Raymond E. Brown *et al.* (Minneapolis: Augsburg Publishing House; and New York/Paramus/Toronto: Paulist Press, 1973), p. 35 and n. 78.
12. C. Brown, "History and the Believer" in *History, Criticism and Faith*, ed. C. Brown (Downers Grove, Ill.: Inter-Varsity Press, 1976), pp. 147–224, esp. pp. 171–177.
13. Most recently see W. Pannenberg, *Basic Questions in Theology I* (Philadelphia: Fortress Press, and London: SCM Press, 1970), pp. 44–50, arguing against the use of the analogy principle to deny the historicity of the resurrection.

CHAPTER ONE

1. R. Bultmann, "New Testament and Mythology," *Kerygma and Myth*, Vol. I, ed. H. W. Bartsch, trans. Reginald H. Fuller (London: S.P.C.K., 1953), p. 39.
2. Cf. M. Dibelius, *Jesus*, trans. C. B. Hedrick & F. C. Grant (Philadelphia: Westminster Press, 1949), p. 141, "a something."
3. James A. Pike with Diane Kennedy, *The Other Side* (New York: Doubleday, 1968), p. 51. Dr. Pike made this "discovery" through reading James McLaren, *Resurrection Then and Now* (London, 1965, and Philadelphia, 1967). Apparently he had never read Samuel Butler.
4. Kirsopp Lake, *The Historical Evidence for the Resurrection of Jesus Christ* (New York: G. P. Putnam's Sons, 1907); P. Gardner-Smith, *The Narratives of the Resurrection* (London: Methuen, 1926).
5. M. Goguel, *La foi à la résurrection de Jésus dans la christianisme primitif* (Paris: E. Leroux, 1933).
6. Cf. the essays translated in *The Significance of the Resurrection for Faith in Jesus Christ*, ed. C. F. D. Moule, SBT N.S. 8 (London: SCM Press, 1968).
7. H. Grass, *Ostergeschehen und Osterberichte* (Göttingen: Vandenhoeck & Ruprecht, ²1962).

CHAPTER TWO

1. The first clear recognition of the non-Pauline words appears in R. Seeberg, *Der Katechismus der Urchristenheit* (Leipzig: A. Diechert, 1903), pp. 63ff. See J. Jeremias, *The Eucharistic Words of Jesus* (New York: Charles Scribner's Sons, 1966), pp. 101–102. Jeremias lists the following un-Pauline words and phrases: "for our sins" (*huper tōn hamartiōn hēmōn*); "he was raised" (*egēgertai*); "on the third day" (*tē hēmerā tē tritē*); "the twelve" (*dōdeka*).
2. Apparently this observation was first made by G. Kittel, *Die Probleme des palästinensischen Spätjudentums und das Urchristentum, BWANT* 3.1 (Stuttgart: W. Kohlhammer, 1926). He has been followed among others by: W. D. Davies, *Paul and Rabbinic Judaism* (London: S.P.C.K., 1948), pp. 248–249, and J. Jeremias, *loc. cit.* In an article criticizing other aspects of Jeremias's argument about our passage H.

Conzelmann, "zur Analyse der Bekenntnisformel I Kor. 15, 3–5," *EvTh* 25 (1965), pp. 1–10, accepts the pre-Pauline character of the formula.

3. Thus recently U. Wilckens, "The Tradition of the Resurrection" in *The Significance of the Message of the Resurrection*, ed. C. F. D. Moule (London: SCM Press, 1968), p. 57, on the general ground that Paul is most likely to have received the tradition from the church which he first joined as a Christian and which was the first base for his missionary activity.

4. *Op. cit.*, pp. 102–103. Jeremias follows a tradition going back to Harnack (1922) in placing the conclusion of the pre-Pauline formula at "twelve." See below, p. 12.

5. In a review article of F. Hahn's *Christologische Hoheitstitel* (Göttingen: Vandenhoeck & Ruprecht, 1963), E.T.; *The Titles of Jesus in Christology* (London: Lutterworth, 1969, cited hereafter), "Ein Weg zur ntl. Christologie?" *EvTh* 25 (1965), pp. 24–72, esp. pp. 57–58, Vielhauer confines himself to the denial that "Christos" without the article is evidence of Palestinian Aramaic.

6. *Art. cit.*

7. "Artikelloses Χριστός. Zur Ursprache von I. Kor. 15:3b–5," *ZNW* 57 (1966), pp. 211–215.

8. R. H. Fuller, *The Foundations of New Testament Christology* (London: Lutterworth, 1965), pp. 160–162.

9. Some analysts have assigned the *whole* of v.6 to Paul, but without reason.

10. "Die Verklärungsgeschichte Jesu, der Bericht des Paulus, I Kor. 15, 3ff.," SBA phil.-hist. KE. (1922), p. 62ff. This article, though frequently referred to, has been inaccessible to me.

11. E.g., even J. Jeremias, *op. cit.*, p. 102.

12. Cf. W. G. Kümmel, *Kirchenbegriff und Kirchenbewusstsein in der Urgemeinde und bei Jesus*, SNU I (Zürich: Max Niehans, and Uppsala: Seminarium Neotestamenticum Upsaliense, 1943), p. 45, n. 12.

13. "Herkunft und Funktion der Traditionselemente in I. Kor. 15:1–11," *ThZ* 11 (1955), pp. 401–419.

14. "Der Ursprung der Überlieferung der Erscheinungen des Auferstandenen" in *Dogma und Denkstrukturen*, ed. W. Joest and W. Pannenberg, Edmund Schlink Festschrift (Göttingen: Vandenhoeck & Ruprecht, 1963), pp. 56–95. This essay is an elaboration of the views already put forth by the same author in *Die Missionsreden der Apostelgeschichte* (Neukirchen: Neukirchner Verlag, 1960), pp. 74–80. Parts of this essay are reproduced in Moule (ed.), *op. cit.*, pp. 71–76.

15. E. Norden, *Agnostos Theos* (Leipzig: Teubner, 1929), p. 271, cited by Wilckens, *Missionsreden*, p. 76, n.

16. On this, see R. H. Fuller, *A Critical Introduction to the New Testament* (London: Duckworth, 1966), p. 91.

17. See H. Tödt, *The Son of Man in the Synoptic Tradition* (London: SCM Press, 1965), pp. 209–210.

18. *Ibid.*; F. Hahn, *op. cit.*, pp. 56–58 *contra* C. K. Barrett, "The Background of Mark 10:45" in *New Testament Essays, Studies in Memory of Thomas Walter Manson, 1893–1958*, ed. A. J. B. Higgins (Manchester: University Press, 1959), pp. 1–18.

19. Cf. R. H. Fuller, *Foundations*, p. 153f.
20. So H. von Campenhausen, *Der Ablauf der Osterereignisse und das leere Grab*, S.H.A. phil.-hist. Kl. (Heidelberg: C. Winter, 1958), p. 27.
21. G. Kittel, "Die Auferstehung Jesu," *Deutsche Theologie* 4 (1937), pp. 133–135, cited by H. Grass, *Ostergeschehen und Osterberichte* (Göttingen: Vandenhoeck & Ruprecht, 1962), p. 146.
22. On the interpretation of this passage, see C. H. Dodd, *The Johannine Epistles*, MNTC (London: Hodder and Stoughton, 1964), *ad loc.*
23. M. Goguel in *La foi à la résurrection de Jésus dans le christianisme primitif* (Paris: Leroux, 1933), p. 215–222, has sought to demonstrate that this apocalyptic conception of the resurrection (and assumption) from the tomb survived in a number of later Christian legends (*Acta Johannis, Transitus Mariae,* etc.) and appears to underlie some of the Jewish apocalyptic ideas about the ascensions of Enoch, Moses and Elijah.
24. Cf. C. F. D. Moule in Moule (ed.), *op. cit.*, pp. 9f.
25. For this interpretation of 1 Cor. 15, see J. Schniewind, "Die Leugner der Auferstehung in Korinth," *Nachgelassene Reden und Aufsätze* (Berlin: A. Töpelmann, 1952), pp. 110–139.
26. *Op. cit.*, p. 146.
27. So, for example, H. Goudge, *The Second Epistle to the Corinthians,* West. Comm. (London: Methuen, 1927), *ad loc.*
28. R. Bultmann, *Theology of the New Testament* (London: SCM Press, 1952), pp. 201–203.
29. R. H. Fuller, *The Foundations of N. T. Christology*, pp. 143–151. This type of Christology is reflected in Acts 3:21, though there the title Son of man has disappeared.
30. See for example, A. M. Ramsey, *The Resurrection of Christ* (London: Bles, 1946), esp. pp. 33–34.
31. See for example, W. Pannenberg, *op. cit.*, pp. 98–99.
32. So R. Bultmann, *Kerygma and Myth* I (London: S.P.C.K., 1953), pp. 38–43, esp. p. 42: "If the event of Easter Day is in any sense an historical event, additional to the event of the cross, it is nothing else than the rise of faith in the risen Lord."
33. By placing "occurred" in quotation marks, we call attention once more to the peculiar character of the Easter event. "Occur" applies in ordinary language to the observable, verifiable events within history. Its use in reference to the decisive eschatological event is strictly analogical.
34. For example from such different scholars as H. Grass, *op. cit.*, pp. 136–138, and B. Linders, *New Testament Apologetic* (London: SCM Press, 1961), pp. 60–61. Grass ascribes the use of Hos. 6:2 to the earliest church, Linders to Jesus himself, on the basis of his saying about the destruction and rebuilding of the temple in "three days" (Mark 14:58 par. 15:29; John 2:19), which he interprets to mean "soon." Linders offers no reconstruction of the history of the tradition.
35. G. Kittel, *op. cit.*, p. 160. Grass had already noted this, p. 137. He admits the disappearance of references to Hos. 6:2 from the early Christian records and seeks (unconvincingly) to give reasons for the alleged disappearance.

36. As we shall see later, Hos. 6:2 does provide a remote clue for the meaning of the phrase.
37. H. Gunkel, *Zum religionsgeschichtlichen Verständnis des Neuen Testaments* (Göttingen: Vandenhoeck & Ruprecht, 1903), p. 20.
38. M. Goguel, *op. cit.*, pp. 166–167.
39. *Ibid.*, pp. 167–169.
40. *Ibid.*, pp. 169ff. (translation mine).
41. For example, J. Jeremias, *op. cit.*, p. 102; E. Bammel, *art. cit.*
42. The textual tradition is not quite unanimous on the use of these particles. The first *eita* (v.5) appears as *epeita* in Sinaiticus, Alexandrinus and several minuscules, and the second *eita* as *epeita* in P⁴⁶, the original reading of Sinaiticus, etc. This shows that the scribes no longer appreciated the reasons for the groupings.
43. Karl Barth, *The Resurrection of the Dead* (New York: F. H. Revell, 1933).
44. *Kerygma und Mythos* I (Hamburg: Reich & Heidrich, 1948), p. 48. Cf. E.T. *Kerygma and Myth* I (New York: Harper, 1961), p. 39, where the German "fatal" is rendered a "dangerous procedure."
45. W. Michaelis, *TDNT* V, p. 331.
46. The attempt to identify the experience of 2 Cor. 12:2 with the Damascus road event is almost certainly ruled out also on chronological grounds (the 14 years of Gal. 2:1 should not be equated with the 14 years of 2 Cor. 12:2). The appointment of 2 Cor. 12:1–9 in the American Book of Common Prayer for the second evensong of the Conversion of St. Paul is thus based on a mistaken exegesis.
47. Professor R. P. C. Hanson has suggested to me that Paul refused to narrate or objectify his call because to do so would be contrary to his doctrine of justification by grace alone. It would be treating his call as a meritorious achievement of his own. I think this is quite probable. But may we therefore assume that the same scruples were operative for the earlier recipients?
48. See E. G. Selwyn, "The Resurrection" in *Essays Catholic and Critical,* ed. E. G. Selwyn (London: S.P.C.K., 1938), pp. 281–319, esp. pp. 296–299; also H. Grass, *op. cit.*, pp. 233–249, esp. 247–249. The "objective vision hypothesis" seems to have originated with T. Keim and his celebrated "telegram from heaven" theory of the appearances: while visionary experiences, they had a transcendental cause. Neither Selwyn nor Grass is happy with the term "objective." Selwyn preferred "veridical visions" (*op. cit.*, p. 310).
49. M. Albertz, "Zur Formgeschichte der Auferstehungsberichte," *ZNW* 21 (1922), pp. 259–269. This judgment is often repeated by supporters of the Jerusalem tradition.
50. C. H. Dodd, *Historical Tradition in the Fourth Gospel* (Cambridge: University Press, 1963), p. 55.
51. In a recent article, I ventured (*cum grano salis*) the suggestion (which at that time I thought was original) that the *Quo Vadis?* legend might have developed out of this tradition. R. H. Fuller, "The 'Thou art Peter' Pericope," *McCormick Quarterly* 20 (1967) [in honor of Floyd V. Filson], pp. 309–315, esp. 314. I have since discovered that a num-

ber of scholars have made this suggestion quite seriously, e.g., F. C. Burkitt, *Christian Beginnings* (London: University Press, 1924), pp. 87f.

52. In the article cited above (see last footnote), I argued, as many others have done, that this passage is part of the narrative of the first appearance to Peter. Since reaching the conclusion that the resurrection appearances were not, in the earliest tradition, *narrated*, I would modify this: Matt. 16:17–19 is the earliest community's *reflection* upon the meaning of the appearance to Peter. This would explain how the tradition came to be detached from its post-Easter appearance context.

53. The suggestion was apparently first put forward by E. von Dobschütz, *Ostern und Pfingsten* (Leipzig: J. C. Hinrichs, 1903). It has received the support of F. C. Burkitt, *op. cit.*, pp. 90ff.; E. Meyer, *Ursprung und Anfänge des Christentums* III (Stuttgart-Berlin: J. J. Cotta, 1923), pp. 221f.; H. W. Beyer, *Die Apostelgeschichte*, NTD 5 (Göttingen: Vandenhoeck & Ruprecht, 1949), p. 18; J. Finegan, *Die Ueberlieferung der Leidens– und Auferstehungsgeschichte Jesu* (Giessen: A. Töpelmann, 1934), p. 109. K. Lake in *The Beginnings of Christianity* I (London: Macmillan, 1933), p. 121, and N. A. Dahl, *Das Volk Gottes* (Darmstadt: Wissenschaftliche Buchgesellschaft, 1963), p. 176, consider it a possibility. It has been opposed by Goguel, *op. cit.*, pp. 255–261, and by Kümmel, *op. cit.*, p. 8.

54. For this view I am indebted to U. Wilckens, *op. cit.* (ed. Moule), pp. 59–60. Both share the same *ōphthē* and are joined by the internal connecting particle *eita*.

55. In the best textual tradition (Gal. 2:9) the name *Iakobos* appears first: the reversal of the order in the Western textual tradition is obviously secondary, and attests the beginnings of the doctrine of the perpetual primacy of Peter.

56. The reference in Acts 12:17, where Peter reports to James after his incarceration, suggests that this marks the point of time when James took over the leadership of the church. Peter exercised the primacy during the initial foundation period. Once the foundation had been laid, the next phase of missionary expansion was conducted under the leadership of James.

57. Later traditions tell us that Mary, the Mother of Jesus, was present at Jerusalem during the Passion (John 19:25–27) and after Easter (Acts 2:14), but it is impossible to test the validity of these traditions.

58. See the article on *stulos* by U. Wilckens, *TWNT* VII, pp. 734f.

59. The question as to whether Paul had been at Damascus prior to the appearance (as this statement seems to imply) or whether (as in Acts) he was on his way from Jerusalem to Damascus, need not concern us here. Even if at the time Paul was based in Damascus, this would not necessarily exclude an earlier Jerusalem residence.

60. So H. von Campenhausen, *op. cit.*, pp. 19f. W. Schmithals, *The Office of Apostle in the Early Church* (Nashville and New York: Abingdon Press, 1969), p. 76.

61. For the various possible meanings of *ektrōma*, see J. Schneider in *TDNT* 2, pp. 465–467.

62. E. Hirsch, "Die drei Berichte der Apostelgeschichte über die Bekehrung des Paulus" in *ZNW* 28 (1929), pp. 305–312. Hirsch was followed among others by H. W. Beyer in the earlier edition of the Commentary on Acts in the NTD series.
63. M. Dibelius, *Studies in the Acts of the Apostles*, ed. H. Greeven (London: SCM Press, 1956), pp. 123–137. The chapter first appeared as an article in German in 1949, having originally been written in 1944.
64. E. Schweizer, in *Studies in Luke-Acts* (Paul Schubert Festschrift), ed. L. E. Keck and J. L. Martyn (Nashville and New York: Abingdon Press, 1966), pp. 183–193.
65. I hope to discuss this further in a work on Early Catholicism in the New Testament.
66. In composing vv.17f. Luke draws upon the language of Isa. 35:5; 42:7,16 and 61:1. Paul also understood his apostolic call in Deutero-Isaianic terms (cf. Gal. 1:15/Isa. 49:1).
67. W. Kümmel, *Röm. 7 und die Bekehrung des Paulus* (Leipzig: J. C. Hinrichs, 1929), p. 147. Grass, *op. cit.*, p. 219, cites this view sympathetically, but with the proviso that it is "uncertain."
68. Grass, *ibid.*

CHAPTER THREE

1. The problem of the ending of Mark will be discussed later (pp. 64–67).
2. Mark calls the figure that appeared at the tomb a "young man" (*neaniskos*, v.5). But there can be no doubt that this is an angel, as is indicated by the description of his "white robe" and by a comparison with Acts 1:10. See V. Taylor, *The Gospel according to St. Mark* (New York: St. Martin's Press, 1966), *ad loc.*
3. So e.g., M. Dibelius, *From Tradition to Gospel* (London: Nicholson & Watson, 1934), pp. 189f.
4. E.g., W. Bousset, cited with approval by R. Bultmann, *History of the Synoptic Tradition* (Oxford: Blackwell, 1963), p. 285.
5. SB are unable to give a single example *ad loc.*
6. For the possibility that the clause "they said nothing to anyone" is redactional, see below, p. 64.
7. Bultmann, *op. cit.*, p. 274.
8. So U. Wilckens, *Missionsreden*, p. 135 (my translation); cf. also M. Goguel, *op. cit.*, p. 129. It may be objected that the attribution of the burial to the Jews fits in with Luke's anti-Jewish apologetic. But even so, would Luke have introduced such an obvious contradiction with what he had written in his Gospel? If anywhere, it is in the kerygmatic formulae of the speeches that we may rightly look for pre-Lucan materials.
9. The Joseph legend continues to develop in the apocryphal Gospel of Nicodemus or Acts of Pilate, and reaches its apogee in the Glastonbury legend of medieval England.
10. So, e.g., V. Taylor, *op. cit.*, *ad loc.*
11. Cf. E. Schweizer, *Das Evangelium nach Markus*, NTD 1 (Göttingen: Vandenhoeck & Ruprecht, 1967), p. 214 (E.T., 1970.) At this point

Schweizer is speaking of historical fact; we are merely seeking to reconstruct the earliest tradition.

12. *Op. cit.* (ed. Moule), pp. 73–74.

13. Cf. the interpretation in M. Goguel, *op. cit.*, pp. 213–233. But while recognizing the primitive conceptions underlying the empty tomb story, Goguel draws the corollary that the appearance tradition is later than that of the empty tomb. This corollary is ruled out by the equally primitive character of the pre-Pauline list of appearances in 1 Cor. 15. Rather, we have two independent traditions (empty tomb and appearances), both presupposing the resurrection kerygma. These two traditions were not brought together until Mark added his redactional verse, 16:7.

14. *Ibid.*, pp. 215–222. See above, p. 201, n. 23.

15. "Die Himmelfahrt vom Kreuz aus" in *Festgabe für Adolf Deissmann* (Tübingen: Mohr, 1927), pp. 187–218.

16. See also E. Bickermann, "Das leere Grab," *ZNW* 23 (1924), pp. 281–292. Bickermann, like Goguel (who is largely dependent upon him), correctly recognizes the primitive apocalyptic background of the empty tomb pericope. But he goes on to draw a distinction between assumptions, which he connects with the empty tomb motif as in Mark 16:1ff., and the resurrection appearances as in 1 Cor. 15:3ff. The latter he designates as Hellenistic and akin to the dying and rising gods of the mysteries. But the sharp distinction between assumptions and resurrections is unfounded (Mark 16:6 actually uses *ēgerthē*, "he was raised"), and both 1 Cor. 15:3ff. and Mark 16:1ff. remain firmly within the framework of Jewish apocalyptic conceptions.

17. So apparently Goguel, *op. cit.*, p. 235, who speaks of "une apparition du Christ devant des disciples et peut-être devant les femmes en Galilée." That the women are to be included is highly improbable: 1) the cross-reference to Mark 14:28 (see below) shows that the "you" of 16:7 is the same as the "you" of 14:28, viz., the disciples; 2) "that" (*hoti*) is a *hoti*-recitative (so rightly Taylor *ad loc.*), citing in direct speech what the women are to say to the disciples, not a direct address to the women; and 3) as will become apparent later, appearances to women are a subsequent modification of the earlier tradition of angelophanies.

18. "Der Ursprung der Ueberlieferungen," p. 80: "Die Formulierung in Mk. 16,7 ordnet Petrus den Jüngern nicht nach, sondern vor, in dem sie Petrus als einzigen namentlich Genannten, herausstellt."

19. In *Die Schriften des Neuen Testaments* (Göttingen: Vandenhoeck & Ruprecht, 1909), p. 197; *idem, Earliest Christianity* I (New York: Harper and Brothers, 1959), p. 18.

20. "Adversaria Exegetica," *Theology* 7 (1923), pp. 147–155. Hoskyns does not mention J. Weiss.

21. "I will go before you into Galilee," *JTS*, N.S. 5 (1954), pp. 3–18.

22. I hope to discuss the more modest role of the Old Testament in the message and self-understanding of Jesus in a later work.

23. Cf. R. H. Fuller, "Some Further Reflections on Heilsgeschichte," *USQR* 22 (1967), p. 100.

24. W. Marxsen, *Mark the Evangelist* (Nashville: Abingdon, 1969), pp. 89f.
25. *Ibid.*, pp. 114–116 agrees that, although the verse is redactional in its present position, it is nevertheless pre-Marcan. However, he identifies it not as an echo of the pre-Pauline list as we have done, but as a reflection of the oracle addressed to the Jerusalem church in A.D. 66 (Eusebius, *Church History* III 5) which instructed them to go to Galilee and await the parousia. But (1) the oracle directs them to Pella in Transjordan, not to Galilee; (2) it says they are "to dwell" there, indicating a permanent settlement, not a temporary waiting for the parousia. It is only fair to mention that Marxsen recognizes the first of these two difficulties (pp. 115f., n. 176) but he does not adequately dispose of it. The oracle has no obvious bearing on the origin of Mark 16:7.
26. "Galilee and the Galileans in St. Mark's Gospel," *BJRL* (1952–53), pp. 334–348.
27. The passages which associate Galilee with Gentiles are Judg. 1:30, 33; Joel 4:4; 1 Macc. 5:21. In addition to Isa. 9:1, we have the phrase *Galilaia tōn allophulōn* in Joel 4:4 and 1 Macc. 5:15. Boobyer adds a second point, not mentioned by Evans, that Galilee was notorious in Mark's day for its mixed Jewish-Gentile population.
28. For a similar approach, cf. M. Karnetzki, "Die Galiläische Redaktion im Markus-Evangelium," *ZNW* 52 (1961), pp. 238ff.
29. J. Schreiber, "Die Christologie des Markus," *ZThK* 58 (1961), pp. 154–183, esp. 171–172; *idem*, *Theologie des Vertrauens* (Hamburg: Furche Verlag, 1967), pp. 170–184.
30. *Op. cit.*, pp. 173–178.
31. *Galiläa und Jerusalem* (FRLANT, N.F. 34) (Göttingen: Vandenhoeck & Ruprecht, 1935), pp. 10–14; *Das Evangelium des Markus*, Meyer Commentary (Göttingen: Vandenhoeck & Ruprecht, 1937), *ad loc.*
32. *Locality and Doctrine in the Gospels* (New York: Harper, 1938), pp. 61, 65, 73ff. In *The Gospel Message of St. Mark* (Oxford: Clarendon Press, 1950), pp. 95–96; 106–116, he is far less clear on the subject, preferring to speak not of the 'parousia' but more vaguely of a reunion with or revelation of the Risen Lord (p. 96). Did Lightfoot intend to withdraw his earlier hesitant acceptance of Lohmeyer?
33. *Die Erscheinungen des Auferstandenen* (Basel: Heinrich Meyer, 1944), pp. 61–76.
34. *Mark the Evangelist*, pp. 83–92; 111–116.
35. See S. Schulz, *Untersuchungen zur Menschensohn-Christologie im Johannesevangelium* (Göttingen: Vandenhoeck & Ruprecht, 1957), pp. 97–103; 168–176.
36. *Rediscovering the Teaching of Jesus* (New York-Evanston: Harper & Row, 1967), pp. 181–185. This is the verse cited in John 19:37; Rev. 1:7. The LXX has *epiblepsontai*, but the two Johannine quotations have *opsontai*.
37. E. Lohmeyer also interpreted this pericope as a parousia scene. See "Mir ist gegeben alle Gewalt" in *In Memoriam Ernst Lohmeyer*, ed. W. Schmauch (Stuttgart: Evangelisches Verlagswerk, 1969), pp. 22–

49. But, as will be argued in the next chapter, this scene, although using the language and scenario of the parousia from Dan. 7:14, is nevertheless intended as a resurrection appearance.

38. U. Wilckens, in Moule (ed.), *op. cit.*, p. 71, had suggested that the statement of the women's silence and the clause assigning its reason to their fear was a redactional insertion of Mark connected with his theory of the messianic secret. Wilckens used this point as an additional argument against the parousia interpretation of *opsesthe*. We agree, except that we would assign verse 7c and d to pre-Marcan tradition. As so often, Mark did not create the secrecy materials, but re-interpreted them in the sense of his theory.

39. We would not deny, as Wilckens, *ibid.*, does, all connection between the messianic secret and the parousia. We hope to develop this point in later work.

40. The best recent discussion of the ending of Mark in English is that of R. H. Lightfoot, *The Gospel Message of St. Mark* (Oxford: Clarendon Press, 1950), pp. 80–97.

41. It is hardly possible that the post-Marcan community should very soon have wished to shift the locale of the appearances from Galilee to Jerusalem, and that since Mark's appearances were located in Galilee they no longer squared with the later view, for Matthew and even the apocryphal *Gospel of Peter* continue to maintain the Galilean tradition. It did not disappear overnight.

42. *Op. cit.*, p. 17: "the mutilation would have to have occurred as soon as the gospel, which was perhaps at first a private work, was received by the church, and before it was circulated to other churches. If we suppose this, what most probably happened was that this reception did not take place until after the death of the author, so that there was a hesitation on the part of Mark's church to undertake a revision of the final story of the work whose author was still revered. The best solution was simply to leave out the offensive conclusion, both in church use and in the multiplication and circulation of the gospel" (my translation). All this is highly speculative and, I believe, unnecessary.

43. See R. H. Lightfoot, *Gospel Message*, p. 86. Lightfoot wrote that "it is said that some further light on the matter will be forthcoming in the fourth edition of Bauer's Wörterbuch." This, of course, has since become available, and in English translation by Arndt and Gingrich. Reference to the relevant article will show that we now have a letter concluding with *gar*.

44. See especially the moving suggestion of R. H. Lightfoot in *Gospel Message*, p. 97.

45. The variant on the deliberate conclusion hypothesis propounded by W. Marxsen, *op. cit.*, to the effect that Mark intended to leave his Gospel open-ended to alert his church ca. 66 to an imminent parousia in Galilee depends on an exegesis of *opsesthe* in v. 7 which we have already seen reason to reject.

46. W. Marxsen, *op. cit.*, pp. 57–95.

CHAPTER FOUR

1. In Mark the Pharisees are absent from the passion narrative. Their insertion in Matt. is consistent with the anti-Pharisaic polemic sustained throughout this Gospel.

2. J. Jeremias, *The Eucharistic Words of Jesus*, pp. 75–79.

3. See R. H. Fuller, *The Foundations of New Testament Christology*, pp. 108–131.

4. For these features, added by Matthew to Mark see below.

5. *Op. cit.*, pp. 24–27.

6. *Op. cit.*, p. 26, following J. Finegan, *op. cit.*

7. So e.g., V. Taylor, *St. Mark, ad loc.*: "On the whole, it seems more probable that the women went to see the grave (Mt., Jn.), rather than to anoint the body." Actually, however, John 20:1 suppresses any motive for the visit.

8. For the likelihood that Matt. 16:17–19 was originally associated with the first appearance to Peter, see above, p. 35 and n. 52.

9. V. Taylor, *St. Mark*, at 16:7 thinks that the Marcan words were "difficult"—it is hard to see why. Goguel (*Foi*, p. 182, n. 2) thinks that Matthew reflects an earlier stage of the tradition which did not yet know the prediction made by Jesus to his disciples in Mark 14:28. But why should Matthew want to return to the pre-Marcan form? Further, our analysis has suggested that the Marcan redaction was the first to connect the tomb story with the appearance tradition.

10. Goguel, *Foi*, p. 185. But he cannot be right in holding that the words of the angel "you shall see" include the women as well as the disciples, since the message which the women are to address to the disciples is given in direct speech (see above, p. 57 on Mark 16:7).

11. See the discussion in P. Gardner-Smith, *St. John and the Synoptic Gospels* (Cambridge: University Press, 1938), pp. 79–81. I would, however, regard the Christophany to the women as a development out of the earlier tradition of an angelophany, not as an alternative explanation of the identity of the "young man" at the tomb in the earliest tradition, as Gardner-Smith does.

12. This Christophany will be further discussed in connection with John 20:11–18, see below, pp. 136ff.

13. A further motive has been at work in Luke, see below, pp. 117f.

14. See G. Barth in G. Bornkamm *et al.*, *Tradition and Interpretation in Matthew* (Philadelphia: Westminster Press, 1963), p. 131, n. 1. He includes "behold" (*idou*) among the Matthean characteristics, but this word is nearly as frequent in Luke.

15. Cf., *Epistula Apostolorum*, 1–10 in which the disciples successively doubt Mary's report of the empty tomb, Sarah's report of the same (so Ethiopic text: the Coptic makes Mary repeat the news only to meet again with incredulity), their own sight of the empty tomb, and the appearance of the Risen One at the tomb. Whereupon the Risen One at last offers to allow Peter to touch his hands, and Thomas to touch his side. This account thus develops further the apologetic motif already present in the Johannine story of the doubting Thomas.

16. *Op. cit.*, p. 30. Grass admits the lack of apologetic motivation in Matt., and equally admits that historically there were certainly those among the disciples who did doubt the Lord's resurrection. Yet he denies that Matt. 28:17 has any historical basis, and concludes that it must have some other *Sitz im Leben*—which, however, he fails to provide. One wonders where he finds the evidence for his historical certainty if every single mention of doubt is attributed to apologetic motifs. This is an excellent example of the determination to be skeptical at all costs.

17. In Bornkamm, *op. cit.*, pp. 132–133, G. Barth calls attention to a difference between the Matthean reference to doubt and that of the other narratives, in that the doubt is removed here (apparently) by the revelatory *word* of the Risen One, rather than by a physical demonstration. This should have opened his eyes to the non-apologetic character of Matthew at this point.

18. "Der Abschluss des Mt.-Evangeliums," *EvTh* (1950–51), pp. 16–27.

19. So E. Klostermann, *Das Matthäusevangelium [HzNT]* (Tübingen: J. C. B. Mohr, ³1938), *ad loc.* (*contra* O. Michel, H. Grass and G. Barth).

20. The disciples "worship" Jesus, but this worship is not prostration before a divine man on earth (contrast vv.9–10 where the women touch the feet of the Risen One). It is the worship of a parousia scene (see below).

21. R. H. Fuller, *The Foundations of N.T. Christology*, pp. 184–186.

22. The association of this passage with Dan. 7:14 is generally accepted (M'Neile, Filson, Fenton, Klostermann, Lohmeyer, Schniewind, G. Barth, Grass). It has, however, been recently denied by A. Vögtle, "Das christologische und ekklesiologische Anliegen von Mt. 28, 18–20" *Studia Evangelica* [TU 87], ed. F. L. Cross (Berlin: Akademie Verlag, 1964), on the ground that the situation, unlike that of Dan. 7:14, is pre-parousia. Vögtle sees its affinities rather with Matt. 16:18f.; 18:15–18; 18:20 and interprets the self-manifestation as a fulfillment of 26:64. This is entirely unconvincing. Numerous instances in the New Testament tradition can be quoted for successive shifts of the parousia Son of man Christology, first to the exaltation and then to the earthly existence of Jesus—the latter especially in the Johannine tradition. A shift from the exaltation to the earthly Jesus has occurred in the first three passages cited by Vögtle, while 26:64 is the case *par excellence* for the shift of a Christology based in part on Dan. 7:13f. from the parousia to the exaltation.

23. F. Hahn, *Mission in the New Testament*, SBT 47 (London: SCM, Press, 1965), pp. 40f.

24. Cf. D. R. A. Hare, *The Theme of Jewish Persecutions of Christians in the Gospel according to St. Matthew*, S.N.T.S. Monograph Series 6 (Cambridge: University Press, 1967), pp. 146–162.

25. *Beginnings* I, p. 340; cf. J. Weiss, *Earliest Christianity* I, pp. 50–51.

26. *Theology of the New Testament* I (London: SCM Press, 1952), p. 39.

27. M. Goguel may be right in thinking that the Johannine tradition (John 4:22–23; 4:1–2) of an earlier period in Jesus' ministry, when he was ministering baptism parallel to John the Baptist, may be authentic (*Life of Jesus* [New York: Macmillan, 1933], pp. 271–273).

The Johannine evidence on this point is usually rejected by the Bultmann school. But since it is obviously an embarrassment for the Evangelist (cf. John 4:1–2), it must surely be pre-Johannine tradition rather than Johannine redaction.

28. Contemporary scholars are rightly hesitant to ground the practice of baptism directly on an actual command of the Risen One. So G. W. H. Lampe, *The Seal of the Spirit* (London: Longmans, Green & Co., 1951), pp. 19, 46; N. A. Dahl, "Origin of Baptism" in *Norsk Theol. Tidskrift* 65 (1955), pp. 36–52, esp. 46f. But more weight should be given to the earliest community's understanding of the implications of the call to evangelize, interpreted in the light of their "Baptist" heritage.

29. Mark 9:37 may be an allusion to the baptism of children, like the similar episode in Mark 10:13–16. On the latter see J. Jeremias, *Die Kindertaufe in den ersten vier Jahrhunderten* (Göttingen: Vandenhoeck & Ruprecht, 1958), pp. 61–68. More cautiously E. Schweizer, *Markus*, p. 118.

30. See R. H. Fuller, "On Demythologizing the Trinity," *ATR* 43 (1961), pp. 121–131.

31. Mark 13:32; Matt. 11:27 and the Fourth Gospel. This Christology seems to be rooted in Jesus' use of Abba. So F. Hahn, *Titles*, pp. 307–315.

32. Thus R. Bultmann, *Theology of the N.T.* I, p. 134.

33. See F. C. Conybeare, "The Eusebian Form of the Text Matt. 28:19" in *ZNW* 1 (1901), pp. 275–288.

34. K. Stendahl, *The School of St. Matthew* (Philadelphia: Fortress Press, ²1968), p. 22. See the literature given *ibid.*, n. 5.

35. P. Carrington, *The Primitive Christian Catechism* (Cambridge: University Press, 1940), C. H. Dodd, "The Primitive Catechism and the Sayings of Jesus," reprinted in *More New Testament Studies* (Michigan: Eerdmans, 1968), pp. 11–29.

36. The saying occurs in P. Ox. 1; also (in reverse order) in *Ev. Thomas* logion 77. See Jeremias, *Unknown Sayings of Jesus* (London: S.P.C.K. ²1964), pp. 106–111.

37. Cited by Jeremias, *ibid.*, p. 107, n.3.

38. Jeremias, *ibid.*, p. 111.

39. G. Barth in Bornkamm, *op. cit.*, p. 135.

40. *Op. cit.*, p. 29.

41. *Art. cit.*, p. 17.

42. For the connection between the Q material and the Easter faith, see H. E. Tödt, *The Son of Man in the Synoptic Tradition*, pp. 250–253.

CHAPTER FIVE

1. R. Bultmann, *History of the Synoptic Tradition*, pp. 314–317.

2. *Jesus and the Son of Man* (Philadelphia: Fortress Press, 1964), p. 82.

3. *dei* ("must") Mark 8:31/Luke 9:22; *paradothēnai* ("be delivered") Mark 9:31/Luke 9:44; Mark 10:33/Luke 18:32; *eis cheiras* ("into the hands") Mark 9:31/Luke 9:44; *anthrōpōn* ("of men") Mark

9:31/Luke 9:44; *harmatōlōn* ("sinful") Mark 14:41 (omitted Luke *ad loc.*); *tē hēmerā tē tritē* ("on the third day") Luke 9:44, an editorial alteration of Mark's "after three days"; *anastēnai* ("rise") Mark 8:31, which Luke alters to *egerthēnai*, Mark 9:31 (omitted Luke); Mark 10:34/Luke 18:33.

4. *TDNT* II, pp. 23–34. Cf. E. Fascher, "Theologische Beobachtungen zu *dei*," *Neutestamentliche Studien für R. Bultmann* (Berlin: Töpelmann, ²1957); H. Flender, *St. Luke, Theologian of Redemptive History* (London: S.P.C.K., 1967), pp. 143–144.

5. Luke 9:22; 17:25; the present passage; 24:7 and 24:26; Acts 1:16; 3:21; 17:3.

6. We here adopt with some modification H. Conzelmann's characterization of Lucan theology in the title of the German original of his work on Luke, *Die Mitte der Zeit* (E.T. *The Theology of St. Luke* [London: Faber & Faber, 1960]. See also H. Flender, *op. cit., passim.*

7. For the relation of this group to the Twelve, see above, pp. 39ff.

8. The translation of RSV margin omits "lying" after "cloths."

9. "The Resurrection Narratives in Luke (XXIV 12–53)," *NTS* 2 (1955–56), pp. 110–114; cf. also *idem, The Gospel according to St. Luke* (New York: Harper, 1958), *ad loc.*

10. This change is evidently redactional, to correspond with the piercing of the *side* in John 19:31–37. See below.

11. Von Campenhausen *op. cit.*, p. 35, n. 139, states that Leaney's arguments for the genuineness of Luke 24:12 "haben mich in keiner Weise überzeugt," an interesting statement of opinion, but with no attempt to offer any refutation of Leaney's arguments!

12. So Hahn, *Titles*, pp. 376–378.

13. So P. Schubert, "The Structure and Significance of Luke 24," *Ntliche Studien für R. Bultmann*, pp. 165–186. Schubert regards the whole dialogue, vv.17–27, as Lucan redaction.

14. E.g., G. Bornkamm, *Jesus of Nazareth* (New York: Harper, 1960), p. 172: ". . . these words seem to express quite accurately the convictions of his followers before his death."

15. Cf. P. Schubert, *art. cit.*, pp. 170f.

16. Cf. the old Gospel prologue which describes Luke as "a Syrian of Antioch." The first paragraph of this prologue (as opposed to the second) contains material which cannot be deduced from the internal evidence of the N.T., and has therefore some claims to be based on genuine historical information. See R. G. Heard, "The Old Gospel Prologues," *JTS* N.S. 6 (1955), pp. 1–16.

17. If, with Codex Sinaiticus, we read "one hundred and sixty" instead of "sixty" the discrepancy would not be so large.

18. The writer has within the past few days listened to a fascinating paper by Professor B. M. Metzger of Princeton, entitled, "Naming the Unnamed," and dealing with the various names that have been given in the above-mentioned sources to unnamed figures in the New Testament. The variety of names given to each figure is bewildering. With occasional exceptions (e.g., possibly Bar-Timaeus in Mark 10:46) the

tendency is for names to be added later, rather than to be worn away in transmission.

19. *Contra* P. Schubert, *op. cit.*, p. 170.

20. See *Early Christian Worship* (London: SCM Press, ¹1953, ⁶1966), pp. 14–16.

21. *Op. cit.*, p. 89.

22. This point has been discussed briefly in R. H. Fuller, *The Foundations of N.T. Christology*, and I hope to elaborate it further in a study of the Christology of the New Testament writers.

23. Fuller, *ibid.*, pp. 244–245.

24. So Hahn, *Titles*, p. 401, n. 176.

25. There was no need for him to continue with the statement of the appearance to the Twelve (eleven), since he had a narrative which could cover that.

26. Some MSS add a reference to a honeycomb. If this reading were more strongly attested, it would be another indication of a eucharistic setting.

27. *History of the Synoptic Tradition*, p. 286.

28. "It is necessary," cf. Mark 8:31; "it is written," Mark 14:21; "suffer," Mark 8:31; 9:12; "on the third day" appears in Luke's redaction of the Marcan predictions in the place of Mark's "after three days," though on the other hand the active "rise" appears in the Marcan predictions, but is consistently altered in the Lucan parallels to Mark to the passive "be raised." "From the dead" appears in the prediction at Mark 9:9 but is omitted by Luke *ad loc.*, since it is there connected with the Marcan messianic secret, which Luke does not wish to develop. The christological title (*Christos* with the article) at Luke 24:26, 46 contrasts with the title, Son of man, in the Marcan passion predictions; "glory" is not found in the Marcan passion predictions although it is rooted in the Son of man Christology (Mark 8:38; 13:26), while, as already noted, the contrast suffering/glory is widespread, and especially prominent in 1 Peter. All this suggests a complicated history of transmission and warrants the conclusion that Luke has in addition to the Marcan passion predictions other (more Hellenistic?) summaries of the passion-resurrection kerygma, which he uses partly in preference to the Marcan predictions in the course of his resurrection-narratives. This non-Marcan form of passion-resurrection summaries is also echoed in the kerygmatic speeches of Acts. From these considerations U. Wilckens, *Missionsreden*, draws the conclusion: "Independently of the three passion predictions which Luke found in his Marcan *Vorlage*, Luke knew a tradition of short summaries of the passion from which he derived not only the Marcan passion predictions but also various other formulae which came down to Luke in the kerygmatic tradition of his time" (pp. 116–117, my translation, italicized in the original).

29. For a different view see Leaney *ad loc.* But where is there evidence for the rise of Christian groups by spontaneous combustion in places like Joppa, Lydda or Damascus, or even Galilee? Luke is surely right in his general picture of Christianity as a movement which began in Jerusalem and after a period of consolidation spread from there. This

picture is confirmed by the evidence of the Pauline Epistles (Gal. 1–2; 2 Cor. 8–9 [the collection]; Rom. 15:19).

30. See F. Hahn, *Mission in the New Testament*, p. 150.
31. For the place of Jerusalem in Luke's salvation-historical theology, see H. Conzelmann, *The Theology of St. Luke*, pp. 113ff.; P. Schubert, *art. cit.*, pp. 183–185; H. Flender, *St. Luke*, pp. 107–117.
32. E.g., E. Meyer, *Ursprung und Anfänge*, pp. 34–42, cf. also 31f.
33. *Beginnings* V (1933), pp. 3–4.
34. *Der Messias und das Gottesvolk* (Uppsala: Alqvist & Wikselis, 1945), pp. 14–18.
35. "Variant Traditions of the Resurrection in Acts," *JBL* 62 (1943), pp. 306–311, esp. 311.
36. "Remarques sur les textes de l'ascension dans Luc-Actes," *Nt.-liche Studien für R. Bultmann*, pp. 148–156.
37. "The Interpretation of the Ascension in Luke and Acts," NTS 5 (1958–59), pp. 30–42. Van Stampvoort's views have been accepted in principle among others by C. K. Barrett, *Luke the Historian in Recent Study* (London: Epworth Press, 1961), pp. 55–58; by P. Menoud, "Pendant quarant jours (Actes i 3)" in *Neotestamentica et Patristica*, Cullmann Festschrift (Leiden: E. J. Brill, 1962), pp. 148–156 (thus correcting his earlier view in the Bultmann Festschrift), and by H. Flender, *St. Luke*, pp. 11–13.
38. Luther's opinion that the ascending Lord delivered the Aaronic blessing (Num. 6:24–26) is on one level fanciful but, on another, exhibits profound theological understanding.
39. RSV translates it also as "was taken up," thus obscuring the difference in the Greek.
40. *History of the Synoptic Tradition*, p. 286.
41. This is the Christology expressed in Acts 3:20–21. For the distinction between ascension and assumption I am indebted to F. Hahn, *Titles*, p. 133, n.4. This distinction has been questioned by P. Vielhauer in his review article on Hahn's book, "Neue Wege zur Christologie des Neuen Testaments?" pp. 47–49, on the ground that OT assumptions (Enoch, Elijah) are of persons still living. This does not seem to have troubled the early Christians, for the ascension narrative in Acts 1:9 is couched in Elijah typology. Some critics have also seen Elijah typology in the brief assertion of Luke 24:51b.
42. The old Latin textual tradition omits *anelēmphthē*. See J. M. Creed, "The Text and Interpretation of Acts 1:11," *JTS* 35 (1935), pp. 176–182.
43. *Op. cit.*, p. 48.
44. Luke would see no contradiction between the christological instruction of Luke 24 and the eschatological instruction of Acts 1.
45. Cf. e.g., E. Haenchen, *Die Apostelgeschichte*, Meyer's Commentary (Göttingen: Vandenhoeck & Ruprecht, ⁵1965), pp. 115–119.
46. *Op. cit.*, p. 133.
47. M. S. Enslin has collected the early references to the ascension outside the New Testament in "The Ascension Story," *JBL* 47 (1928), pp. 60–73, esp. 68–73.

CHAPTER SIX

1. Cf. R. H. Fuller, *Critical Introduction to the New Testament*, p. 170.
2. See above, p. 55, for the suggestion that John or pre-Johannine tradition has combined two separate versions of the burial. This need not imply John's direct dependence on Mark, but only the confluence of the pre-Marcan tradition with another version in which Nicodemus figured.
3. So Finegan, *op. cit.*, p. 93.
4. So Grass, p. 54 following Bultmann, *Das Evangelium des Johannes*, Meyer's Commentary (Göttingen: Vandenhoeck & Ruprecht, [16]1959).
5. Note that John knows nothing of the Emmaus story, a possible indication that he does not derive the material in 20:3–10 from Luke. This would also lend color to Bultmann's view that the Beloved Disciple is an "ideal figure" and an artificial creation. However, the Beloved Disciple appears earlier in the passion narrative as an eyewitness to the distinctive Johannine tradition. It is in passages like the present which portray rivalry between Peter and the Beloved Disciple that we have the artificial creation of a Johannine theme.
6. *The Gospel of the Hebrews*, fragment 7, Hennecke-Schneemelcher, p. 165. See below, pp. 189ff.
7. So Grass, *op. cit.*, p. 57.
8. *Op. cit.*, p. 32. He offers no primary references, but cites S. Kraus, *Das Leben Jesu nach jüdischen Quellen* (1902), pp. 170ff. In a later article cited with approval by von Campenhausen, Kraus maintained that "Judah the gardener" was intended for Judas Iscariot.
9. John 3:13; 6:62. The katabasis-anabasis pattern is characteristic of Johannine Christology. See R. H. Fuller, *The Foundations of N.T. Christology*, pp. 229–230.
10. The removal of all references to Galilee is an indication that the appendix is not part of the original Gospel.
11. Some MSS add (in assimilation to John 20:19), "and said, 'Peace be to you.'"
12. On the textual problem, see above, p. 102. Even those who regard verse 40 as an interpolated assimilation to the text of John 20:20 must admit verse 39 indicates an affinity of tradition between the Lucan and Johannine pericopes.
13. This thesis will be strengthened if we view the appearance to the +500 as the origin of the Lucan Pentecost narrative. If Eph. 4:7–10 reproduces an early Christian use of Ps. 68:18 as a testimonium (so Lindars, *N.T. Apologetic*, pp. 52–54), we have additional indirect evidence of the close connection between the gift of the Spirit, and the resurrection-ascension. If the appearances were originally conceived as manifestations of the Resurrected and Ascended One, and if the gift of the Spirit is also the gift of the Resurrected and Ascended One, then the gift of the Spirit and the appearances must coincide. The earliest summary of the appearances in 1 Cor. 15:5ff. says nothing about the gift of the Spirit, but the Pauline theology of the Spirit recognizes the close connection. For Paul, the Spirit is "the Spirit of him who raised Jesus from the dead" (Rom. 8:11).

14. See F. Büchsel in *TDNT* II, p. 60, "The customary meaning of the Rabbinic expression is . . . to declare forbidden or permitted, and thus to impose or remove an obligation, by a doctrinal decision."
15. See R. H. Fuller, "The 'Thou art Peter' Pericope," pp. 311–312.
16. This form was first established by Käsemann in an article "Sätze heiligen Rechtes im Neuen Testament," first published in *NTS* 1 (1954–55), pp. 248–260. (E.T. in *New Testament Questions of Today* [London: SCM Press, 1969], pp. 66–81). See also N. Perrin, *Rediscovering the Teaching of Jesus*, pp. 22f., who succinctly definies the form thus: "a two-part pronouncement with the same verb in each part, in the first part referring to the activity of man and in the second to the eschatological activity of God."
17. Note the apocalyptic overtones in the saying; cf. E. Käsemann, *New Testament Questions of Today*, pp. 106f.
18. This disappearance of the doubt motif in the course of transmission lends weight to our conclusion that this motif is not necessarily always a later feature.
19. Thus Finegan, Hirsch, Bultmann, Grass.
20. The meaning of Rom. 9:5 is controverted. Contrast the RSV margin with RSV text: the RSV text gives the more probable rendering. Such doxological outbursts addressed to God are characteristically Jewish. See the commentaries *ad loc.*
21. See Bultmann, "The Christological Confession of the World Council of Churches," *Essays Philosophical and Theological* (London: SCM Press, 1955), pp. 273–290, esp. pp. 286–290.
22. *TNT* II, p. 56: "It is not surprising that the evangelist, following the tradition, narrates some Easter stories. The question is, what do they mean to him? The original close of the Gospel (20:31) just after the Easter stories says, 'Now Jesus also did many other signs.' Evidently then, the resurrection appearances just like the miracles of Jesus are reckoned among his signs. . . . So far as they are actual occurrences— and the evangelist need not have doubted their reality—they resemble the miracles in that ultimately they are not indispensable; in fact, there ought to be no need for them, but they were granted as a concession to man's weakness. The Thomas-story is used to make this idea clear: his wish to see the risen Jesus in the body, even to touch him, is granted. But at the same moment he is reprimanded." John could perhaps have dispensed with Easter *stories* (the earlier traditions probably had none), but not with the Easter *proclamation*. And by John's time the Easter stories were accepted as vehicles of the Easter proclamation.
23. *Der Augenzeuge* (Zollikon-Zürich: Evangelischer Verlag), p. 270.
24. Hennecke-Schneemelcher, p. 197. See below, pp. 192ff.
25. This Johannine school may have had several members who contributed to the Johannine writings. As well as the authors of John 1–20 and John 21, there are the author(s?) of the Johannine epistles. Bultmann also would include the ecclesiastical redactor who added the references to futurist eschatology and to the sacraments in the body of the Gospel and in 1 John. One might even include the author of Revelation as a somewhat "way out" member of the school.

26. H. Grass, *op. cit.*, p. 80.
27. So Bultmann, *History of the Synoptic Tradition*, pp. 217f.; C. H. Dodd, *More N.T. Studies*, pp. 118f.; K. H. Rengstorf, *Das Evangelium nach Lukas*, NTD 3 (Göttingen: Vandenhoeck & Ruprecht, 1962), *ad loc*; Finegan, p. 96.

CHAPTER SEVEN

1. The MS evidence for this ending is traceable back to the second century, to which date it is usually assigned.
2. *More New Testament Studies*, pp. 18f., 32f.
3. *Foi*, p. 305.
4. Cf. our analysis of the Great Commission in Matthew, above; also O. Michel, "Der Abschluss . . . ," p. 25.
5. Despite the agreement between Ps.-Mark and John in recording the visit of Mary Magdalene alone at the tomb, Dodd does not think that Ps.-Mark is here dependent on the Fourth Gospel. If he is correct, this would strengthen our contention that in the original tradition only Mary Magdalene visited the tomb and found it empty (see above, p. 56). In that case we have two independent survivals of the earliest tradition.
6. Two eighth-century uncials and several minuscules. Still other MSS give this ending after the canonical ending.
7. D. E. Nineham, *Mark, ad loc.* aptly compares 1 Clem. 5:16.
8. Cf. C. H. Dodd, *More New Testament Studies*, p. 104.
9. *History of the Synoptic Tradition*, p. 126.
10. R. H. Fuller, *The Foundations of N.T. Christology*, pp. 167–173.
11. See Bultmann, *History of the Synoptic Tradition*, pp. 259–261 and the literature cited, p. 259, n.2. In this footnote Bultmann argues further that 2 Pet. 1:17 knew the transfiguration as a resurrection appearance. This is the one transposition that Goguel (*Foi*, pp. 317–330) is prepared to take seriously.
12. *Op. cit.*, pp. 171f.
13. *History of the Synoptic Tradition*, p. 259.
14. R. H. Fuller, *op. cit.*, p. 109.

CHAPTER EIGHT

1. See above, pp. 48f.
2. 2. Cor. 4:16.
3. See O. Cullmann, "Immortality of the Soul or Resurrection of the Dead?" in *Immortality and Resurrection*, O. Cullmann *et al.* (New York: Macmillan, 1965), pp. 9–53, esp. pp. 33f.
4. "If the event of Easter Day is in any sense an historical event additional to the event of the cross, it is nothing else than the rise of faith in the risen Lord" (R. Bultmann in *Kerygma and Myth* I, p. 42).
5. Cf. Mark 16:7.
6. See above, pp. 32f.
7. 1 Cor. 15:20. See above, pp. 21f.
8. A relation has been established above, p. 35 and p. 153, between

the primary and church-founding appearance to Cephas, the *Tu es Petrus* pericope in Matt. 16:18 and the *Pasce oves* pericope in John 21:15ff.

9. See above, pp. 153f.
10. For their late character see above, pp. 139ff. and pp. 104ff.
11. See above, pp. 139f. and p. 145.
12. E.g., the passing through closed doors, the lack of immediate recognition, the vanishing out of sight.
13. For the Pauline christological formulae containing the earthly name Jesus see W. Kramer, *Christ, Lord, Son of God*, SBT 50 (London: SCM Press, 1966), pp. 133–150, 151–159.
14. I hope to develop this Lucan change of perspective on salvation history in a later book on "Early Catholicism in the New Testament."
15. See above, p. 35 and n. 52.
16. John 20:30f. The writer of the first epistles makes the same claim: 1 John 1:1–3.
17. See R. H. Fuller, *The Foundations of N.T. Christology*, pp. 244f.
18. Cf. esp. Acts 2:36.
19. The earlier character of Mark 16:15 is argued above, p. 157.
20. See above, pp. 42ff.
21. Bultmann in *Kerygma and Myth* I, pp. 9f.; H. W. Bartsch in *Kerygma and Myth* II (1962), pp. 1–82, esp. pp. 8f.
22. *Kerygma and Myth* I, pp. 38–43.
23. *Ibid.*, p. 46.

Biblical References

BOLDFACE TYPE INDICATES MAJOR REFERENCES.

Ancient Authors and Anonymous Ancient Writings

Index of References to Modern Authors